THE 50 GREATEST PLAYS
in GEORGIA BULLDOGS
Football History

PATRICK GARBIN

TRIUMPH
BOOKS

Library of Congress Cataloging-in-Publication Data

Garbin, Patrick, 1975–
 The 50 greatest plays in Georgia Bulldogs football history / Patrick Garbin.
    p. cm.
 ISBN-13: 978-1-60078-119-3
 ISBN-10: 1-60078-119-5
 1. University of Georgia—Football—History. 2. Georgia Bulldogs (Football team)—History
 3. Football players—Georgia. I. Title. II. Title: Fifty greatest plays in Georgia Bulldogs football history.
 GV958.G44G364 2008
 796.332'630975818—dc22

                                        2008009638

This book is available in quantity at special discounts for your group or organization. For further information, contact:
 Triumph Books
 542 South Dearborn Street
 Suite 750
 Chicago, Illinois 60605
 (312) 939-3330
 Fax (312) 663-3557

Printed in U.S.A.
ISBN: 978-1-60078-119-3
Design by Sue Knopf
Page production by Patricia Frey

*For my family and the University of Georgia football coaches
and players who made this book a possibility*

CONTENTS

FOREWORD

During my 1941 freshman season, Coach Butts was determined that Georgia must develop a new tradition in football. In those days the practice field was located adjacent to Sanford Stadium. If the team's practice did not suit Coach Butts, he would move us to the stadium to practice at night under the lights. Sometimes we would not eat dinner until 8:00! The practices were long, hard, and very physical. Coach Butts was a tough taskmaster, demanding excellence at all times. If you gave 100 percent, he wanted an additional 10 percent. As it turned out, all of our hard work eventually paid off.

Against Auburn that season, the score was tied 0–0, and there was time for Georgia to run only one more play. Usually freshmen sat in the stands, but for that game I was on the bench in my street clothes. Frank [Sinkwich] was a tremendous runner from tackle to tackle, but he was also an excellent passer. We also envied another teammate of ours, Lamar "Racehorse" Davis, because he had so much speed. Whenever Frank wanted to throw a long pass, he usually looked for Davis because he could get open and no one would be able to catch him. When the two connected on a long pass in the game's final play to beat Auburn, it was the beginning of a new tradition.

It is amazing how sometimes one play can change the complexion of an entire game. I frequently noticed this during my years playing football and many times since. Often, a single play also determines who wins or losses the game—as was the case against Auburn my freshman year.

In my 19 years of playing organized football, I was fortunate to be a part of several memorable and great plays, two of which are featured in Pat's book.

My long punt return against Tulsa in the 1946 Oil Bowl was somewhat unique because of the method I used to score. In a close game, I remember catching the punt and starting to my left, but I was trapped. So, I reversed my field toward the right, and I was in the same unfortunate situation. Reversing for a second time toward the left, I finally began to get some blocking and started to head down the sideline. Suddenly, two Tulsa men converged on me, and the only thing I could do was lower my shoulder. When I did, the three of us collided, but fortunately the two Tulsa defenders fell off me, and I went into the end zone for a touchdown.

In another close game against Alabama the following season, we decided to quick-kick near our own goal line. Alabama's Charley Compton came through and blocked my kick. We both chased the football, and I was able to recover it close to our end zone. With many yards to go, I had no alternative but to punt, and I was able to kick the football out of dangerous territory and keep the Crimson Tide from having a short field. My recovery and long punt, as was the case with my return in the Oil Bowl, probably changed the outcomes of those games, resulting in Bulldogs victories.

I have always been very proud to be associated with Georgia football, even during the intermittent tough times the program has experienced in the past. I am extremely proud now, as the Bulldogs have a tremendous program. And speaking of great plays and victories, Georgia has definitely had its share since Coach Richt's arrival.

When I played for Georgia, half of our team was from Ohio or Pennsylvania. Now, Georgia seems to be able to recruit from anywhere it desires. Recruiting is the key to winning football. I have always said that you don't win games in the fall; you win them in the winter or spring when you recruit your players. Most people do not realize that.

What a privilege it must be today to be a part of the University of Georgia's extraordinary football program and to use its first-class facilities. And what a thrill it must be to run out and play in front of more than 92,000 people at Sanford Stadium in Athens, Georgia. That's more spectators than were in attendance at my first bowl game, and we played in the Rose Bowl in Pasadena, California!

—Charley Trippi

Acknowledgments

This book, my third on University of Georgia football, would not have been possible without the support and assistance of several individuals. I have many fond memories of my father, mother, sister, and I spending precious time with one another, including at my first Georgia football game—a 44–0 win over Tennessee in the season opener of 1981. I want to thank the three of them for, among many other things, their love, inspiration, and encouragement, and for introducing Georgia Bulldogs football to me.

I feel extremely fortunate that Triumph Books requested that I write a book on UGA football for the second consecutive year. Last year, they took a chance on an unknown author when they asked me to write *"Then Vince Said to Herschel…"*. The publishing of my first book had a major impact on my life in many ways. I have Triumph Books to thank for making it possible for me to become a three-time author on a subject that has been a passion of mine since I was a child.

Based on a handful of freelance sports articles, the *Gwinnett Daily Post* hired me as a staff correspondent in 2004 to cover high school football. If not for this valuable experience, the chances of me securing any of my publishing contracts were highly unlikely. I am very grateful for this opportunity given to me by the newspaper's Todd Cline and Will Hammock—excellent and accomplished writers in their own rights and, more importantly, admirable people.

Although countless photographs exist depicting past and present Georgia football players, coaches, etc., few are readily available related to the greatest plays in Georgia's history. I want to thank the sports information departments at Georgia Tech and the universities of Pittsburgh and Tennessee for contributing photos to this project. Additionally, Nelson Morgan and the staff at the Hargrett Rare Book and Manuscript Library at the University of Georgia were more than generous in helping me find and obtain scarce and seldom-seen photographs. In particular, I want to express my gratitude to photographer Wingate Downs. Fortunately for me, Wingate photographed Georgia games for nearly 20 years and was able to contribute a number of photos to this book. Wingate is regarded as one of the best, if not the best, photographer in Athens, Georgia, and was more than a pleasure to work with.

A special thanks goes to Charley Trippi for writing the foreword to this book. He is not only one of the greatest Bulldogs to ever play football but one of the most premier players to grace any gridiron. It was truly wonderful to meet and spend time with Charley, and I appreciate his willingness to contribute to this book.

First and foremost, I am forever grateful for my wife, Elizabeth, and our one-year-old son, Trip. For the past five years, I have attempted to establish a career as a freelance journalist along with working a full-time job. During the many days when I have been absent from our household while researching and writing, my wife has been my principal supporter. Elizabeth, thank you for allowing me to realize my dream and for giving me the greatest gift I have ever received: our son.

INTRODUCTION

For more than a century, University of Georgia football has been synonymous with stellar accomplishments surpassed by few other college programs. Sixty-six Georgia players in 82 seasons have been named first-team All-American, 14 times the Bulldogs have captured conference championships, and five Georgia teams have been selected national champions by at least one recognized poll. During the most recent seasons, the reputation of the Georgia football program has been enhanced significantly as the Bulldogs have achieved a 9–2 bowl record since 1997, five out of their last six teams have won 10 or more games, and 11 consecutive squads have finished in the final Associated Press national rankings.

Much of the Bulldogs' recent success can be attributed to coach Mark Richt and his assistant coaching staff. Prior to Coach Richt's arrival in 2001, for more than a decade, Georgia was considered a second-rate team in the Southeastern Conference. During his relatively short tenure, Richt has altered this perception; the Bulldogs are now one of the most highly regarded teams not only in the conference but in all of college football. Richt's Bulldogs have accomplished in three of the past six seasons what no Georgia squad achieved in 17 successive campaigns from 1984 to 2000—they earned an upper-tier or major bowl appearance. Richt now rightly belongs to a group of outstanding Georgia coaches who experienced similar successes, namely, Alex Cunningham, Harry Mehre, Wally Butts, and, of course, Vince Dooley.

These coaching icons have coached some of the most outstanding players in all of college football. Georgia greats who left indelible marks on the program include Bob McWhorter, Vernon "Catfish" Smith, Frank Sinkwich, Charley Trippi, Fran Tarkenton, Bill Stanfill, Jake Scott, Herschel Walker, Terry Hoage, Eric Zeier, David Greene, and David Pollack, to name only a few. These players and many others have been involved in a countless number of remarkable plays since the program's beginning in 1892. The greatest of these plays are counted down and presented in the following pages of this book.

The most important, memorable, or amazing plays in Georgia football history are recounted, starting with what is considered the 50th greatest play and working up to the one deemed the greatest ever. Each play is intricately detailed while the game in which it occurred is also summarized. Also included is an explanation as to why the play is so important or memorable in Bulldogs football lore. Besides the main text, each chapter contains a variety of additional material. There are profiles of players and coaches involved in the plays and quotes from individuals who participated in or observed the plays as they unfolded. As an added feature, some plays are diagramed, presented with the *Xs* and *Os*.

From the spectacular, like Greene's touchdown pass to Michael Johnson against Auburn in 2002, to the unusual, such as the shoestring play run against Vanderbilt in 1975, to the heartbreaking, like Jasper Sanks's "nonfumble" that eventually led to a Georgia Tech defeat of the Bulldogs in 1999, a wide variety of plays are featured. The 50 greatest plays presented cover the entire history of Georgia football, from the sport's first forward pass thrown in 1895, when the Red and Black faced North Carolina, to the Bulldogs' excessive touchdown celebration against Florida in the most recent season of 2007.

Of the many great plays in the history of Georgia football, it was extremely difficult to arrive at a selection of 50 such plays and to rank them in terms of their relative importance. It is acknowledged that there may be many other plays that arguably could be substituted for some of the 50 highlighted in this book. Some examples are the "water boy" reception by Georgia's Alonzo Awtrey against Alabama in 1912, Charley Trippi's electrifying 87-yard jaunt through Georgia Tech's defense 30 years later, and in 2003, Odell Thurman's 99-yard touchdown return off an Auburn interception. Notwithstanding, some general criteria were employed in the selection and ranking process. More often than not, Georgia's greatest plays selected were those that were both extraordinary and aided in winning games and/or championships in the contest's final minutes. Remarkable plays that achieved team or player milestones and those that transpired in critical situations having implications for winning or losing games were also considered as my evaluative rationale. Also, the decision was made to consider trick plays, those plays fans may not easily recall (i.e., special teams and defensive plays), and plays executed by opposing teams that were defined as great

because, after all, they also help to make up the history of Georgia football. Understandably, it was a most challenging task to measure these rather loose criteria for the selection and ranking process. Hence, it must be acknowledged that to a considerable extent, the play selection and especially the rankings of such plays are the end result of an extremely subjective and somewhat arbitrary evaluative process.

In researching and writing this book, I was reminded of all the great Georgia football plays I have witnessed since I began attending Bulldogs games in the early 1980s. As an example, I will never forget Kevin Butler's 60-yard field goal that defeated Clemson in 1984. After Butler's kick went through the uprights, I remember a drink in a cupful of ice being thrown from the upper deck onto me, my family, and others in the section where we were sitting. But no one really cared. Georgia had just defeated the No. 2–ranked team in the country on a miraculous field goal. As I looked up toward the seats to see where the dropped drink came from, an elderly man sitting near me commented the drink smelled like it had something in it besides Coca-Cola. Sanford Stadium appeared to me, at nine years of age, to literally swing and sway and nearly collapse in excitement. I knew then what Larry Munson meant when he said "the girders are bending now," following another outstanding Georgia play that occurred nearly a decade prior. Butler's field goal was the first great Bulldogs play that brought me to tears of euphoria, but not the last.

It is my hope that many readers of this book will relive and reexperience some of the plays described as I did during my research. If *The 50 Greatest Plays in Georgia Bulldogs Football History* is able to realize this goal, its author will consider it a success.

October 27, 2007

EXCESSIVE BUT EFFECTIVE CELEBRATION

Penalty called on Georgia following a Knowshon Moreno touchdown unifies young Bulldogs squad

In 2007 a favored Georgia squad traveled to face Tennessee in Knoxville, where it was surprisingly dominated and defeated by three touchdowns. It next survived a scare in Nashville only when a late fumble by Vanderbilt saved the Bulldogs from losing for a second consecutive week. Georgia needed a field goal by Brandon Coutu in the final seconds to defeat the Commodores, 20–17.

A much-needed week off followed for Georgia before its yearly journey to Jacksonville to meet the Florida Gators. Since 1990 the Bulldogs had lost 15 of 17 games to Florida. The Gators were nationally ranked in the top 10 and coming off a national championship in 2006. A loss to Florida by Georgia's young and inexperienced squad seemed certain, and some Bulldogs backers were already looking past the seemingly disappointing 2007 season and ahead to '08.

Florida took the opening kickoff and quickly moved from its 29-yard line to Georgia's 33 before losing a fumble to cor-nerback Asher Allen. After Allen's return to the Gators' 39, the Bulldogs executed eight consecutive running plays, seven by tail-back Knowshon Moreno, to Florida's 1-yard line. On third down and goal, quarterback Matthew Stafford turned to his right and handed the ball to Moreno for the eighth time. Moreno ran directly up the middle and dove for the end zone, barely breaking the plane of the goal line for a touchdown. With six minutes remaining in the opening quarter, the Bulldogs had struck first.

Suddenly, most of Georgia's sideline emptied onto the field to join the offensive unit. There were approximately 70 Bulldogs celebrating the game's first touchdown as Florida players looked on in bewilderment. Many witnesses, including Florida coach Urban Meyer, thought a fight had broken out, but on the contrary, a party had started. The highlights of Georgia's jubilation were left tackle Trinton Sturdivant's dancing and center Fernando Velasco pretending to take photos of Moreno posing in the end zone. The exuberant end zone celebration was

Nearly every Bulldog stormed the field to celebrate in the end zone following the first score of the 2007 Georgia-Florida game. Georgia's celebration resulted in a couple of penalties but arguably revitalized its season. *Photo courtesy of AP Images.*

Mark Richt

After achieving an 8–4 record in his inaugural season as a head coach in 2001, Mark Richt's next four Georgia teams (2002–2005) each won 10 or more games and finished ranked 10th or higher in both major polls. After not appearing in the SEC Championship Game for 10 years, the Bulldogs played for the title three times during the four-year span, winning twice. In 2006 Georgia rebounded from a 6–4 start to end the season with three consecutive victories over ranked opponents and to finish with a 9–4 record and a No. 23 ranking. Richt's 2007 team was similar to the previous year's version as the Bulldogs struggled during the middle of the season but finished extremely strong, beginning with a victory over Florida.

The usually conservative and mild-mannered Richt certainly acted out of character with his motivational directive against the Gators. Soon afterward, the coach's integrity was exhibited when he contacted SEC commissioner Mike Slive to apologize for his actions.

Relieving himself of play-calling duties since the 2006 Georgia Tech game, Richt has had more time to spend on the intangibles of football and is likely more acquainted with his team than in the past. Richt knew exactly what might be instrumental in enhancing the intensity level of his squad. It can be argued that the coach's ordered celebration was a major factor in Georgia achieving one of its best seasons; only one other time in history has the Bulldogs' 2007 No. 2 national ranking in the AP poll been matched or exceeded—the 1980 national championship.

> That's what everybody [the team] did [following the game's first touchdown]. They just ran out there and formed a big, old Dog Pile.
>
> —MARCUS HOWARD, GEORGIA DEFENSIVE END

GAME DETAILS

Georgia 42 • Florida 30

Date: October 27, 2007

Site: Jacksonville Municipal Stadium

Attendance: 84,481

Records: Georgia 5–2; Florida 5–2

Rankings: Georgia: No. 20 (AP)/ No. 19 (USA Today); Florida: No. 9 (AP)/ No. 11 (USA Today)

Series: Georgia 46–37–2 (Florida two-game winning streak)

> **I** told them [the team] we are going to liven it up and create some excitement.
> —MARK RICHT, GEORGIA HEAD COACH

certainly a first at Georgia, if not in all of organized football.

With several penalty flags strewn across the field, most of the Bulldogs retreated back to the sideline for Coutu to attempt the extra point. After Coutu's successful kick, Georgia was forced to kick off from its 7½-yard line instead of the 30. The 22½ yards in penalties were well worth it.

Following the game, some questioned Georgia's discipline, class, and poise. One member of the media went so far as to call it "foolishness."

The Bulldogs' hoopla following the game's first score did not secure victory for Georgia. In fact, the Gators would tie the score only three plays and 1:21 later on a 40-yard pass from quarterback Tim Tebow to Louis Murphy. What the celebration did was unify and motivate a young Bulldogs team. This particular Georgia squad wanted to demonstrate it was different from the previous ones the Gators were used to dominating.

Coach Mark Richt had ordered the celebration, telling his offense that if they did not receive a penalty after their first touchdown, he would run them at 5:45 AM the following week. Richt wanted to fire up his young

players and generate greater intensity; however, he did not realize nearly the entire team would participate in the celebration.

After Florida had tied the game at 7–7, Georgia answered two plays later on an 84-yard touchdown pass from Stafford to Mohamed Massaquoi. The Bulldogs would go on to shock the seven-and-a-half-point-favored Gators 42–30. Moreno was outstanding, rushing for 188 yards and three touchdowns on 33 carries. Georgia's defense recorded six sacks of Tebow, who had been sacked just five times all season.

Moreno's first touchdown against Florida and the excessive celebration that followed arguably turned around a season that had appeared to be heading nowhere fast. Beginning with the Florida victory, the Bulldogs played like a different team through the end of the year, finishing with seven consecutive victories, winning the Sugar Bowl, and ranking second in the nation in the final Associated Press Poll.

Sometimes unexpected occurrences can unite and motivate young men to overcome apparently insurmountable obstacles to succeed. For the Bulldogs in 2007, it seems "foolishness" led to greater successes.

THE CELEBRATION

Quarterback Matthew Stafford signaled with his left foot, and fullback Shaun Chapas went into motion from his left to right. Stafford turned and handed the football to Knowshon Moreno, who got the football at the 6. Moreno took three steps and leaped from the 3 over a pile of players. Moreno's outstretched football barely broke the plane of Florida's goal line for the first score of the contest. Suddenly and unexpectedly, almost the entire Georgia team ran from the sideline and gathered with the offense in the end zone for a celebration unlike anything ever witnessed before in football.

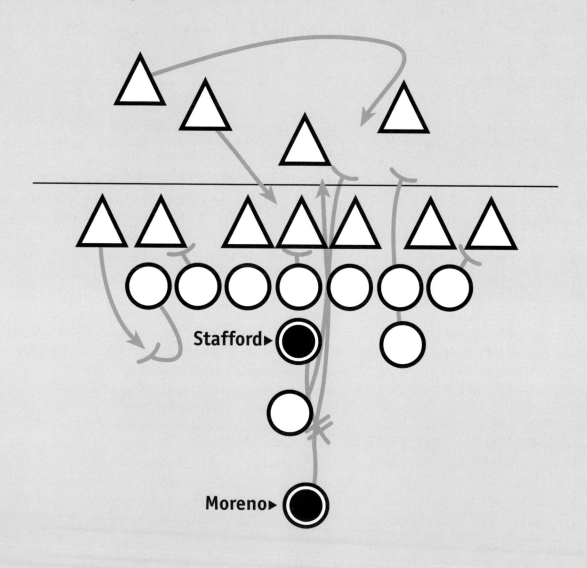

KNOWSHON MORENO

Although considered Georgia's third-string tailback during the summer of 2007, Knowshon Moreno was being compared, even by Coach Richt, to Georgia great Garrison Hearst. However, only Herschel Walker—not Hearst—had a better and more impactful freshman campaign than the New Jersey native Moreno did in 2007.

Moreno was not Georgia's third tailback for long after carrying the ball 20 times and catching two passes in the season opener against Oklahoma State. His 22 touches against the Cowboys would be his most until Georgia's seventh game, versus Vanderbilt.

For the Bulldogs' next five games, Moreno was one of college football's premier backs, averaging more than 153 rushing yards on 26 carries per game while scoring a total of nine touchdowns. He finished the season with 1,334 rushing yards, a 5.4 rushing average, 14 touchdowns, and 20 catches. Despite starting only six games, Moreno's rushing total is the fifth highest single-season total in Georgia history and fourth most for a freshman in the Southeastern Conference. He was the only Bulldog in 2007 named to both the Associated Press and Coaches All-SEC first teams, and he was also selected to several freshman All-American first teams.

Knowshon Moreno scores his first touchdown against the Gators on a one-yard run. He would account for two additional touchdowns while rushing for 188 yards on 33 carries. *Photo courtesy of AP Images.*

November 6, 1913

Fairground Gallantry

Red and Black escape upset with Bob McWhorter's late touchdown pass

The eighth annual Georgia-Carolina State Fair was 11 days of corn, kennel, livestock, and poultry shows, automobile and motorcycle races, and an "auto-polo game: one of the most thrilling events ever witnessed on earth." Held at Augusta, Georgia's fairgrounds, the fair was considered one of the best agricultural festivals in the South.

Played on the second day of the gala, the 1913 Georgia-Clemson contest was thought to be only a small part of the celebration; however, the football game, a specific touchdown pass in particular, turned out to be one of the most thrilling events in Georgia football history at that point in time.

Losing 15–12 with only a few minutes left in the game, Georgia All-American Bob McWhorter lofted a long pass to newcomer Roy "Scrapper" Smith, who caught the ball on the 1-yard line and crossed Clemson's goal for the game-winning score. The pass play ended any hopes for a Clemson upset, added to McWhorter's illustrious career as perhaps the most valuable Georgia football player of all time, and was the pinnacle in the football career of Smith, a little-known end at Georgia until his acclaimed scoring catch.

In large part because of coach Alex Cunningham's stellar guidance and half-back McWhorter's outstanding play, by 1913 Georgia was considered one of the best teams in the South. After nearly two decades of mediocrity since they began playing football in 1892, the Red and Black had contended for the Southern Intercollegiate Athletic Association (SIAA) championship every year since 1910. Unsuccessful in capturing the SIAA title since 1896, Georgia had only lost to an excellent Virginia team in '13 and was believed to be able to easily handle an average Clemson squad.

From the onset, Clemson was shockingly able to move the ball easily against Georgia while holding McWhorter and the rest of the Red and Black offense to short gains. Soon after Clemson's J.P. Jeter missed a field goal, teammate Johnny Logan booted one from the 25-yard line to give the underdogs a 3–0 lead.

Shortly thereafter, McWhorter caught a missed field goal on his goal line and ran 20 yards before fumbling and losing the ball. On the next play, Clemson's quarterback, Jimmie James, ran for a touchdown. The extra point was missed, but Clemson held a commanding 9–0 advantage.

In 1913 Bob McWhorter was selected as Georgia's first All-American. Known primarily as a gifted runner, McWhorter helped defeat Clemson that season by throwing two long touchdowns to Roy Smith, the second coming in the closing minutes of the ballgame. *Photo courtesy of Hargrett Rare Book & Manuscript Library/University of Georgia Libraries.*

After a scoreless second quarter, Georgia quarterback Dave Paddock broke loose for one of his four runs of 20 yards or more during the game; he would finish with an impressive 165 yards on 11 carries. On the next play, McWhorter scored on a short run, and Georgia finally had some points.

Into the final quarter, Clemson had scored again. Georgia trailed 15–6 and was seemingly to lose only its sixth of 32 games since Cunningham and McWhorter's arrival. It seemed that it would take a miracle for the Red and Black to snatch victory out of the jaws of defeat, something McWhorter had accomplished before.

Clemson had limited McWhorter's rushing; he would finish the game gaining only 75 yards on 21 carries with just two runs greater than five yards. However, Clemson had yet to face his passing prowess. Although Clemson allowed Georgia only one completion in its first nine passing attempts, only two of the tosses were thrown by McWhorter.

Facing third down on Clemson's 30-yard line, McWhorter connected with

ROY "SCRAPPER" SMITH

Roy Smith's first and only season at the University of Georgia was in 1913. Playing from his end position, he weighed a scant 145 pounds but reportedly was extremely fast. Although Smith started in six of the Red and Black's eight games (three at left end, three at right end), he is scarcely mentioned in Georgia's football archives. The only points he scored in 1913 were 12 on the two come-from-behind touchdown receptions from Bob McWhorter against Clemson. While playing football at Georgia, Scrapper was a true "two-hit wonder."

GAME DETAILS

Georgia 18 • Clemson 15

Date: November 6, 1913

Site: Augusta Fairgrounds

Attendance: 6,000 (attendance at Georgia-Carolina State Fair)

Records: Georgia 4–1; Clemson 2–2

Series: Clemson 8–7–1 (Georgia two-game winning streak)

Smith for a touchdown, and Georgia had pulled within three points.

In the last few minutes of the contest, Tanny Webb punted to McWhorter, who was immediately tackled. On the next play, McWhorter threw again to Smith and again got the same result. Smith caught the pass on the 1-yard line and crossed Clemson's goal for a 45-yard touchdown, giving Georgia an 18–15 lead. The Red and Black missed the extra-point attempt, but it would not matter.

Clemson had one last possession, but on Georgia's kickoff, Logan fumbled and the Red and Black recovered on the 40-yard line. Georgia ran five plays, gaining 15 yards, before the game ended.

At perhaps the grandest agricultural exhibition in the South, behind the arm of McWhorter and the hands of Smith, the Red and Black's fierce rally was one of the most illustrious comebacks ever witnessed on a Southern gridiron.

DAVE PADDOCK

Dave Paddock, a New Yorker tired of northern winters, came to the University of Georgia and tried out for football in 1912. Barely making the squad, he moved positions from halfback to quarterback by the end of the season. It was at Paddock's new position that he starred with his quickness and shifty moves.

Although he was not directly involved in Georgia's memorable, game-winning touchdown pass to defeat Clemson in 1913, if it were not for Paddock, the Red and Black likely would have lost. Paddock gained 165 of Georgia's 318 rushing yards, averaged 15 yards per carry, and had two runs of 40-yard gains.

In 1914 Paddock scored his first touchdown at Georgia against North Carolina. At the conclusion of the season, he was named the school's second All-American by the *New York Herald*.

Paddock scored four touchdowns in 1915, including one in his final game at Georgia, a 13–0 win over Clemson. He was later selected the first-team quarterback for Georgia's all-time team prior to World War I (1891–1916).

September 29, 1956

RECORD-BREAKING WINNER

Ken Cooper's field goal sets mark and defeats 'Noles in '56

There were few memorable plays or moments in Georgia football for most of the 1950s. By 1956 the Bulldogs' gridiron play was vastly inferior to that characteristic of their glory years of 1941–1948. In the '56 season-opening game against Vanderbilt, Georgia was shut out 14–0, never getting the football closer than the Commodores' 38-yard line.

Only nine years since it was known as the Florida State College for Women, Florida State University was reviving its football program after a 43-year layoff. It defeated a reputable Ohio University squad by 40 points in its first game. For several years, Florida State had been seeking admission into the Southeastern Conference but had been turned away. In promoting their program, the Seminoles had scheduled five SEC opponents through 1955, all losses, including defeats to Georgia in 1954 and 1955 by a 23.5-point scoring margin. Florida State was led by quarterback Lee Corso and was given a good chance of defeating the Bulldogs.

For most of the game, it appeared the Seminoles would beat Georgia for the first time in history. However, a late interception by the Bulldogs led to a memorable and "long" 36-yard field goal by Ken Cooper that broke a scoreless tie and resulted in a Georgia victory. Cooper's field goal was one of only a handful kicked at Georgia to that point in time, one of only 53 made successfully in all of college football in 1956, and one of the most memorable plays in Georgia football history during the 1950s.

Late in the scoreless affair, Corso attempted a pass to end Ronnie Schomburger, but Billy Hearn, leaping over the intended receiver, made an interception on Georgia's

> [Quarterback Billy] Hearn steered a course back into scoring range where Ken Cooper could come in and boot one snapped from the 26 to save a game that had been all but washed down the drain.
>
> —ED DANFORTH, SPORTS EDITOR OF THE *ATLANTA JOURNAL*

The 1956 Bulldogs experienced a disappointing 3–6–1 campaign. One of the few highlights of that season was Ken Cooper's (No. 83) game-winning field goal that defeated Florida State. *Photo courtesy of Hargrett Rare Book & Manuscript Library/University of Georgia Libraries.*

38-yard line. With five and a half minutes remaining, quarterback Hearn began moving the Bulldogs down the field.

Hearn first passed to Roy Wilkins for a 10-yard gain. Two rushes by fullback Knox Culpepper carried the ball into Seminoles territory, where Gene Littleton picked up 12 yards on a run. After a Ken Schulte incompletion, Georgia's Cooper lined up to kick a field goal from the 26-yard line with 1:30 left on the clock.

Cooper's field goal was described as "beautiful" as it sailed successfully through the uprights. Kicked from Cooper's encased shoe, the 36-yard game winner broke the Sanford Stadium record for longest made field goal and would defeat the upset-minded Seminoles, 3–0.

Hearn's critical interception and leadership under center for the winning Bulldogs was sweet revenge for the junior quarterback. Several months prior, Hearn was the ace pitcher for Georgia's baseball team and won his first seven decisions before losing to Florida State. The loss occurred when a Seminoles batter tripled

LEE CORSO

Prior to becoming what he is presently well known for, an analyst and personality on ESPN's *College Gameday*, Lee Corso was an accomplished athlete at Florida State and later a head football coach. From 1969 to 1982 and 1984 to 1985, he coached at three different colleges and the Orlando Renegades of the defunct United States Football League.

Corso was one of the most highly recruited football players in Florida history. A standout on offense and defense at Florida State from 1953 to 1956, he was responsible for 19 touchdowns via the pass, rushing, receiving, and on punt returns. In 1956 he was named Associated Press All-American Honorable Mention and was elected to the Florida State University Hall of Fame in 1978. His 14 career interceptions were a school record for 32 years until 1988. However, the interception he threw to Billy Hearn in 1956 will probably be best remembered in Georgia football annals.

Lee Corso was a star quarterback and halfback at Florida State during the 1950s. He was later a head coach for 16 years at both the collegiate and professional levels and then went on to work for ESPN. *Photo courtesy of AP Images.*

GAME DETAILS

Georgia 3 • Florida State 0

Date: September 29, 1956

Site: Sanford Stadium

Attendance: 25,000

Records: Georgia 0–1; Florida State 1–0

Series: Georgia 2–0 (Georgia two-game winning streak)

> **I** was afraid I hadn't kicked it [the ball] hard enough.
>
> —KEN COOPER, GAME-WINNING KICKER

off Hearn, knocking in two runs. The Seminoles batter who ultimately defeated Hearn was Corso. It was Hearn, however, who would now turn the tables on Corso with his timely, leaping interception.

Besides Cooper's record-breaking, game-winning kick, another noteworthy event in Georgia football history occurred on September 29, 1956—the introduction of mascot Uga (pronounced "Uh-guh"). Although he was never intended to go to the Florida State game, Uga, a white English bulldog, left a fraternity party earlier that day with an excited group of students for Sanford Stadium. The ticket takers allowed Uga through the gate because of "his pugnacious attitude and the big *G* on his chest." Later that season and after a chain of unexpected events, Uga became the official mascot of the University of Georgia.

Georgia's victory over Florida State was one of the few highlights in an otherwise disappointing '56 season. The Bulldogs finished with a 3–6–1 record, including just 1–6 in conference play—the only Wally Butts Georgia team to finish last in the SEC in his 22 seasons as head coach. If not for Hearn's interception leading to Cooper's "beautiful" boot, the 1956 campaign would have been even more dismal

KEN COOPER

In all three of his varsity seasons at Georgia, Ken Cooper would do most of the Bulldogs' place kicking during a time when no player was solely designated for the position. While playing end, Cooper made three of nine field goals and 24 of 34 extra points from 1955 to 1957. Included was Georgia's last drop kick for a score following a bad snap after a touchdown against Texas in 1957. Cooper also averaged 33.2 yards on 21 career punts and caught seven passes, including a touchdown against Kentucky in 1957.

Besides his game-winning field goal against the Seminoles, Cooper is most recognized for his coaching career. Following an 11-year stint as an assistant coach at Georgia and the University of Mississippi, he compiled a 21–23 record as the Ole Miss head coach from 1974 to 1977.

November 2, 1946

A One-Man Show

Highlighted by a recovery of his own blocked punt, Charley Trippi nearly single-handedly defeats 'Bama in '46

Prior to the arrival of Herschel Walker, the greatest football player ever at the University of Georgia was arguably Charley Trippi. Trippi made several remarkable runs, passes, returns, and plays on defense during his three years on Georgia's varsity (1942, 1945–1946). Nevertheless, the greatest play he ever pulled off, according to some, including author John Stegeman, is rather unconventional to say the least.

In the second quarter of the 1946 Georgia-Alabama game, the Bulldogs led 7–0; however, Georgia was backed up toward its own goal line, and Trippi was set to punt on third down. His quick kick was blocked by Alabama tackle Charley Compton, and the ball bounded toward the Bulldogs' end zone. Both Charleys ran toward the goal line in mad pursuit and, once inside the 10-yard line, dove simultaneously for the ball. Georgia's Charley made an extraordinary recovery of his own blocked quick kick at the Bulldogs' 6-yard line. Because Georgia had elected to punt on third and not fourth down, it retained possession. On the next play, Trippi lofted a lengthy punt out of his own end zone

and bailed the Bulldogs out of anticipated danger. It was the third consecutive punt by Trippi from behind his own goal line; he averaged 51 yards per kick.

For only the second time in 32 meetings since 1895, Georgia and Alabama faced off in Athens. The 52,000 in attendance at Sanford Stadium were the most to witness a sporting event in the state of Georgia. On a rain-drenched field, Georgia's Dick McPhee intercepted star Harry Gilmer on the quarterback's first pass of the game. Three plays later, the Bulldogs faced third down and 6 on the Crimson Tide's 9-yard line. Trippi passed into the end zone, and end Dan Edwards made a diving catch of a tipped ball for a touchdown.

In the following quarter, Trippi, besides his punt return against Tulsa in the 1946 Oil Bowl, might have executed his greatest play as a collegian. If he had not recovered his own blocked kick, Alabama, regarded as one of the best teams in the nation, likely would have scored a touchdown soon afterward. Instead, the Crimson Tide began their next drive near midfield, where they could not generate any offense.

Prior to halftime, Trippi ran a toss sweep to his right for 46 yards, "tight roping down the sideline to the end zone." As he had accomplished several times before during his two and a half seasons at Georgia, Trippi had given the Bulldogs a comfortable lead nearly by himself. He was attributed the ultimate respect when Alabama's Million Dollar Band spelled out "T-R-I-P-P-I" in his honor at halftime.

Trippi's towering kicks held off the Crimson Tide during the final two quarters. Two of his second-half punts were downed inside Alabama's 10-yard line. Trippi's 38-yard punting average for the game was achieved in booting a soaked football.

Alabama finished with only 163 total yards (zero passing on nine attempts) in its 14–0 shutout loss to the Bulldogs. Georgia rushed for 139 yards, 98 by Trippi on 16 carries. The Bulldogs' superstar halfback also completed five of 11 passes, throwing for 109 of the game's 110 passing yards. Performing a one-man show, Trippi was responsible for 207 of Georgia's 249 yards, while his punts kept the Crimson Tide from nearing the Bulldogs' goal line, including one that was blocked.

Trainer Harry "Squab" Jones applies a towel to star halfback Charley Trippi in 1946. Trippi's recovery of his own blocked punt that season against Alabama has been called his greatest play. *Photo courtesy of AP Images.*

HARRY GILMER

Just as significant as Charley Trippi's performance against the Crimson Tide in 1946, Alabama's Harry "the Arm" Gilmer's performance, or a lack thereof, was also significant. As a sophomore in '45, Gilmer was named SEC player of the year, finished fifth in the Heisman Trophy voting, and led the Crimson Tide to a perfect 10–0 record, including a 28–14 victory over Georgia in late October. Against the Bulldogs, Gilmer completed 14 of 20 passes for 146 yards and three touchdowns. A year later in '46, the Arm was grounded at Georgia. Although Gilmer led Alabama with 55 rushing yards on 12 carries, he did not complete a single pass in eight attempts and was intercepted twice. Gilmer was recognized as probably the best passer in college football. In more than two and a half seasons at Alabama, he never had a game in which he had not successfully completed at least one pass. The 6', 160-pound quarterback completed 69 passes for the 1946 season—fourth best in the nation.

Gilmer rebounded against the Bulldogs as a senior in 1947. In a 17–7 victory, he completed five of 10 passes and scored the game's first points on an 80-yard punt return. The 52 touchdowns he accounted for while at Alabama still remain a school record after 60 years. Gilmer played eight seasons in the NFL, was a head coach for two years with Detroit in the mid-1960s, and was inducted into the College Football Hall of Fame in 1993.

Alabama's Harry Gilmer was considered one of the best passers in college football during the 1940s. However, against Georgia in 1946, he did not complete a single pass in eight attempts during a 14–0 loss.
Photo courtesy of Getty Images.

GAME DETAILS

Georgia 14 • Alabama 0

Date: November 2, 1946

Site: Sanford Stadium

Attendance: 52,000

Records: Georgia 5–0; Alabama 5–1

Rankings: Georgia: No. 5 (AP); Alabama: No. 15 (AP)

Series: Alabama 15–13–3 (Alabama one-game winning streak)

> Trippi was certainly the difference [in Georgia's victory].
>
> —VAUGHN MANCHA, ALABAMA'S ALL-AMERICAN CENTER

> Trippi's scramble with Compton for that blocked kick was really great. Charley's recovery sure pulled us out of a hole.
>
> —WALLY BUTTS, GEORGIA HEAD COACH

CHARLEY TRIPPI

Charley Trippi's successful football career continued after his playing days at Georgia. Trippi played for nine seasons in the NFL from 1947 to 1955, all with the Chicago Cardinals. For at least one season, Trippi led Chicago in rushing, passing, receiving, punting, kick returns, and/or punt returns. In 99 career games, he passed for 2,547 yards, rushed for 3,506 and a 5.1 average, caught 130 passes, intercepted four, averaged 13.7 yards per punt return, and averaged 22.1 per kick return. Trippi was responsible for 53 touchdowns during a professional career similar to his stint at Georgia—a "do-it-all" type player. He is only one of three Georgia players to be the first overall selection in the NFL draft (Frank Sinkwich and Harry Babcock are the others) and just one of two inducted into the Pro Football Hall of Fame (Fran Tarkenton).

After retiring from playing, Trippi was an assistant coach in Chicago for two seasons. He then returned to Georgia and held the same position with the Bulldogs from 1958 to 1962. Trippi finished his coaching career with a second stretch with the Cardinals for three seasons through 1965. He left coaching and became a highly successful businessman in the city where he first flourished. The 85-year-old living legend still resides in Athens, Georgia.

October 30, 1993

THE TIMEOUT

Disputed timeout called by Florida negates Georgia's potential game-winning score

The Bulldogs at 1–4 were absolutely dreadful during the first half of the 1993 campaign, losing twice as many games as they had lost the entire season before. However, behind one of the best quarterbacks in the nation, junior Eric Zeier, and a set of gifted receivers, "Air Georgia" finally reached its full potential and won three consecutive games by the end of October.

Next on the schedule was Steve Spurrier's Florida Gators and their feared offense, the "Fun 'n' Gun." The Gators were an overwhelming favorite to defeat Georgia with an offense averaging an eye-popping 40 points and 514 yards per game for the season. In three consecutive wins over the Bulldogs, the "Fun 'n' Gun" averaged more than 36 points per contest while defeating Georgia by more than three touchdowns per victory. It certainly appeared the '93 Georgia senior class would be the first to lose four straight to Florida in 30 years (1960–1963).

To the astonishment of practically everyone, the Bulldogs trailed by only one touchdown late in the game. In the final seconds, Zeier completed a 12-yard touchdown pass to Jerry Jerman to pull

Georgia within a point, 33–32. Just as a game-winning two-point conversion for Georgia was envisioned, the Bulldogs faithful received some disappointing news. Supposedly, Florida cornerback Anthone Lott called timeout just before Zeier took the snap on the negated scoring pass. The play was called dead with five seconds left in the game, and Georgia still trailed by seven points instead of one. The Bulldogs had two shots at the end zone but could not score and lost to the Gators once again.

The day was as dreary as the first five games of Georgia's season, as swirling winds and a steady rain drenched the Gator Bowl. Down 13–3 in the first quarter, the Bulldogs rallied to take a 20–13 lead in the second quarter. "Air Georgia" was in full effect as Zeier would attempt a whopping 65 passes for the game, one shy of an SEC record, while the Bulldogs would attempt only 14 rushes in the entire contest. Of Zeier's 36 completions, tight end Shannon Mitchell caught 15—a school record that still stands today.

Spurrier benched quarterback and freshman phenom Danny Wuerffel and abandoned the pass; the 21 pass attempts were a low for Florida since Spurrier's arrival. The "Fun 'n'

Gun" turned to the running game and Errict Rhett, who finished with 183 rushing yards on a school-record 41 carries.

Florida regained the lead, 23–20, before halftime and held a 10-point advantage late in the game. Nonetheless, Georgia's Kanon Parkman kicked his fourth field goal with 5:06 remaining, and the Bulldogs trailed only 33–26. Georgia would get the ball back on its own 36-yard line with just 1:36 left on the clock and time for one last possession.

The Bulldogs reached Florida's 12-yard line with only seconds remaining. Just as the ball was snapped, Lott noticed the Gators sideline was screaming for a timeout because Florida had only 10 players on the field. Lott asked a nearby judge for the timeout, and Georgia's potential winning play was waved off by the official.

Pass interference on Florida was the call on an incomplete Zeier pass, and the Bulldogs advanced to the Gators' 2-yard line with no time on the clock and were granted one final play. Zeier threw behind and incomplete to Jeff Thomas, and Florida escaped with a 33–26 victory.

Against Florida in 1993, Eric Zeier's touchdown pass to Jerry Jerman with only seconds remaining was negated by the officials. The call cost Georgia the game, but replays revealed the touchdown should have counted. *Photo courtesy of Wingate Downs.*

STEVE SPURRIER

Known as the "Ol' Ball Coach" and the "Evil Genius," Steve Spurrier seemingly has had a longtime disdain for Georgia football, and vice versa. As Florida's quarterback, he faced the Bulldogs three times (1964–1966), defeating Georgia in '65 on a touchdown pass in the final minutes.

As the first-year head coach at Florida in 1990, Spurrier's Gators were leading the Dogs 38–7 toward the end of the game. Georgia's reserve offense was on the field and close to making one of the team's few first downs for the game. Spurrier's reaction was to take out his reserve defensive unit and insert the first team during the blowout. In subsequent years, Spurrier often made snide and ridiculing remarks about Georgia football, occasionally during postgame interviews when Florida had soundly defeated the Bulldogs.

Even Spurrier's own players have admitted in the past that their coach did not think too much of Georgia. Supposedly, the dislike stems from a 27–10 Bulldogs victory over Florida in Spurrier's Heisman Trophy–winning campaign of 1966. Spurrier won just one of three games against Georgia as Florida's quarterback—the identical record he has against the Bulldogs since becoming South Carolina's head coach in 2005.

Florida quarterback Steve Spurrier confers with his coach, Ray Graves, in 1967. Although Spurrier was extremely successful as the Gators' head coach against Georgia, he only defeated the Bulldogs once as a player. *Photo courtesy of AP Images.*

GAME DETAILS

Florida 33 • Georgia 26

Date: October 30, 1993

Site: Gator Bowl

Attendance: 80,392

Records: Georgia 4–4; Florida 5–1

Rankings: Florida: No. 10 (AP)/ No. 10 (CNN)

Series: Georgia 44–25–2 (Florida three-game winning streak)

While the Gators rejoiced, several Georgia players were dazed, staggering, and crying uncontrollably, still disbelieving their earlier touchdown had been waved off and six points had been taken off the scoreboard.

The Bulldogs were correct in their assessment. Television replays clearly proved that Zeier had taken the snap and was dropping back with the ball prior to the official calling the touchdown play dead. Instead of Georgia scoring and possibly upsetting the Gators, because of a judge's error, Florida kept the Dogs out of its end zone and defeated them for the fourth consecutive time.

The setback was one of many disappointing defeats for Georgia in what has been a Gators-dominated series since 1990. Unfortunately, a chance at victory was taken away from the Bulldogs in '93, a possible victory over Florida that has been hard to come by for nearly two decades.

ERIC ZEIER

When the action was not nearly as commonplace as it is today, Eric Zeier enrolled early at Georgia out of high school and participated in spring drills prior to his freshman season of 1991. He was regarded as one of the better quarterbacks in the SEC as a freshman and sophomore. In 1993 the Bulldogs were without running back Garrison Hearst and an adequate running game and were forced to throw the ball more often. Over his final two seasons, Zeier eclipsed most school and many conference passing and total offense records.

Zeier is regarded by many as the greatest quarterback ever at Georgia. Since Fran Tarkenton in 1960, Zeier is the only Bulldogs signal caller chosen first-team All-American (1994). Besides Ray Goff (1976), Zeier is the lone Georgia quarterback to finish in the Heisman Trophy's top 10 voting, and he did it twice (10th in 1993, seventh in 1994).

Since playing in the NFL from 1995 to 2000, Zeier has enjoyed a successful business career. In addition, at the start of the 2007 season, he was selected as Georgia's new color analyst on its radio broadcast team for road games.

During the regular-season finale of 1993, his junior season, quarterback Eric Zeier passes for some of his 328 yards in a 43–10 victory over Georgia Tech. Sixteen days later he finished 10th in the Heisman Trophy voting, and he finished seventh the following year. To date, Zeier is only one of three Bulldogs, along with Frank Sinkwich and Herschel Walker, to finish in the Heisman's top-ten voting in two or more seasons. *Photo courtesy of AP Images.*

October 26, 1968

GREAT SCOTT!

Jake Scott intercepts Kentucky in '68 and twists and whirls his way to a touchdown

Despite having only a subpar record, the '68 Kentucky Wildcats were called "the best 2–3 football team in America" by their head coach, Charlie Bradshaw. The football team was perhaps the school's best since the Bear Bryant–coached Wildcats bowl squads of the early 1950s. For the Georgia game, however, Kentucky's starting quarterback, Stan Fortson, would not be able to play because of appendicitis. Backup Dave Bair, who led the SEC in 1967 with 21 interceptions thrown, would be filling in for Fortson and facing a Bulldogs defense ranked second in the conference, on a chilly night in Lexington, Kentucky.

Georgia had one of the nation's best defenses and, in the opinion of many, the very best safety-man in all of college football in Jake Scott. Scott displayed his excellence against the Wildcats with two interceptions returned for touchdowns; the second return was especially praiseworthy.

With the Bulldogs holding a two-touchdown lead in the final quarter, Scott intercepted a pass by Bair intended for all-purpose star Dicky Lyons at the Kentucky 35-yard line. Scott was hemmed in and trapped by Lyons, and it appeared that Scott was soon to be tackled. However, the All-American safety planted his feet, completely turned around, and left a falling Lyons grasping for air. Scott dashed down the right sideline on an unbelievable return for a score.

Scott scored the first points of the game on an interception return with 3:49 remaining in the first quarter. Defensive tackle Bill Stanfill deflected a Bair pass into Scott's arms, who then returned the deflection 33 yards for a touchdown.

Georgia led Kentucky 21–0 at halftime. The Bulldogs defense dominated the 'Cats in the first two quarters of play, yielding no first downs and only 32 total yards.

With just under eight minutes left in the game, Kentucky trailed 21–7 and had the ball on its own 17-yard line. Bair's pass was intercepted by Scott, and for the second time, Georgia's standout safety returned the ball for a touchdown on, according to writer Furman Bisher, "an even more special run [than Scott's first return]." For the game, Scott led a Georgia defense that allowed the Wildcats to score only in the final quarter in a 35–14 win.

Following his interception against Kentucky in 1968, it appeared that Jake Scott would be tackled. However, the junior safety-man escaped from his would-be tackler and ran 35 yards for a touchdown. *Photo courtesy of AP Images.*

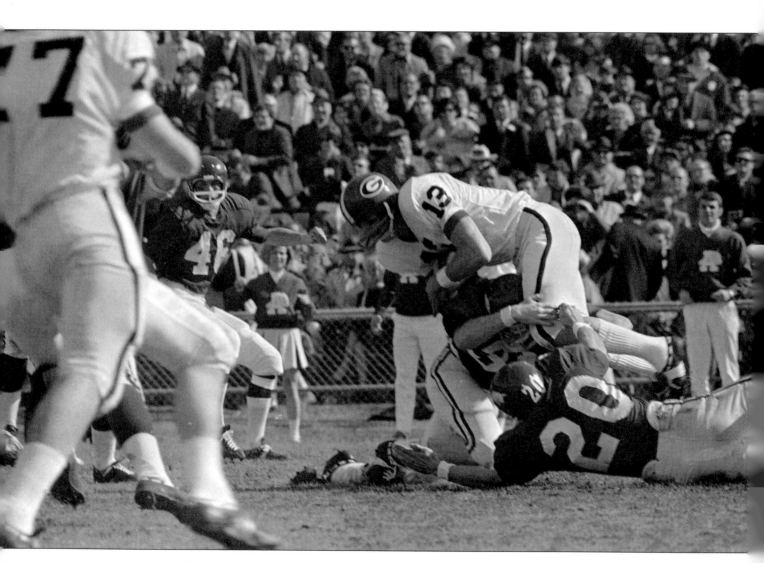

Jake Scott (No. 13) attempts to break a tackle in the 1969 Cotton Bowl, his final game as a Bulldog. Scott ended his college career with 16 interceptions in only two seasons, which remains the school record. *Photo courtesy of AP Images.*

GAME DETAILS

Georgia 35 • Kentucky 14

Date: October 26, 1968

Site: Stoll Field/McLean Stadium

Attendance: 32,000

Records: Georgia 4–0–1; Kentucky 2–3

Rankings: Georgia: No. 8 (AP)/No. 8 (UPI)

Series: Georgia 14–5–2 (Georgia two-game winning streak)

> **Y**ou don't ever think you're going to score [after making an interception]. You just run where there ain't nobody.
>
> —JAKE SCOTT, SAFETY

To date, no other Georgia player in the modern era has returned two interceptions for touchdowns in a single game. It has been done only one other time in SEC history, by Florida's Joe Brodsky versus Mississippi State in 1956. In fact, only once in NCAA annals has a player returned three interceptions for scores in a game—Houston's Johnny Jackson versus Texas in 1987.

It seems safe to contend that no interception return in Georgia football and few in college football history were as spectacular as Scott's second against Kentucky in 1968. As he turned and churned through the Kentucky offense after making the interception, Scott later admitted he did not think he would score. Nevertheless, nothing could stop the great Scott as he journeyed down the sideline for a 35-yard touchdown.

BILL STANFILL

Bill Stanfill first made a name for himself at Georgia as the only non-junior and non-senior defensive starter on the Bulldogs' 1966 SEC title team. Against Florida that season, Stanfill harassed eventual Heisman Trophy winner Steve Spurrier the entire game, sacking the quarterback several times and forcing turnovers in a 27–10 Georgia victory.

Standout performances in 1968, like in the Kentucky game, led to Stanfill being chosen first-team consensus All-American and Georgia's only Outland Trophy recipient as college football's most outstanding interior lineman.

Against Kentucky in '68, Stanfill, as he did much of his Georgia and eight-year professional football career, played injured. As was the case with other teammates, Stanfill was suffering from boils on his leg. It seems that six weeks before, when Georgia faced Tennessee on its Tartan Turf, small slivers of the synthetic grass were imbedded into the legs of several Bulldogs players, causing the painful inflammation.

JAKE SCOTT

As one of only two sophomore starters, along with left guard Steve Greer, on Georgia's 1967 defense, Jake Scott demonstrated an outstanding ability to both defend the pass and return punts. He would soon display his knack for returning interceptions and punts for touchdowns.

Against Florida in '67, the varsity newcomer returned a Gator interception 32 yards for a score. Prior to Scott's two touchdown returns against Kentucky in 1968, Scott's final year at Georgia, he took a Tennessee punt back 90 yards for a score, although in the process he endured three hits by would-be Volunteers tacklers. In 1970, as a rookie for the Miami Dolphins, Scott returned a punt 77 yards for a touchdown in a 34–17 win over Baltimore.

Following only two years at Georgia and a stellar nine-season career in the NFL, Scott, for personal and unacknowledged reasons, disassociated himself from Georgia football until he acted as the Bulldogs' honorary captain for a 2006 game against Georgia Tech.

Besides defending the pass, Jake Scott was also an excellent punt returner. Here he returns a Tennessee punt 90 yards for a touchdown in the season-opening game of 1968. *Photo courtesy of Hargrett Rare Book & Manuscript Library/University of Georgia Libraries.*

November 25, 2006

Tony Takes It to the House

Tony Taylor takes fumbled football away from Georgia Tech in 2006 and scampers 29 yards for a score

Following a 5–0 start to the 2006 season, Georgia lost four of its next five games; the Bulldogs' 6–4 record was their worst after 10 games in 10 years. The chance for a satisfactory season seemed doubtful, as Georgia was to finish the year against Auburn and Georgia Tech.

Surprisingly, the Bulldogs stunned the fifth-ranked Tigers 37–15 on the road and returned home to host the Yellow Jackets. The Bulldogs had defeated their intrastate rival five consecutive times; however, No. 16 Georgia Tech had its best team in years, having already clinched a playoff spot in the Atlantic Coast Conference Championship Game for a bid to play in the Orange Bowl.

In a defensive standoff, the Bulldogs trailed the Yellow Jackets 3–0 late in the third quarter. Georgia Tech lined up in a shotgun formation on its own 27-yard line, facing third down and 15. Quarterback Reggie Ball took the snap, dropped back to his 15-yard line, and then rolled to his right. He decided to keep the football, turned upfield, and

ran by Georgia's Marcus Howard. Howard trailed Ball and tackled him from behind, knocking the ball loose close to the 30-yard line. Seconds later, approximately 15 players were fighting for the fumbled ball or peering into the pile. As most of the players nonchalantly stood around, Georgia's Tony Taylor emerged from the massive huddle with the football. The senior linebacker raced to the right of the pile toward the goal line and then dove from the 2-yard line into the end zone, completing a 29-yard fumble return for a touchdown.

Most of the players and coaches on both teams and the sellout crowd in Sanford Stadium had hardly seen what had taken place. The play was reviewed by the replay booth. Surely, the play had been stopped prior to the touchdown return, or Taylor was down before snatching the football out of the pile. Nevertheless, the call on the field, a Georgia touchdown, was confirmed. The Bulldogs added the extra point and led for the first time, 7–3, with 3:10 remaining in the quarter.

> I didn't know [what was happening] when I first picked it [the football] up.... I just kept running.
>
> —TONY TAYLOR, GEORGIA LINEBACKER

Tony Taylor's 29-yard fumble return for a touchdown against Georgia Tech in 2006 is capped with a celebratory dive into the end zone. *Photo courtesy of AP Images.*

MATTHEW STAFFORD

Quarterback Matthew Stafford from Dallas, Texas, was perhaps the second-most highly recruited player in Georgia football history behind only Herschel Walker. An injury to Joe Tereshinski forced Stafford into significant playing time amidst the Bulldogs' four losses in five games during the 2006 season. Stafford struggled until the Auburn game, when he finally came into his own, passing for 219 yards and rushing for 83 against one of college football's best defenses in a 22-point Georgia upset.

Against Georgia Tech, Stafford played opposite Yellow Jackets quarterback Reggie Ball. Ball, a senior looking for his first win over Georgia, suffered mightily, completing just six of 22 passes for 42 yards and turning the ball over on three occasions. Stafford, a true freshman, led the Bulldogs to the game-winning score in the final minutes. In the final game of his freshman campaign, Stafford was named Offensive Most Valuable Player in a 31–24 win over Virginia Tech in the 2006 Chick-fil-A Bowl.

Stafford rode the momentum of the end of his initial year at Georgia into the 2007 season. After a 4–2 start, the sophomore was instrumental in the Bulldogs winning their final seven games, including the 2008 Sugar Bowl, and finishing ranked second in the nation in the Associated Press Poll. Despite only starting 20 career games (16–4 record) in two seasons at Georgia, Stafford's 4,272 career passing yards entering the 2008 season already rank sixth in school history.

True freshman quarterback Matthew Stafford guided the Bulldogs 64 yards in 12 plays for a touchdown to defeat the Yellow Jackets in the final minutes. *Photo courtesy of AP Images.*

GAME DETAILS

Georgia 15 • Georgia Tech 12

Date: November 25, 2006

Site: Sanford Stadium

Attendance: 92,746

Records: Georgia 7–4; Georgia Tech 9–2

Rankings: Georgia Tech: No. 16 (AP)/No. 15 (USA Today)

Series: Georgia 57–36–5 (Georgia five-game winning streak)

> **I** got nothing to say on that, dog [in regard to his fumble returned for a touchdown by Taylor].
>
> —REGGIE BALL, GEORGIA TECH QUARTERBACK

The Yellow Jackets would build a 12–7 advantage late in the final quarter. Freshman quarterback Matthew Stafford responded by directing the Bulldogs on a 12-play, 64-yard drive that culminated with a four-yard touchdown pass to Mohamed Massaquoi with only 1:45 left to play. A two-point conversion gave Georgia a 15–12 lead. On the ensuing drive, Paul Oliver intercepted Ball to clinch the Bulldogs' eighth win of the year and the sixth consecutive victory over the Yellow Jackets.

Taylor, who grew up just outside of Athens, Georgia, and whose father also played linebacker for Georgia, brought excitement to an otherwise drudging ballgame. His fumble return also added to the long line of controversial plays in the series' nearly 100-game history.

As Ball fumbled forward, it appeared that Georgia Tech right guard Nate McManus had fallen on the ball. The Yellow Jackets said it was clear that McManus's knee was down; however, the officials (an ACC officiating crew) saw differently. As time seemed to stand still, the referees gazed into the pile, looking to see who recovered Ball's fumble, but they never blew a whistle or marked the ball dead. While Tech exclaimed that Taylor pried or yanked the football from a downed McManus, the Georgia linebacker stated the football was lying "two centimeters" from the leg of a Yellow Jacket. Taylor, who later admitted he thought for certain the officials would blow his fumble return dead, simply picked up the ball and headed for the end zone.

In 1978 Georgia was given a second chance to defeat Georgia Tech on a contestable pass interference called on a two-point conversion. In 1997 a pass-interference penalty on the Yellow Jackets negated a game-clinching interception and led to Mike Bobo's winning touchdown pass to Corey Allen. In both 1998 and 1999, a controversial fumble and nonfumble were the deciding factors in Georgia Tech victories over Georgia.

One of the greatest plays in Georgia football history, Taylor's touchdown return may be added to the list of questionable calls that helped determine the winner in this bitter rivalry.

Tony Taylor is mobbed by teammates Tra Battle (No. 25) and Brandon Miller (No. 12) after his touchdown gave Georgia a third-quarter lead. *Photo courtesy of AP Images.*

TONY TAYLOR

When Tony Taylor arrived in Athens as a freshman from nearby Watkinsville, Georgia, he had much to live up to. Tony's father, Nate, was an undersized but overachieving linebacker at Georgia from 1979 to 1982. Nate started all four seasons as a Bulldog and still ranks fifth at Georgia in career tackles.

Tony was also a smaller but tenacious linebacker for the Bulldogs, starting as only a sophomore in 2003. After missing the '04 season because of an injury, Taylor returned to start at middle linebacker in 2005 and would then lead the team in tackles the following year as a senior. Taylor's nine tackles and two interceptions earned him the Defensive Most Valuable Player Award of the 2006 Chick-fil-A Bowl. His 272 career tackles and 10 interceptions are tied for 20th and 12th, respectively, for all time at Georgia. Taylor's seven interceptions in 2006 were the most in the nation of all nondefensive backs, while his 10 career interceptions are the most ever among nondefensive backs at Georgia. Importantly, Taylor, like his father, played on Bulldogs teams that were a perfect 4–0 against Georgia Tech (like father, like son).

An undrafted free agent by Atlanta of the NFL, Taylor played in all of the Falcons' 16 games in 2007, recording 12 tackles (11 solo).

In 2006, against Ole Miss, Tony Taylor (No. 43) is on the verge of recording one of his 11 tackles against the Rebels n a 14–9 victory. He finished his senior season with a team-high 96 tackles. From his linebacker position, Taylor also intercepted seven passes, leading the nation among nondefensive backs.. *Photo courtesy of AP Images.*

November 9, 1985

No Longer No. 1

Tim Worley's dazzling 89-yard run caps Bulldogs' stunning defeat of top-ranked Florida

In 1985 Georgia made its annual trek to Jacksonville, Florida, for the "World's Largest Outdoor Cocktail Party" and met a University of Florida team like no other before. The Gators were on an 18-game nonlosing streak and were ranked No. 1 in the nation for the first time in school history.

Florida had no apparent weaknesses. It had a dominating defense and a highly productive offense. The Gators' quarterback, sophomore Kerwin Bell, was the second-highest-rated passer in the nation and a Heisman Trophy candidate. Florida's massive and preeminent offensive line was nicknamed the "Great Wall of Florida."

A victory over Georgia seemed so certain that, days before the contest, the Jacksonville Gator Club printed and distributed flyers advertising a postgame victory party at the Jacksonville Coliseum immediately following Florida's win. The Gators were aiming for a national championship, and the Bulldogs were expected to be their next opponent to fall by the wayside.

However, it would be the Gators suffering defeat and falling from the Associated Press Poll's pinnacle spot. Freshman Tim Worley's spectacular 89-yard touchdown jaunt capped an improbable three-touchdown victory for the Bulldogs. Worley's lengthy run tied a school record and was the highlight of the tailback's outstanding career at Georgia, one that included a run for the Heisman Trophy in 1988 as a junior.

In the opening stanza, freshman fullback Keith Henderson streaked up the middle through Florida's dominating defense for a 76-yard score. In the next quarter, Henderson did the same thing, on the exact same play, for a 32-yard touchdown, and Georgia surprisingly led 14–0 and later 17–3 at halftime. Florida's Bell drove the Gators all over the field but could never cross Georgia's goal line. He finished the game with a school-record 408 passing yards on 33 of 49 passing; however, he lost a fumble and also threw an interception. As far as Florida's "Great Wall," it allowed Bell to get sacked five times while paving the way for Gators rushers to gain a meager 28 yards on 30 carries.

Late in the game, Florida was threatening to score, but John L. Williams lost a

Tim Worley outraces Florida's Curtis Stacy into the end zone, completing an 89-yard touchdown run. Worley's lengthy jaunt clinched an upset victory over the Gators and still remains tied as the longest scoring rush in school history. *Photo courtesy of Wingate Downs.*

fumble. Linebacker Steve Boswell recovered the ball on Georgia's own 8-yard line. On first down, Henderson carried for three yards to the 11-yard line.

On the next play, the Bulldogs ran a toss sweep with Worley to the right side. He ran through a huge hole created by the offensive line. Suddenly, a Gators defender grabbed at Worley's leg and nearly tore his shoe off. The shoe slipped from the heel but luckily slipped back on the foot with the next running stride. Distancing himself from Florida's defense, Worley ran down the sideline and then cut back around the

Gators' 40-yard line toward the middle of the field. Here, the tailback outran the last would-be tackler, cornerback Curtis Stacy, for an 89-yard touchdown with 3:58 left on the clock.

Worley's magnificent, 89-yard sprint is still tied with Johnny Griffith's run in 1946 versus Furman for the longest rushing touchdown at Georgia. Most importantly, Worley's accomplishment put the final nail in the top-ranked Gators' coffin in a 24–3 upset victory for the Dogs in what remains the lone win in Georgia football history over a No. 1–ranked team.

TIM WORLEY

As a freshman in 1985, Tim Worley, along with Keith Henderson, Lars Tate, David McCluskey, and James Jackson, was part of a dynamic quintet of Bulldogs rushers who each entered the Florida game averaging at least 40 rushing yards per game for the season. Worley would finish the year second on the team with 627 rushing yards and first with 10 touchdowns.

> **T**he defensive end skated outside [during the 89-yard touchdown run], and after that it was just a matter of beating one guy.
>
> —TIM WORLEY, TAILBACK

Against Florida in 1985, Worley carried the ball just seven times for 104 yards, 89 of which came on his memorable run. According to Georgia's offensive coaching staff, Worley's long jaunt was more important than Henderson's two scoring sprints. Before the 89-yard score, the Gators were only one play from cutting their deficit to a touchdown. In addition, Worley's late touchdown clinched Georgia's only win ever over a top-ranked team.

Worley's 1986 season was cut short because of an injury, and he was redshirted as a junior. In '88 Worley rebounded to rush for 1,216 yards, was responsible for 20 touchdowns, was named first-team All-American, and was a Heisman Trophy candidate until the final couple weeks of the season. He still ranks high in several all-time career categories at Georgia despite playing in only 26 regular-season games.

Crossing Florida's goal line, Worley celebrates as his spectacular run increases the Bulldogs' lead to three touchdowns. *Photo courtesy of Wingate Downs.*

GAME DETAILS

Georgia 24 • Florida 3

Date: November 9, 1985

Site: Gator Bowl

Attendance: 82,327

Records: Georgia 6–1–1; Florida 7–0–1

Rankings: Georgia: No. 17 (AP)/ No. 15 (UPI); Florida: No. 1 (AP)

Series: Georgia 40–21–2 (Florida one-game winning streak)

> **G**eorgia played one of its greatest games ever today.... I don't know how you play any better. Everybody was superb.
>
> —VINCE DOOLEY, GEORGIA HEAD COACH

KEITH HENDERSON

For the 1985 season freshman Keith Henderson led the Bulldogs in rushing, including 145 yards on nine carries and the two long scoring runs against Florida. Against the Gators, he spearheaded a rushing attack that gained 344 yards and averaged 7.3 yards per carry. Entering the game, Florida had the 10th-best rushing defense in the nation, allowing just 105 yards per game and 2.8 yards per carry.

Like Tim Worley, Henderson missed part of the '86 season with an injury, was redshirted in 1987, and left one year early for the NFL following the '88 season. Despite playing fewer than three seasons and leaving the school two decades ago, Henderson remains ranked 15th at Georgia in career all-purpose yardage.

Due primarily to Keith Henderson's 145 rushing yards and two touchdowns, Florida was upset 24–3 in 1985 and fell from its No. 1 ranking.
Photo courtesy of Wingate Downs.

PUNT PINS DOWN GREENIES

Bill Hartman's 44-yard boot against Tulane in 1937 leads to Vassa Cate's scoring return and a victory

The 1937 season began auspiciously for the Georgia Bulldogs as they started 4–1 with only a one-point loss keeping them from perfection at Holy Cross, which would finish the season undefeated and ranked 14th in the nation. However, injuries began to take their toll on the Bulldogs squad, and Georgia suffered shutout losses in its next two ballgames.

The Georgia-Tulane game had been advertised as a battle between the teams' fullbacks: captain Bill Hartman of Georgia and Tulane's "Honest" John Andrews. This was no longer the case, as the veteran Hartman was forced to play quarterback for the first time as a Bulldog because of the rash of injuries.

It was a 44-yard punt by Hartman, however, in the opening quarter that led to Georgia's lone touchdown and a Bulldogs victory. Hartman had several marvelous punts on that day versus Tulane, but none was better than the one pinning Tulane near its own goal line—the greatest punt in the history of Georgia football.

Late in the first quarter, Georgia faced fourth down and 1 on the Green Wave's 46-yard line. The Bulldogs were having considerable difficulty moving the football, so coach Harry Mehre elected to punt the ball instead of going for the first down. Precision punting by Hartman resulted in the 44-yard kick going out of bounds at Tulane's 2-yard line.

Seventy or so years ago, before most football offenses began utilizing a passing attack and sustaining long offensive drives via the run and pass, teams would often punt prior to fourth down if backed up close to their goal line. On first down on its own 2-yard line, Tulane's Stanley Nyhan punted to Vassa Cate. Cate, a 165-pound sophomore, took the punt on the Green Wave 37-yard line, twisted and wove his way through would-be tacklers, and headed down the left sideline abetted by excellent blocking for a touchdown. Billy Mims's point-after try was successful, and the Bulldogs had an early 7–0 lead. Cate's return was one of only two Bulldogs touchdowns in five games from October 30 until December 10.

Tulane missed out on several scoring opportunities during the contest. Just before halftime, Tulane's Bill "Dub" Mathis was dropped for a three-yard loss by Marvin Gillespie on fourth and goal from inside Georgia's 1-yard line. In the third quarter, Tulane again reached inside the Bulldogs' 4-yard line but came up empty.

With 12 minutes remaining in the game, Tulane finally scored on a touchdown pass; however, Mathis's point after was blocked by John Davis, preserving Georgia's one-point lead. The Green Wave's two final possessions ended with interceptions: Jim Cavan picked off a pass in his own end zone, and Walter Troutman clinched the upset win with an interception at his own 20-yard line.

The Bulldogs offense struggled, gaining only four total yards and one first down during the entire game. In comparison, Tulane, in a losing effort, had 228 yards and 12 first downs.

Without a doubt, it was Hartman's punting that won the game for the Bulldogs. He averaged 40 yards per kick on 17 punts, including a long punt of 72. Most importantly, it was Hartman's first-quarter, 44-yard punt that went out of bounds at the 2-yard line that led to an eventual 7–6 Georgia victory.

Prior to becoming an assistant coach at Georgia for 36 seasons through 1994, Bill Hartman was a standout fullback for the Bulldogs. An All-American in 1937, Hartman's extraordinary punting against Tulane led to a 7–6 Georgia win. *Photo courtesy of AP Images.*

Hartman was a Deadeye Dick with his kicks. He placed the ball expertly out on the Tulane 2. Such kicking was slowly wearing Tulane out.

—JACK TROY, *ATLANTA JOURNAL*

HARRY MEHRE

The 1937 season was the final of 10 years spent by Harry Mehre as Georgia's head coach before he left to coach Ole Miss from 1938 to 1942 and 1944 to 1945. Although the '37 campaign was not one of his most successful years at Georgia, it was arguably Mehre's best coaching effort.

The Bulldogs entered the last month of the season marred with injuries and facing superior opposition. Mehre's squad responded without a loss, defeating Tulane and Miami of Florida and tying Auburn and Georgia Tech to finish 6–3–2 for the season.

Mehre still ranks fourth at Georgia in all-time coaching victories with 59. Importantly, he was known as a coach who always had his Bulldogs well prepared for the big games. During his tenure, Georgia achieved a 6–2–2 record against Georgia Tech and was 8–3–1 against the eastern elite: Fordham, New York University, and Yale.

Soon after Hartman's great punt, Vassa Cate (No. 25) returned a Tulane kick 37 yards for a touchdown.
Photo courtesy of Hargrett Rare Book & Manuscript Library/University of Georgia Libraries.

Game Details

Georgia 7 • Tulane 6

Date: November 13, 1937

Site: Sanford Stadium

Attendance: 13,000

Records: Georgia 4–3; Tulane 4–2–1

Series: Tied 5–5–1 (Georgia two-game winning streak)

> It is the best game I have ever seen a Georgia team play against a superior team.
>
> —HARRY MEHRE, GEORGIA HEAD COACH

Bill Hartman

In 1937 fullback Bill Hartman was selected first-team All-American; it would be four seasons later before a Georgia player, Frank Sinkwich, earned the same recognition. Considered one of college football's most underrated players at the time, the versatile Hartman played quarterback against Tulane because of injuries and won the game with his punting.

Two weeks later against Georgia Tech, it was Hartman again who was responsible for the Bulldogs' points. He returned the second-half kickoff 93 yards for a touchdown in a 6–6 tie with the favored Yellow Jackets. Georgia Tech certainly would have scored more if not for Hartman's punting. Kicking a rain-soaked, heavy football, he averaged 42 yards on 15 punts.

Hartman played one season in the NFL and returned to Georgia in 1939 as an assistant and volunteer kicking coach for 36 seasons through 1994. Hartman is well remembered as one of the most beloved Bulldogs ever and as a man who put the University of Georgia and its football program ahead of his personal interests.

THERE GOES HERSCHEL!

Freshman Walker outraces entire Gamecocks defense for a breathtaking 76-yard touchdown

Georgia and South Carolina both had surpassed most expectations by November 1980. The Bulldogs were undefeated and ranked fourth in the nation. Unranked in the preseason, the Gamecocks had lost only to Southern California and were positioned at No. 14 by the pollsters. The Georgia–South Carolina meeting had garnered enough attention around the country to televise the event—only the third game ever nationally televised in Athens. Although the Dogs and 'Cocks were considered an appealing matchup, most of the national media would not have come to Athens if not for the clash between players who were probably college football's best two running backs.

South Carolina's George Rogers was primarily responsible for the Gamecocks' best record since 1924. Rogers, a Georgia native, had already rushed for more than 1,000 yards in only seven games and was the odds-on favorite to receive the Heisman Trophy. The senior running back had always performed well against Georgia, rushing for 310 yards on 66 carries in three games since 1977. He was also the key reason why South Carolina had defeated the Bulldogs two consecutive years.

The highly recruited Herschel Walker chose Georgia over the rest of the nation and instantly made a tremendous impact. Although he had played sparingly in the fourth and fifth games of the season, Walker had rushed for 877 yards in seven contests, ranking ninth in the country in rushing. Herschel quickly made a name for himself by scoring on long runs. He had already rushed for four touchdowns of 48 yards or more, including a 76-yarder against Texas A&M. However, the freshman phenom's best run was yet to come.

Early in the third quarter, with Georgia leading 3–0, the Bulldogs had possession on their own 24-yard line. Walker took a delayed handoff from quarterback Buck Belue on a play designed to be run through the right portion of the offensive line. Instead, Walker slid off right tackle. Aided by fullback Jimmy Womack's crushing block on a Gamecocks linebacker, Walker headed toward his right sideline and was off to the races. As he dashed down the sideline, three different South Carolina defenders had perfect angles

Herschel Walker slides off right tackle, heading toward the sideline against South Carolina in 1980. The freshman tailback outraced the entire Gamecocks defense, gaining 76 yards for a touchdown. *Photo courtesy of Wingate Downs.*

to intercept the fast-moving freshman. However, never before had college football seen a back combine such speed, size, and power. Walker was not to be caught, leaving the last would-be tackler 15 yards behind him on his way to a 76-yard touchdown.

At halftime, the Bulldogs held a 3–0 lead. According to Coach Vince Dooley, it should have been by more, but poor coaching decisions and a missed 22-yard field-goal attempt had cost Georgia a wider scoring margin.

Georgia took the second-half kickoff and, from its own 20-yard line, gained four

yards in two plays. Faced with third down and 6, Tailback Draw 22 was the play called, and Walker responded with his long jaunt to pay dirt. What makes Walker's run so remarkable was the fact that he outran three Gamecocks who each could have taken him down—that is, if he was any other ordinary running back.

The fact that Walker first outran left cornerback Harry Skipper, South Carolina's fastest player, should have been indicative that no one would catch him. Next, free safety Robert Perlotte had an angle to catch him but could not. Finally,

GEORGE ROGERS

Almost as big a story as George Rogers playing in Athens in 1980 was the fact that his dad would be watching him in Sanford Stadium. After nearly eight years of imprisonment for nonpremeditated murder, George Rogers Sr. recently had been paroled and released from a Georgia prison. Having been a free man for only 10 days, the father was able to witness his electrifying son play football for the first time.

Rogers would eventually win the Heisman Trophy on December 1 and would later be the first pick of the 1981 NFL draft. In his first season with New Orleans, Rogers would rush for nearly 1,700 yards on a dreadful team and would be chosen NFL Rookie of the Year. His seven-year NFL career featured four 1,000-yard rushing seasons.

Since retiring from professional football, Rogers has returned to South Carolina for his degree, worked at the university's Blatt Physical Education Center, and has been South Carolina's color analyst for its television replays on Charter Sports Southeast (CSS).

South Carolina's George Rogers eludes defenders Jimmy Payne (No. 87) and Tim Crowe (No. 91) for several of his 168 rushing yards. Rogers eventually captured the Heisman Trophy in 1980, but against Georgia he was outshined by freshman Herschel Walker in a 13–10 Bulldogs victory. *Photo courtesy of Wingate Downs.*

right cornerback Mark Bridges was left in the tailback's dust.

Georgia would lead 13–0 before the Gamecocks stormed back and trailed by only three points late in the third quarter. With 5:22 left in the contest and South Carolina threatening to at least tie the game, Rogers, who finished with 168 yards on 35 carries, lost a fumble that was recovered by the Bulldogs on their own 16-yard line. Georgia would eventually run out the clock and defeat the 'Cocks, 13–10.

Walker outdid Rogers by rushing for 219 yards on a school-record 43 carries. When asked after the game which player, Walker or Rogers, he would rather have on his team, Dooley replied: "They are both great backs, but I'll take Herschel. For one thing, he has three more years to play."

Herschel would play two more seasons following 1980 before departing early for the professional ranks. In becoming perhaps college football's greatest player ever, Walker had several lengthy touchdown runs that helped distinguish his outstanding collegiate career. None of them were more memorable than his 76-yarder against South Carolina in 1980.

GAME DETAILS

Georgia 13 • South Carolina 10

Date: November 1, 1980

Site: Sanford Stadium

Attendance: 62,200

Records: Georgia 7–0; South Carolina 6–1

Rankings: Georgia: No. 4 (AP)/ No. 4 (UPI); South Carolina: No. 14 (AP)/ No. 14 (UPI)

Series: Georgia 26–6–2 (South Carolina two-game winning streak)

> There was not another back in the game who could have scored on that play.
>
> **—VINCE DOOLEY, GEORGIA HEAD COACH**

HERSCHEL WALKER

Herschel Walker's 219-yard rushing performance against South Carolina in 1980 instantly propelled him into the running for the Heisman Trophy. After rushing for a combined 315 yards against Florida and Auburn, Walker would finish third in the trophy's voting. His 205 yards and three touchdowns against Georgia Tech in the regular-season finale were unfortunately not considered because the votes had already been submitted. If Walker's performance against Georgia Tech had been considered prior to the voting, he might have been accorded the Heisman, even though he was only a freshman.

Walker followed up his sensational freshman season with second- and first-place Heisman Trophy finishes in 1981 and 1982, respectively. His third-second-first Heisman finishes are unprecedented and one of many reasons why he is Georgia's greatest

> I surprised myself [with the 76-yard scoring run]. I didn't know I had that kind of ability.
>
> **—HERSCHEL WALKER, TAILBACK**

player ever, if not college football's greatest. Most importantly, Walker was the catalyst for the Bulldogs' success from 1980 to 1982, when they achieved a 33–3 record and won three Southeastern Conference titles and a national championship.

Since retiring from professional football after the 1997 season, Walker has been involved in a variety of business opportunities. Currently, he owns and operates Renaissance Man Food Services, LLC.

October 31, 1942

Poschner Propels Bulldogs to No. 1

George Poschner's acrobatic reception from Frank Sinkwich defeats Alabama in '42

After nearly a decade of mediocrity, Georgia football began making great strides in the early 1940s. In 1942 Coach Wally Butts had a stellar senior class, featuring All-Americans Frank Sinkwich (halfback) and George Poschner (end), that led the Bulldogs to an unblemished record through six games and a No. 2 national ranking. Playing at the neutral site of Atlanta's Grant Field because gas rationing was in effect during World War II, Georgia faced third-ranked Alabama. The undefeated Crimson Tide had been chosen national champions by the Houlgate System the previous season and looked to duplicate this achievement in 1942. Georgia hoped to defeat Alabama for the first time in 13 years in a game that had been sold out for nearly a month.

In the fourth quarter, the Bulldogs had rallied and cut their deficit to three points, 10–7. The Crimson Tide defense had slowed the great Sinkwich's running (he finished with only 39 rushing yards on 20 carries), but the eventual Heisman Trophy recipient's aerial attack suddenly could not be stopped. Georgia

had a second down and 11 on Alabama's 15-yard line. Sinkwich fired a pass down the middle near the goal line. Just as Poschner made a leaping catch between two Crimson Tide defenders, he was hit both high and low. Georgia's magnificent left end completely turned a flip in the air and came down on his head and one shoulder. Poschner rolled into the end zone, clutching the football to his chest. It was an extraordinary, acrobatic catch for a touchdown made by one of the best ends in football.

Georgia had dedicated the game to its former center, Tommy Witt, who had died during the early stages of the war. In the second half and with Alabama holding a 10–0 lead, someone sarcastically stated in Georgia's offensive huddle how proud Witt must have been of his Bulldogs teammates' performance thus far. The remark "was like a message from God," Sinkwich said years later. "The effect was electrical—everyone felt it."

Georgia's offense suddenly came alive as Sinkwich completed five of six passes for 77 yards. The final completion was a five-yard touchdown toss early in the final quarter to Poschner, who made the scoring catch just beyond the reach of defensive back Al Sabo.

Later in the quarter, Alabama's Norm "Monk" Mosley was forced to quick kick from his own territory. Earlier in the game, Mosley's first quick kick had traveled 78 yards and pinned Georgia near its own goal line. However, Mosley's second kick, the turning point of the contest, landed on the Bulldogs' 30-yard line, but instead of rolling for additional yardage, bounced straight up in the air and backward two yards. Georgia took over on its own 32-yard line, trailing 10–7.

On first down, Sinkwich passed to Van Davis, who lateraled to Ken Keuper, who streaked to the Crimson Tide's 48-yard line. From there, "Fireball" Frankie Sinkwich completed a 24-yard pass to Poschner. From Alabama's 24-yard line, Sinkwich threw incomplete but followed it up with an eight-yard completion to Davis. On third and two from the 16-yard line, Sinkwich rushed for two yards and a critical first down. On first down, Sinkwich lost a yard back to the 15.

Next, Poschner made his second touchdown reception while "standing on his head." How Poschner held on to the football, no one knows, but it gave Georgia its first lead of the ballgame.

All-American George Poschner caught two touchdown passes from Frank Sinkwich—including one while "standing on his head"—in a 21–10 victory over Alabama in 1942. *Photo courtesy of Hargrett Rare Book & Manuscript Library/ University of Georgia Libraries.*

On the ensuing possession, Georgia added an additional score for good measure. Alabama's Russ Craft was hit by Walter Maguire and fumbled. Andy Dudish of Georgia grabbed the midair fumble and ran 19 yards into the end zone.

Although he had his worst rushing performance in quite some time in the 21–10 win, Sinkwich completed 17 of 32 passes for 222 yards, including nine of 11 for 154 yards on Georgia's two rallying touchdown drives.

Author Loran Smith describes the 1942 Alabama game as Sinkwich's greatest thrill at Georgia. Following the contest, a tearful Wally Butts proclaimed that the victory was the biggest thrill of his life. They both experienced additional excitement when, on the following Monday, Georgia was ranked the No. 1 team in the nation. Poschner's bewildering touchdown catch had not only stunned a packed Grant Field but placed the Bulldogs into college football's top ranking for the first time in history.

GEORGE POSCHNER

If not for Frank Sinkwich, George Poschner would not have been a Georgia Bulldog. A skinny, 150-pound recruit one year removed from high school, Poschner grew to a 180-pound All-American end by 1942. After breaking his arm against the University of Alabama as a junior, Poschner retaliated against the Crimson Tide with his two-touchdown performance in 1942. The Youngstown, Ohio, native was also an outstanding defender. On Alabama's possession after Poschner's unbelievable touchdown grab, he sacked Norm "Monk" Mosley for a seven-yard loss, which led to Andy Dudish's fumble return for a score. In the same game, writer Bill Cunningham wrote that when Poschner "hit his man you could see Crimson legs in the air."

In three seasons (1940–1942) on Georgia's varsity, Poschner scored 10 touchdowns, nine receiving and one by recovering a nonreturned kickoff, and he scored 61 career points. Six of his touchdowns were scored in his senior All-American campaign.

Poschner followed his friend Sinkwich from high school to Georgia and then again to the NFL when he too was drafted by the Detroit Lions in 1943 (eighth round, 61st overall pick). However, he never played professionally. Poschner was soon partially paralyzed and lost both legs because of injuries sustained in the Battle of the Bulge in World War II. Nevertheless, one of college football's greatest ends during his time lived to be 85 years old until his death in 2005.

Led by Frank Sinkwich and George Poschner, Georgia earned a bid to play UCLA in the 1943 Rose Bowl. His head down, Sinkwich picks up yardage through the Bruins defense. *Photo courtesy of AP Images.*

GAME DETAILS

Georgia 21 • Alabama 10

Date: October 31, 1942

Site: Grant Field

Attendance: 32,000

Records: Georgia 6–0; Alabama 5–0

Rankings: Georgia: No. 2 (AP); Alabama: No. 3 (AP)

Series: Alabama 14–11–3 (Alabama four-game winning streak)

> We stopped 'em [the Bulldogs] running, but we couldn't check that passing attack.
>
> —FRANK THOMAS, ALABAMA HEAD COACH

FRANK SINKWICH

Frank Sinkwich's performance on the gridiron is well documented. He finished fourth in the Heisman Trophy voting as a junior when he became the first player in the history of college football to amass 2,000 yards of total offense. As a senior, he was the Heisman recipient and ended a collegiate football career that still remains one of the very best at the University of Georgia.

Few realize that Sinkwich almost did not come to Georgia but nearly attended Ohio State University. When coach Wally Butts recruited the prep star from Youngstown, Ohio, Sinkwich insisted that Butts also give a scholarship to his hometown friend, George Poschner. Butts was not overly impressed with Poschner but wanted Sinkwich so badly, he offered scholarships to both Youngstown natives.

After a short stint with the U.S. Marines, Sinkwich was the first selection of the 1943 NFL draft. By his second season in the professional ranks, Sinkwich was named the NFL's Most Valuable Player in 1944, playing for the Detroit Lions. However, by 1947, because of a knee injury, his football career had ended. Sinkwich was a successful businessman for years until his death in 1990.

> You're the greatest bunch of battlers I have ever seen.
>
> —WALLY BUTTS, GEORGIA HEAD COACH, TO HIS PLAYERS AFTER THE VICTORY

September 20, 1980

THE RETURNER'S LONG JAUNT

Scott "the Returner" Woerner intercepts Clemson's Homer Jordan and runs 98 yards down the sideline

Professional scouts came to Athens for the Georgia-Clemson game in 1980 primarily to observe Bulldogs senior Scott Woerner. The All-American candidate at cornerback was selected defensive captain for the game; however, there was a slight issue. Woerner was not starting and had been demoted to back up Greg Bell. By his own admission, Woerner had played poorly in Georgia's first two games of the season. Bell, on the other hand, had played well in a reserve role. Woerner had started every game since the 1978 season opener but had to surrender his starting left corner-back position for the Clemson contest.

Clemson sophomore quarterback Homer Jordan was returning home to square off against former high school teammates Amp Arnold and Jimmy Payne and the rest of the Georgia Bulldogs. An all-state player at Athens's Cedar Shoals High School, Jordan chose Clemson over Georgia when he was told he would play a position other than quarterback for the Bulldogs. The strong-armed, quick-footed Jordan had seen limited playing time as a freshman for the Tigers, completing three of 11 passes for 28 yards in 1979. Nevertheless, Homer was named Clemson's starter in '80 and passed for 142 yards and rushed for another 68 in the Tigers' season-opening victory a week prior to facing the Bulldogs.

Late in the opening quarter, Georgia held a 7–0 advantage, but Jordan had driven the Tigers to the Bulldogs' 11-yard line. On third down and nine, Jordan threw over the middle into the end zone. Woerner, who had recently entered the game, picked off the Athens native's pass a couple of yards behind his goal line. As he gained his footing in the end zone, Woerner noticed down the sideline that just one Tiger stood between him and the opposite goal line. "The Returner" Woerner, who had run a punt back for a touchdown earlier in the game, decided to return the interception out of his end zone.

Woerner headed to his right and began dashing down the sideline. The lone would-be tackler he had spotted between him and the goal line and been taken out of the play

Scott Woerner streaks down the sideline after intercepting a Clemson pass in his own end zone. He was not tackled until reaching the Tigers' 2-yard line. *Photo courtesy of Wingate Downs.*

with a beautiful block by roverback Chris Welton. Woerner was not stopped until he had raced 98 yards and was caught from behind by tailback Chuck McSwain.

Herschel Walker rushed for one yard, and then Buck Belue followed with a one-yard sneak for a touchdown. Despite having run only five plays for minus-two yards in the first quarter, Georgia had jumped out

to a 14–0 lead on two magnificent returns by Woerner. At halftime, the Bulldogs still led 14–10, despite the Tigers having a 16–0 advantage in first downs and a 25:10–4:50 upper hand in time of possession.

After rushing for only 12 yards in the first half, Walker gained 109 in the final two quarters, leading to two Georgia field goals. The Tigers kicked two field goals also and trailed 20–16 late in the game. Clemson quarterback Mike Gasque, filling in for a benched Jordan, brought the Tigers to the Bulldogs' 10-yard line. On second and goal, with approximately two minutes remaining, Gasque's pass was tipped by linebacker Frank Ros and intercepted by safety Jeff Hipp to preserve Georgia's undefeated season.

On the first drive of the game, Clemson was forced to punt to Woerner, who returned the Tigers' kick 67 yards for a score. On Clemson's third possession, the Tigers moved 49 yards to Georgia's 11-yard line. After a Clemson timeout following a Jordan incomplete pass on second down, the Tigers lined up in a flanked-left offensive formation opposite of the Bulldogs' man-to-man pass coverage. Woerner's responsibility was to cover the tight end, who, on the play, blocked for Jordan instead of running a pass route. Woerner responded by running into the passing lane, intercepting the pass, and ruining Homer's homecoming.

HOMER JORDAN

In his homecoming return to Athens, Georgia, Homer Jordan spent much of the day on the sideline watching backup quarterback Mike Gasque. Jordan was ineffective against the Bulldogs, losing four yards on eight carries and throwing for just 50 yards on five of 11 passing, including Scott Woerner's interception. Jordan's performance nearly lost him his starting job to Gasque; however, Jordan would eventually start every game for the Tigers in 1980.

As a junior in 1981, Jordan became a household name when he directed Clemson to a perfect 12–0 record and a national championship. In earning All–Atlantic Coast Conference honors, Jordan gained 2,116 yards of total offense, including 194 in a 13–3 upset win over Georgia. In 1982 Jordan threw four interceptions against the Bulldogs on his second return to Athens in a 13–7 Georgia victory. However, although he spent much of the season injured, Homer was instrumental in Clemson's 9–1–1 record and No. 8 national ranking. Jordan played four seasons from 1983 to 1986 in the Canadian Football League for three teams.

Jordan has been an assistant football coach at either Clarke Central or Cedar Shoals high school in Athens since 2004.

Clemson quarterback Homer Jordan did not fare well on his two return trips to his native Athens, losing in both 1980 and 1982. *Photo courtesy of Wingate Downs.*

GAME DETAILS

Georgia 20 • Clemson 16

Date: September 20, 1980

Site: Sanford Stadium

Attendance: 60,800

Records: Georgia 2–0; Clemson 1–0

Rankings: Georgia: No. 10 (AP)/ No. 9 (UPI)

Series: Georgia 32–13–3 (Clemson one-game winning streak)

> What a day he [Woerner] had.... He gave us the [first] 14 points of the game, really.
>
> —VINCE DOOLEY, GEORGIA HEAD COACH

SCOTT WOERNER

Scott Woerner, considered Georgia's top college prospect out of high school, was a standout running back and defensive back at Jonesboro High School, coached by Weyman Sellers—cocaptain of Georgia's 1948 Southeastern Conference championship team.

While at Georgia, Woerner displayed a combination of skills at both defensive back and returning punts better than any Bulldog before him or since, other than perhaps Jake Scott. Woerner's 13 interceptions during his career tie him for fourth place in school history, his 839 kick return yards rank him fifth, and his 1,077 punt return yards were a Georgia record until 2003. Woerner was chosen first-team All-American in 1980.

Woerner is best remembered for his dazzling punt return for a touchdown against Georgia Tech in 1978; his two interceptions against Notre Dame in the '81

> Once I got around the corner [after the interception], it was just a foot race.
>
> —SCOTT WOERNER, GEORGIA CORNERBACK

Sugar Bowl, when he was runner-up behind Herschel Walker in the MVP voting; and the two significant returns against Clemson in '80, without which the Bulldogs would have been defeated.

Woerner was an NFL third-round selection of Atlanta in 1981, leading the Falcons in punt returns as a rookie. He was a standout defensive back from 1983 to 1985 with the United States Football League's Philadelphia/Baltimore Stars, and he played for New Orleans' scab team during the 1987 NFL strike.

September 14, 1968

38 Trapped on the Tartan Turf

Tennessee's game-tying touchdown catch on fourth down in '68 is later declared an incomplete pass

It was undetermined what the '68 Bulldogs dreaded more—opening the season on the road against highly favored Tennessee or playing on its new and controversial field surface, Tartan Turf. The Volunteers, who finished the previous year ranked second in the nation, returned most of their squad and were considered to have no weaknesses entering the season. During the summer, without asking permission from the Southeastern Conference, Tennessee had removed its natural grass and become only the second college football team in the country to install artificial turf. Tennessee's disputed action enraged Georgia, especially athletics director Joel Eaves, who pointed out that the Volunteers would have an unfair advantage over opponents because no visiting teams had played or practiced, for that matter, on an artificial surface.

The Bulldogs unexpectedly held a 17–9 advantage with only four seconds remaining in the game. An upset victory for Georgia was all but clinched as Tennessee

encountered fourth down and goal from the Bulldogs' 20-yard line. Quarterback Bubba Wyche dropped back in the pocket, set himself, and fired a pass over the middle to Gary Kreis. Just as Kreis tried to make the catch near Georgia's goal line, cornerback Penny Pennington tackled the receiver, jarring the ball loose. Kreis rolled into the end zone and, in the process, gained possession of the football. To Georgia's disbelief, officials ruled a Tennessee touchdown.

With time expired, Wyche passed to tight end Ken DeLong for a two-point conversion to end the game in a 17–17 tie. Tennessee celebrated on the field, acting as if it had won the game. Head coach Doug Dickey later stated that he had never been prouder of a team in his life. On the contrary, several Bulldogs were brought to tears as Georgia felt as though it had suffered a defeat.

With an eight-point lead late in the game, Georgia, attempting to run out the clock, committed a five-yard penalty that forced a punt by Spike Jones. Following the kick into the end zone, Tennessee started from its own 20-yard line with only 2:41 left in the contest. Wyche, who would pass for six of his 14 completions on the drive, began moving the Volunteers toward the Bulldogs' goal. Tennessee faced a second and goal on Georgia's 4-yard line with approximately 30 seconds remaining, but successive eight-yard sacks by Billy Payne and Bill Stanfill pushed the Volunteers back to the 20-yard line.

Kreis was instructed in the huddle to simply "get into the end zone." On his pass route, he ran downfield and came back across the middle, where he was thrown the ball and greeted by Pennington. Kreis later admitted that he did bobble the ball as he was being tackled, but he had not dropped it as he rolled into the end zone. Two days later, it would be revealed that the receiver was inaccurate in his assessment.

Rumors and unconfirmed reports were disclosed the following Monday morning that Kreis had actually trapped the football as he rolled over Georgia's goal line. Members of the media examined game film and concluded that Wyche's pass

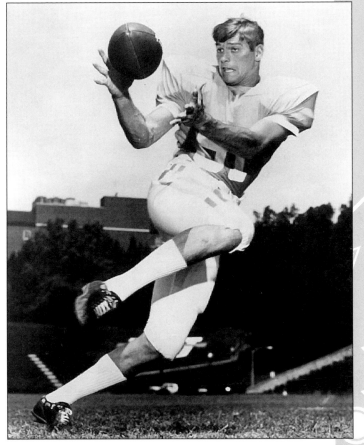

Against Georgia in 1968, Tennessee's Gary Kreis caught a touchdown pass on the final play of the game that, after reviewing game film, was determined an incomplete pass. *Photo courtesy of the University of Tennessee Athletics Department.*

definitely bounced from Kreis's hands to the turf and then rebounded directly back into his arms as he rolled into the end zone. As Pennington and Kreis rolled over the goal line, the receiver was still trying to gain possession. Four officials had mistakenly taken victory away from Georgia; what was ruled a touchdown was actually an incomplete pass.

Y**ou don't win football games on Sunday.**

—VINCE DOOLEY, GEORGIA HEAD COACH,
IN RESPONSE TO GAME FILM LATER PROVING KREIS TRAPPED HIS CATCH

Billy Payne

The son of Porter Payne, an all-conference tackle on Georgia's Southeastern Conference championship team of 1948, Billy Payne is one of the University of Georgia's most prominent graduates. On the gridiron, he started at offensive end for the Bulldogs in 1966 and 1967, leading the team in receiving as only a sophomore. In two seasons, he caught 22 passes for 288 yards, including a 13-yard touchdown reception in a win over Kentucky in '66. In addition, he made three catches for 49 yards and a touchdown against Southern Methodist in the 1966 Cotton Bowl.

Labeled by Vince Dooley as "the best 60-minute player I ever coached," Payne was abruptly moved exclusively to defensive end for his senior year of 1968. He responded by making several notable sacks, intercepting three passes, and was one of four Bulldogs named All-SEC by both the Associated Press and United Press International.

Payne received his law degree from Georgia in 1973. After practicing law in Atlanta, Payne spearheaded Atlanta's effort to bring the 1996 Olympic Games to the city and was the top administrator for the Games. In 2006 Payne was chosen chairman of the Augusta National Golf Club, home of the Masters.

In 1968, his first and only season playing defense at Georgia, Billy Payne (left) was an All-SEC performer. He later played a key role in bringing the Olympic Games to Atlanta in 1996. *Photo courtesy of AP Images.*

Vince Dooley

When game film reportedly established that Tennessee had trapped instead of completed its last-ditch pass to tie the Bulldogs in '68, the University of Georgia released only one comment. Whereas many coaches, especially today, would have ranted and raved about their teams being cheated out of a victory, Coach Dooley simply responded that games are not won on Sunday; looking at film after a game was not going change its outcome. It was an honorable reaction by a young coach who, at the time, was only in his mid-thirties.

Rebounding from the bitter tie with the Volunteers, Dooley's 'Dogs won eight of their next nine games. Included was a 10–10 tie with Houston where, unlike its first tie, Georgia was extremely fortunate not to lose.

The Bulldogs ended the 1968 regular season with an 8–0–2 record—one of only six regular-season campaigns Georgia has finished undefeated. Despite a loss to Arkansas in the Sugar Bowl, the Bulldogs were still declared national champions by the Litkenhous ratings.

GAME DETAILS

Georgia 17 • Tennessee 17

Date: September 14, 1968

Site: Neyland Stadium

Attendance: 60,603

Records: Georgia 0–0; Tennessee 0–0

Rankings: Tennessee: No. 9 (AP)

Series: Tied 6–6–1 (Tennessee three-game winning streak)

> **I** wasn't going to drop that one. No way.
> —GARY KREIS, TENNESSEE WIDE RECEIVER,
> ON HIS GAME-TYING CATCH

Tennessee quarterback Bubba Wyche threw the controversial touchdown to Gary Kreis and subsequently tossed a two-point conversion to tie the Bulldogs 17-17.
Photo courtesy of University of Tennessee Athletics Department.

October 12, 1929

CATFISH—CATCH OF THE DAY

Catfish Smith's touchdown catch highlights a 15-point effort in Sanford Stadium's dedication

Dr. Steadman Sanford, the University of Georgia's faculty chairman of athletics, had worked diligently and aggressively to bring a new stadium to Georgia football and to bring a formidable opponent. By the 1929 season, Sanford's dream had become reality as Sanford Stadium had been built and its dedicatory game had been scheduled on the third home date versus eastern power Yale.

Days prior to the stadium's dedication, thousands began filling the streets of Athens, Georgia. Patrons representing every section of the country came by 40 special trains, airplanes, and 9,000 automobiles. In a town of only 15,000 residents, 35,000 spectators filled the new stadium, including governors of five states. During what was said to be the greatest weekend ever in the city of Athens, a "Catfish" had one of the greatest single-game performances in Bulldogs history.

Georgia led slightly favored Yale, 9–0, late in the game and had the ball on the Elis' 22-yard line. Spurgeon Chandler took a snap from center, started to his right, and drifted back a couple of yards. Sophomore Vernon

"Catfish" Smith, playing at left end, was running wide-open down the middle of the field. Chandler looped a high pass toward Smith, who caught it over his right shoulder and fell in the end zone for a Georgia touchdown. The scoring reception by Smith, who had also been responsible for the Bulldogs' previous nine points, was remarkable and incited the already crazed, sold-out crowd into an unbridled frenzy.

The 1929 Georgia Bulldogs were an extremely young squad, with eight of its 11 regulars only sophomores. The "Flaming Sophs" demonstrated their inexperience by getting upset by Oglethorpe in the season opener. Yale, on the other hand, had defeated Georgia five of the previous six years at its Yale Bowl in New Haven, Connecticut, but was playing football in the South for the first time ever.

During a scoreless second quarter, Yale's Donald McLennan was forced to punt from his own 9-yard line. Sophomores Jack Roberts and Red Maddox swarmed McLennan and blocked the kick behind the Blue and White's goal line. Smith came out of a pile in the end zone with the football, and Georgia had scored a touchdown. Smith also kicked the extra point to give the southern Bulldogs a 7–0 lead.

In the third quarter, a Smith punt went out of bounds on the Yale 14-yard line. The Eli promptly lined up to punt the football back to Georgia; however, the snap went over Yale star Albie Booth's head into the end zone. Booth retrieved the ball and attempted to run it out over his goal line but fell just short. Smith forced Booth out of bounds before he could get out of his own end zone, scoring a safety for Georgia.

In the closing minutes of play, Georgia's Bennie Rothstein intercepted his second pass of the game. Starting from Yale's 30-yard line, Georgia moved eight yards on two plunges. This set up Chandler's capping and noteworthy touchdown pass to Smith. Catching the arching spiral from Chandler on the Eli 2-yard line, Smith crossed Yale's goal line and calmly placed the football on the ground.

Sanford Stadium's first crowd was all but calm as they went absolutely crazy following the Chandler-to-Catfish touchdown. They had become part of history in witness-

Playing in just his third game on Georgia's varsity, Vernon "Catfish" Smith was responsible for every one of the 15 points scored in the 1929 Georgia-Yale game. His final six points came on a remarkable over-the-shoulder, 22-yard touchdown catch. *Photo courtesy of Hargrett Rare Book & Manuscript Library/University of Georgia Libraries.*

ing Georgia easily handle Yale, 15–0, on a special date in history for both Georgia football and the city of Athens. In doing so, the spectators witnessed "Catfish" Smith score every single one of the dedicatory game's 15 points, including the final six on a towering touchdown toss.

Pictured here is a ground-level view of Sanford Stadium's dedicatory game on October 12, 1929—a 15–0 Georgia victory. *Photo courtesy of Hargrett Rare Book & Manuscript Library/University of Georgia Libraries.*

THE CATCH

Georgia's center snapped the football directly to left halfback Spurgeon Chandler, moving from his left to right. On the snap of the ball, left end Vernon "Catfish" Smith ran straight toward Yale's end zone. After Chandler received the snap, he dropped back a couple of steps near the 30 and flung a high pass toward a wide-open Smith. Smith caught the ball on the 2 and easily crossed the goal line, scoring the final six of his 15 points in the first game ever played in Sanford Stadium.

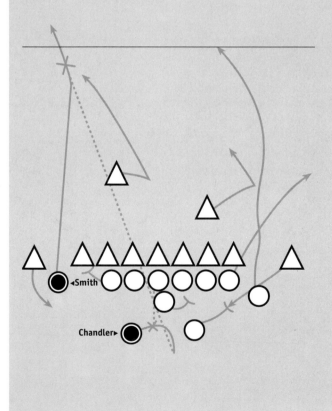

VERNON "CATFISH" SMITH

Vernon "Catfish" Smith's 15-point performance against Yale in 1929 began a brilliant collegiate career. He was selected All–Southern Conference in all three of his seasons at Georgia (1929–1931) and named consensus All-American from his end position in 1931.

In a time when southern football players were not held in the same regard as ones from the East, North, or Midwest, Catfish was well known and highly respected all throughout college football. Smith's three performances against powerhouse Yale netted him considerable national exposure. In three Georgia wins over Yale, Catfish scored 22 of the Bulldogs' 59 combined points and nearly 30 percent of his career points at Georgia. He was also outstanding on defense as the Elis averaged only seven points per game in their three losses.

Three years prior to being inducted into the College Football Hall of Fame in 1979, Smith returned to the stadium where he had been the star of its dedication 47 years earlier. Smith came to the '76 Georgia-California game to watch his son Vern Jr., a defensive back for the Cal Bears.

GAME DETAILS

Georgia 15 • Yale 0

Date: October 12, 1929

Site: Sanford Stadium

Attendance: 35,000

Records: Georgia 1–1; Yale 1–0

Series: Yale 5–1 (Yale one-game winning streak)

STEADMAN SANFORD

Steadman Sanford came to the University of Georgia in 1903 to accept a position teaching English. Never having played athletics as an undergraduate at Mercer University, Sanford later agreed to serve as Georgia's physical director.

Sanford Field, named for the professor because he was chiefly responsible for raising money for its construction, opened in 1911. The field was a combined football gridiron and baseball diamond, exhibited a covered grandstand, and was considered one of the best fields in the South.

After witnessing Georgia get upset by Georgia Tech in 1927 in a driving rain on Sanford Field's "sea of mud," Sanford started a movement to bring a modern stadium to the university. In 1929, his dream of huge crowds at a state-of-the-art stadium against "big" teams was realized when Georgia hosted Yale.

Sanford also served as dean (1927–1932) and later president (1932–1935) of the University of Georgia.

Barely visible from high above newly constructed Sanford Stadium, Georgia and Yale players and game officials gather at midfield for the coin toss. *Photo courtesy of Hargrett Rare Book & Manuscript Library/University of Georgia Libraries.*

CAROLINA CALLS IT QUITS

South Carolina captain pulls team off field, and Georgia is awarded forfeited win

At the turn of the 20th century, football in America was relatively new and a much different sport than it is more than a century later. The field was 110 yards long, touchdowns were worth five points each, and it would not be until 1906 that passing was permitted. Peculiar events also transpired, as in the 1900 Georgia–South Carolina contest, events that would most likely never occur in today's game.

South Carolina had six weeks to prepare for Georgia. Its coach, I.O. Hunt, was considered to be a "good" instructor and had his squad fully prepared for the skirmish in Athens. With a groomed team guided by an excellent coach, it is surprising what resulted toward the end of the game. South Carolina, because of a couple controversial calls made by the referee, suddenly quit and left Herty Field in a tied game. The end result was a 5–0 forfeited victory for Georgia.

After paying the 50¢ admission fee, patrons witnessed the Red and Black score first. Behind the running of Marvin Dickinson, Georgia drove to Carolina's 3½-yard line. With 13 minutes remaining in the opening half, fullback Samuel Hewlett scored, giving Georgia a 5–0 lead. Hugh

Gordon's point after was topped off and never got off the ground.

Toward the end of the first half, South Carolina threatened to score by driving to Georgia's 5-yard line. Two running attempts moved the ball to a half-yard from the Red and Black's goal. Just as South Carolina was lining up to run another play, referee Rowbotham blew his whistle, indicating the end of the first half. Carolina captain T.J. Bell was irate, openly accusing the two judges of cheating and being "incompetent, dishonest, and determined to defeat his team."

For most of the second half, South Carolina possessed the ball in Georgia's territory. With nine minutes elapsed in the half, Carolina tied the score with a touchdown and missed the extra-point attempt.

A series of lost fumbles ended the next four possessions, including Georgia right end Julian Baxter's disputed recovery on South Carolina's 5-yard line with only four minutes remaining in the game. As the Red and Black lined up to attempt to drive for the game-winning score, they realized there was no defense to oppose them. Captain Bell had ordered his team off the field, charging

Georgia's 1900 squad was victorious in only two of six contests. Its second and final win came via a forfeit by South Carolina. *Photo courtesy of Hargrett Rare Book & Manuscript Library/University of Georgia Libraries.*

the officials with "robbery" and indicating the game could be given to Georgia.

The two controversial calls by the referee, ending the first half with South Carolina on Georgia's half-yard line and later awarding Baxter with a disputed fumble recovery, had provoked Bell to pull his team and quit the contest. With the game tied 5–5 the officials had no choice but to award the Red and Black their second and what would be their final win of the season.

College football has certainly evolved over its nearly 140 years of existence. The game's field, scoring values, and rules have undergone numerous changes. In addition, it is apparent that a team's desire for victory constitutes a top priority. In a sport that often features controversial calls, it is doubtful that any dispute would cause a team to suddenly leave the field and forfeit the game. This was not the case for South Carolina and its captain against Georgia in 1900.

MARVIN DICKINSON

After transferring from Mercer University, Marvin Dickinson made an immediate impact at halfback for Georgia. In 1900 he starred in the Red and Black's 5–0 win over South Carolina, and a season later he scored Georgia's only points in a 16–6 loss to Davidson with a touchdown (worth five points) and a successful point after. His rushing was the highlight in an upset, scoreless tie against Auburn.

In 1902 Dickinson's plunge accounted for the only points in a 5–0 victory over Alabama. He also scored a touchdown and converted two extra points in Georgia's 20–0 victory over Davidson.

Dickinson expected to play again in 1903 but was instead appointed Georgia's new head coach. Billy Reynolds, the Red and Black's previous coach, had suddenly resigned. Only one veteran returned from the 1902 squad, and Georgia struggled to a 3–4 record. After playing professional baseball in 1904, Dickinson returned to the University of Georgia in 1905. Again, the Red and Black returned only one veteran from the previous season, and Georgia won only one of six games that year. Following a 29–0 loss to Auburn, Dickinson told a reporter he was tired of football and never coached again.

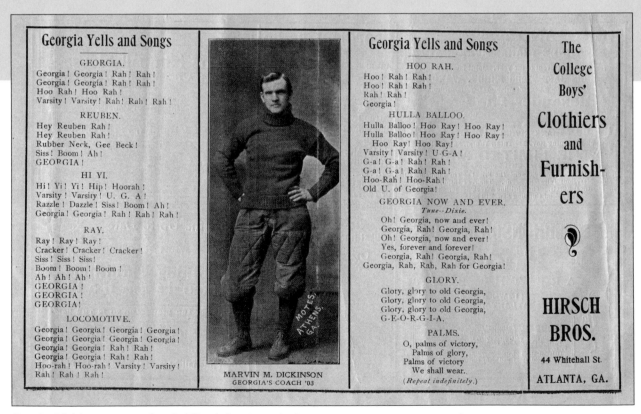

Marvin Dickinson starred at halfback for Georgia from 1900 to 1902. He was the Red and Black's head coach in 1903 and 1905—Georgia's ninth coach in only 12 seasons of football. *Photo courtesy of Hargrett Rare Book & Manuscript Library/University of Georgia Libraries.*

GAME DETAILS

Georgia 5 • South Carolina 0

Date: October 20, 1900

Site: Herty Field

Records: Georgia 1–0; South Carolina 0–0

Series: Georgia 1–0 (Georgia one-game winning streak)

E.E. JONES

E.E. Jones became Georgia's seventh head coach in its first nine years of football by recommendation of, according to author John Stegeman, "the immortal Arthur Poe." Poe was a teammate of Jones at Princeton University, an All-American end in 1899, and became a member of the College Football Hall of Fame in 1969. Poe was also the great-nephew of the well-known writer, Edgar Allen Poe.

While several Georgia coaches have been victorious over Georgia Tech in the final regular-season game of a campaign, Jones is the only coach to defeat Tech in a season-opening game. Prior to facing Georgia Tech in 1900, Jones, according to author Bill Cromartie, told the press he thought he had the game "inside [his] pocket." The Red and Black defeated Georgia Tech, 12–0, and South Carolina the following week. However, Jones's squad would drop its final four games of the season by a combined score of 159–11. It would be not only the first but also the final year for Jones as a collegiate football coach.

November 25, 1971

Shirer's Turkey Day Catch

Jimmy Shirer's key reception against Georgia Tech on Thanksgiving in 1971 leads to game-winning score

Due in large part to the play of sophomores Andy Johnson and Jimmy Poulos, newcomers on Georgia's varsity, the Bulldogs emerged from two mediocre campaigns of 1969 and 1970 as one of the nation's elite teams in 1971. Georgia was not defeated until its 10th game, against Auburn. Quarterback Johnson, much more of a runner than a passer, led a ground-oriented offense that averaged 303 rushing yards and only completed approximately five passes per game. A steadily improving Georgia Tech, the Bulldogs' final regular-season opponent, had won four games in a row, exhibiting one of college football's best defenses, in particular, against the run. The Georgia seniors had never defeated the Yellow Jackets, losing the previous two seasons by a combined 23–7 score and in the 1968 freshman game three years earlier.

What most remember about the '71 Georgia–Georgia Tech game played on Thanksgiving is a young Johnson bringing the Bulldogs down the field in the final minute and a half when they were down by three points. Georgia's acclaimed scoring and game-winning drive was capped by a one-yard dive by tailback Poulos. However, if not for the play prior to Poulos's winning plunge, the drive would have likely resulted in a tie or even a loss, instead of a 28–24 Georgia victory.

The Bulldogs trailed the Yellow Jackets by three points with 24 seconds left in the game, and Georgia was on Tech's 13-yard line with no timeouts remaining and facing second down and goal. Kicker Kim Braswell was warming up on the sideline just in case he had to attempt a game-tying field goal. Flanker Jimmy Shirer, who caught a 23-yard touchdown in the second quarter, returned to the huddle after getting "knocked out on his feet" a few plays before for the second time in the game. Johnson dropped back and threw a pass toward the right sideline. His toss was low, but Shirer made the catch, going out of bounds around the goal line. A few seconds elapsed before the referee signaled whether or not Shirer scored, caught the ball in bounds short of the end zone, or

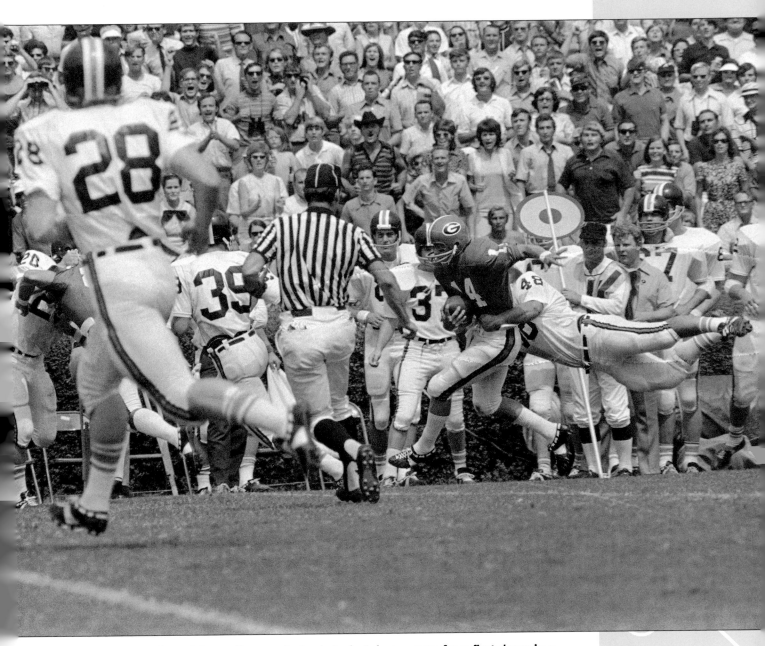

In his first game on Georgia's varsity, quarterback Andy Johnson runs for a first down in a 56–25 win over Oregon State. By the end of the 1971 season Johnson had already shared in several memorable Bulldogs moments, including his critical sideline-pass completion to Jimmy Shirer against Georgia Tech, which led to the Bulldogs' winning touchdown. *Photo courtesy of AP Images.*

ANDY JOHNSON

After leading Georgia in its 11-play, 65-yard winning drive against Georgia Tech in 1971, Andy Johnson commented to the media that it reminded him of two years prior, when he played at Athens High School. In the 1969 Georgia state championship game, senior Johnson guided the Trojans down the field for a late score and a two-point conversion to tie Valdosta High School 26–26. Johnson would direct a few other comebacks before his playing days at Georgia ended, most notably, a 35–31 victory over Tennessee as a senior.

On Georgia's freshman team in 1970, Johnson averaged 215.6 total offensive yards per game and was forecasted as college football's sophomore of the year in '71 by *Playboy* magazine. Labeled a "running-only" quarterback, Johnson finished the 1971 season with 870 rushing yards (second in the SEC) despite missing two games with a bruised thigh. Ironically, it was Johnson's passing (nine of 19 for 107 yards, one touchdown, no interceptions) that ultimately defeated Georgia Tech. As only a sophomore, Johnson was selected second-team All-SEC by the Associated Press.

caught the ball out of bounds for an incompletion. The ruling was Shirer made the catch between the 1-yard line and the goal line with 18 seconds remaining. On the next play, Poulos hurtled into the end zone for a touchdown. Tech had time for a final play, but quarterback Eddie McAshan was intercepted by Don Golden. Tears were shed by the Yellow Jackets and hearts were broken as the Bulldogs defeated their intrastate rival for the first time in three years.

Georgia, which was missing three starters because of injuries, including All-American offensive guard Royce Smith and All-SEC linebacker Chip Wisdom, had trailed Georgia Tech 14–0 and 17–7; however, the Bulldogs scratched their way back into the ballgame. Holding a 24–21 advantage, the Yellow Jackets were

forced to punt from their own end zone. Tech's booming kick backed Georgia to its own 35-yard line with only 1:29 left to play.

The calm and cool Johnson promptly went to work. After throwing incomplete on first down, he was forced to run on a passing play and netted 22 yards to Georgia Tech's 43-yard line. Nevertheless, Johnson followed with three straight incomplete passes, and Georgia was confronted with fourth and 10 with 57 seconds remaining in the game. The season had come down to one play, and Johnson responded by passing on target to tight end Mike Greene over the middle for 18 yards and a critical first down. Consecutive completions to split end Lynn Hunnicutt for nine and seven yards followed, and the Bulldogs had a first and goal on the Jackets' 9-yard

That [Shirer's catch] was the play of the game.... He made a terrific catch, and we won.

—FRED PANCOAST, GEORGIA OFFENSIVE COORDINATOR

Game Details

Georgia 28 • Georgia Tech 24

Date: November 25, 1971

Site: Grant Field

Attendance: 60,124

Records: Georgia 9–1; Georgia Tech 6–4

Rankings: Georgia: No. 7 (AP)/ No. 7 (UPI)

Series: Georgia 31–29–5 (Georgia Tech two-game winning streak)

> **A**ndy Johnson can pass, in case anybody is interested.
>
> —VINCE DOOLEY, GEORGIA HEAD COACH

line with 31 seconds left. On the next snap, Johnson lost four yards and was forced to call Georgia's final timeout. On the sideline, the sophomore quarterback conferred on the next play with his coaches—a sideline pass to Shirer.

Following the game, Shirer admitted he probably could have scored after making the catch but went out of bounds on purpose. He did not want to cut back in bounds after his reception and take the chance of losing yardage. Shirer said he went out of bounds because he knew Georgia could score from inside the 1-yard line on the next play. Offensive coordinator Fred Pancoast later confessed that if Shirer did not make the catch, Braswell likely would have attempted a field goal and "one of the greatest comebacks in Georgia history" would have ended, at best for the Bulldogs, in a tie game.

Jimmy Shirer

Shirer was a four-sport standout at Elloree High School in Elloree, South Carolina. He was chosen all-state in football for two years, all-conference in basketball for two seasons, and a two-time state champion in track.

As a sophomore at Georgia in 1969, the one-time high school star halfback was only a backup punter, punting just one time for 42 yards. However, in 1970, Shirer caught 11 passes for 202 yards as a reserve receiver and had a 39.1 punting average as the Bulldogs' starting punter. Shirer was Georgia's most versatile player on its 11–1 and Gator Bowl champion squad of 1971. He was first on the team with 188 receiving yards on 13 catches and two touchdowns, rushed for 96 yards and a touchdown from his flanker position on 21 carries, and averaged 38.3 yards on 55 punts.

October 10, 1981

A Rebel-Rouser

Herschel Walker leaps, spins, and runs over Ole Miss for six yards and a touchdown in 1981

To some Georgia fans, sophomore Herschel Walker was somewhat of a disappointment through the first four games of the 1981 season. After averaging nearly six yards per carry as a freshman and scoring 12 touchdowns in the season's final seven games, Walker was rushing for only 4.8 yards per attempt and had scored but three touchdowns. His longest run from scrimmage was just 22 yards after having seven rushes of 48 yards or more in 1980. Most importantly, Walker had lost three crucial fumbles in a 13–3 loss to Clemson—Georgia's first defeat in 16 games, dating back to 1979. Once a favorite for the Heisman Trophy, Walker was now considered only a slight possibility to win the award.

Walker was not expected to break out of his "slump" against Ole Miss. Nursing a weak ankle, Herschel had rushed for only 44 yards on 11 carries versus the Rebels as a freshman. The week of the '81 meeting with Ole Miss, he suffered a bruised foot and would be running on AstroTurf for the first time all season. Georgia had not fared well on Hemingway Stadium's turf, losing in

1975 and 1976 and winning by only a field goal in 1979.

As the game began, Ole Miss coach Steve Sloan was placing eight men on the line of scrimmage to stop Walker, and it seemed Walker's lackluster performances would continue. However, it was one rushing effort by Walker in particular, a short run at that, that jump-started his day's stellar performance and is considered perhaps his best run as a Bulldog.

Trailing 7–3, Georgia faced fourth down and inches on Ole Miss's 6-yard line midway through the second quarter. Quarterback Buck Belue turned and handed the ball to Walker, who leaped high into the air and came down around the 3-yard line for a first down. However, Walker was still on his feet as he had landed not on the ground but on the shoulders of Ole Miss's Thomas Hubbard. Walker rolled off Hubbard and another Rebel defender, maintained his balance by placing his hand on the turf, and strolled into the end zone for a touchdown.

Following an early Kevin Butler field goal, Georgia had fallen behind in the second quarter on a touchdown run by

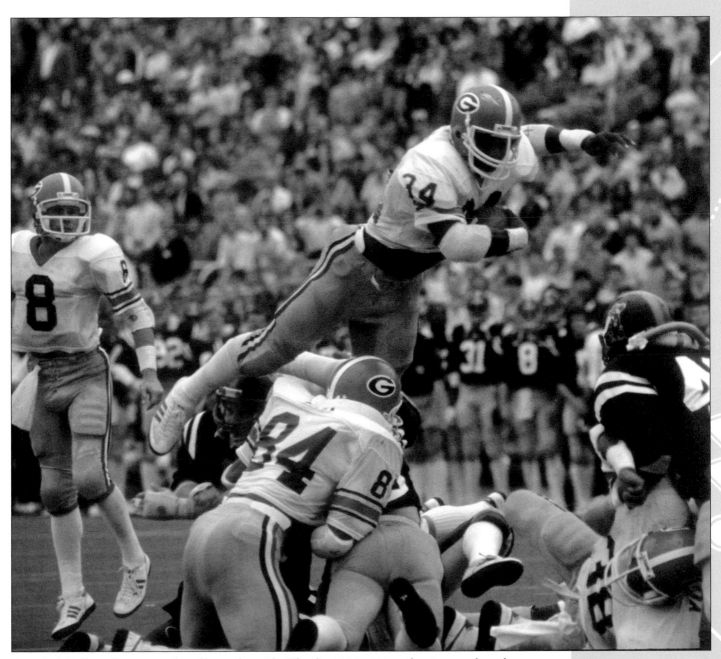

Herschel Walker dives over the pile against Ole Miss in 1981 attempting to merely gain a first down. Walker landed on the shoulders of a linebacker, spun off him and another defender, and walked into the end zone for a six-yard score. *Photo courtesy of Wingate Downs.*

Herschel Walker

Prior to playing football at Georgia, Herschel Walker had already established himself as a man of many hats. He was valedictorian of his high school senior class, an award-winning cook, a first-class runner, an excellent dancer, and a black belt in karate, to name a few interests.

The week of the Ole Miss game in 1981, Georgia practice reports never revealed how Walker actually bruised his foot. Although denied by Walker, rumor was that he had been practicing karate kicks in the shower when he accidentally kicked a fixture. Neither an injured foot nor Steve Sloan's eight-man defensive front could stop Walker's 265-yard performance against the Rebels.

Because of his extremely outstanding three seasons at Georgia and because he might not have lived up to every expectation in the NFL, almost forgotten is Walker's exceptional career in the professional ranks. In three years with the United States Football League's New Jersey Generals (1983–1985), Walker gained 7,046 combined rushing and receiving yards, scored 61 touchdowns, and was named the league's Most Valuable Player in 1985. With Dallas, Minnesota, Philadelphia, and the New York Giants of the NFL for 12 seasons (1986–1997), Walker rushed for 8,225 yards, had 4,859 yards receiving, and 5,084 yards on kickoff returns. Unfortunately, Walker was often used as a secondary or even a blocking back during much of his time in the NFL and was on only three teams that made the playoffs. His professional career is remembered by many as not the all-time professional football (USFL and NFL combined) leader in all-purpose yardage with 25,283, but as the player dealt from Dallas to Minnesota in 1989, which ultimately yielded 19 players to the Cowboys and eventually three Super Bowl championships. Just as he is perhaps the greatest college football player ever, it can be argued that Walker is the most underappreciated professional football player in history.

Walker's 265 rushing yards on 41 carries against the Rebels still remain ranked second and third, respectively, in school history for single-game accomplishments. *Photo courtesy of AP Images.*

GAME DETAILS

Georgia 37 • Ole Miss 7

Date: October 10, 1981

Site: Hemingway Stadium

Attendance: 41,125

Records: Georgia 3–1; Ole Miss 3–2

Rankings: Georgia: No. 11 (AP)/ No. 9 (UPI)

Series: Georgia 11–7–1 (Georgia four-game winning streak)

> They [Ole Miss's defense] hit me, spun me around, and let go. I just kept running.
>
> —HERSCHEL WALKER, TAILBACK

Rebel quarterback John Fourcade. Soon afterward, Fourcade left the game with injured ribs, and the Ole Miss offense would struggle from that point on.

Down by four points, the Bulldogs' offense moved from their 36-yard line to the Rebels' 6 in 13 plays. It was at this point Walker performed his acrobatic run—a leap that was designed to only gain a first down, but Walker added a spin off of two Rebels defenders and a trot into the end zone for a head-scratching score.

After Walker's touchdown, Georgia began to throttle Ole Miss in every phase of the game. Due in large part to Walker's 150 rushing yards at halftime, the Bulldogs had a 24–7 lead at the break. Walker added 115 more in the second half before being taken out early in the final quarter of Georgia's easy 37–7 win over the Rebels.

As the final seconds ticked off the clock, Walker was paid the ultimate compliment as the opposing fans began chanting his name, not in sarcasm but in appreciation. He finished with 265 yards on 41 carries; this would be Walker's best rushing performance in his final two years at Georgia. Thrust back into the race for the Heisman Trophy, Walker had several great runs against the Ole Miss defense, including nine covering more than 10 yards and a season-long of 32. No run, however, was greater than the mere six-yarder.

> As great a six-yard run as you will ever see. File it away in the already bulging folder of Walker's legendary runs.
>
> —BLAKE GILES, *ATHENS BANNER-HERALD* SPORTS EDITOR

October 18, 1975

33 SHOESTRING SINKS 'DORES

Ray Goff and Gene Washington execute the shoestring play, double-crossing the Commodores in 1975

Entering the '75 Vanderbilt meeting, Georgia had a 3–2 record for the season and had lost five of its last eight contests, including the final three games of 1974. Desperately needing a win in Nashville, the Bulldogs had sustained several key injuries, including all-conference standouts running back Glynn Harrison and offensive guard Joel Parrish.

On a wet and chilly day at Dudley Field, Georgia led the Commodores 7–3 in the second quarter. Vanderbilt's Paul Izlar lost a fumble on his own 36-yard line recovered by Georgia defensive end Lawrence Craft. On first down, quarterback Ray Goff was stopped for no gain. Suddenly, coach Vince Dooley, considered unimaginative by some for his years of running a "three yards and a cloud of dust" style of offense, became uncharacteristically innovative.

On second down, Goff approached the football, spotted on the right hash mark, as Vanderbilt stood in its defensive huddle. Goff knelt in front of the ball and pretended to tie

his shoe as the other 10 Bulldogs nonchalantly gathered at the left hash mark on the wide side of the field. Instantly, Goff, acting as the offense's center, flipped the football to junior flanker Gene Washington. Acting as a running back, Washington raced down the left sideline with a convoy of nine blockers. Only one Commodores defender had the possibility of reaching Washington, but he was quickly blocked out of the play by split end Steve Davis. As a confused Vanderbilt defense chased to no avail, Washington easily galloped 36 yards for a touchdown with 4:58 remaining until halftime.

The Goff-to-Washington "shoestring play" jump-started a struggling squad. the Bulldogs would eventually hammer Vanderbilt 47–3 as 11 different ball carriers combined to rush for 297 yards. The Junkyard Dogs defense forced six turnovers, constantly giving Georgia's offense favorable field position.

The key to Georgia's shoestring deception was its preceding play, the 68-sweep,

After taking a pitch from quarterback Ray Goff, Gene Washington, aided by a number of blocks, runs 36 yards for a touchdown, completing the "shoestring" play against Vanderbilt in 1975. *Photo courtesy of AP Images.*

where Goff ran a sweep to the right hash mark. Despite not gaining any yardage, Goff's sweep set up the entire left side of the field for the Bulldogs offense to run one of the most unusual plays in football.

The play was suggested to Dooley by Georgia's offensive line coach, Jimmy Vickers, when Vickers noticed on game film that Vanderbilt's defense often held hands while calling signals in its huddle, paying little attention to the opposing offenses. In addition, Dooley was aware of the shoestring play because it was used by Duke University for a touchdown against his brother Bill's North Carolina team in 1969. Georgia ran the play three times during Thursday's practice, two days prior to the game.

RAY GOFF

Ray Goff was a star quarterback at Georgia from 1974 to 1976, alternating at the position with Matt Robinson as situations dictated. Known more as the running quarterback (Robinson the passer), Goff's 1,434 career rushing yards and 19 touchdowns are both second to Andy Johnson among quarterbacks in school history. A gifted passer as well, Goff's 136.55 career passing rating ranks sixth in school history of those completing just 10 career passes or more, trailing only D.J. Shockley, Charley Trippi, David Greene, Mike Bobo, and Eric Zeier. Besides Zeier, Goff is the only Georgia quarterback to finish in the Heisman Trophy's top 10 voting, placing seventh in 1976.

Following three seasons as an assistant coach at the University of South Carolina, Goff returned to Georgia, where he held the positions of recruiting coordinator, tight ends coach, and running backs coach from 1981 to 1988. When Vince Dooley retired as Georgia's head coach, the 33-year-old Goff was surprisingly named his successor prior to the '89 season. Although an excellent recruiter, it was evident from the outset that Goff was in over his head guiding the Bulldogs. It took Goff three years before he achieved a winning season; Dooley had only one losing year in 25 campaigns. After an unsatisfactory seven-year stint, during which Georgia had only three winning campaigns and received four bowl bids, Goff was fired following the 1995 season. Since patrolling Georgia's sideline more than a decade ago, Goff has continued to live in the Athens area, where he has become a successful businessman.

Ray Goff was perhaps the best running quarterback ever to play for Georgia. There were only a handful of occasions to cheer, however, when Goff was the Bulldogs' head coach from 1989 to 1995. *Photo courtesy of AP Images.*

GAME DETAILS

Georgia 47 • Vanderbilt 3

Date: October 18, 1975

Site: Dudley Field

Attendance: 20,538

Records: Georgia 3–2; Vanderbilt 3–2

Series: Georgia 19–15–1 (Georgia one-game winning streak)

> The more I thought about it [the shoestring play], the less I thought it would work.
>
> —RAY GOFF, QUARTERBACK

The Bulldogs initially were going to attempt the chicanery on the second play of the game. However, the Georgia coaches decided to wait just a little longer to make sure the Commodore defenders would continue their inattentive huddles. The play was designed for Georgia's quarterback to lateral the ball to Harrison or Washington, but because Harrison was out with an injury, Washington, by default, would be on the receiving end of the shoestring. With little more than five minutes remaining in the second quarter, offensive coordinator Bill Pace called for the trickery, Dooley consented, and Washington executed it into the end zone as Vanderbilt's defense stood in bewilderment.

GENE WASHINGTON

Gene Washington arrived in Athens, Georgia, in 1973 as a small, 5'9", 165-pound freshman, but one with dazzling speed. In his second game as a Bulldog, "Lean Gene" tied a school record with a 96-yard kickoff return for a touchdown against Clemson. During the fourth game of his freshman season, Washington broke his arm against Alabama, but not before accounting for 384 all-purpose yards on only 14 touches (27.4 average) and three touchdowns in only three and a half games. Despite missing most of the 1973 season, Washington was named All-SEC freshman first team and led the conference in kickoff return average.

In his four seasons (1973–1976) at Georgia, Washington gained 2,791 all-purpose yards—second most in school history upon his graduation and 13th currently. Washington, who was named second-team All-SEC in 1974 and 1976, was recognized for making big plays. Along with the 36-yard shoestring touchdown in 1975, "Gino" also caught five touchdowns of 74 yards or greater at Georgia and returned three kickoffs of 52 yards or more.

A ninth-round selection (235th overall) of the San Diego Chargers in the 1977 NFL draft, Washington played in two games with the New York Giants in 1979.

September 3, 1983

POST-HERSCHEL HOUNDS BITE BRUINS

Charlie Dean's touchdown return in final seconds clinches season opener of 1983

Both Georgia and UCLA entered their season-opening meeting in 1983 seemingly less competitve compared to their previous seasons. The Bruins, Pac-10 and Rose Bowl champions in 1982, had lost quarterback Tom Ramsey—an all-conference performer and college football's highest-rated passer the year before. Replacement Rick Neuheisel, a fifth-year senior, had played sparingly in college and was one of 10 UCLA players making their initial start ever as a Bruin. Georgia had lost seven starters on defense, including All-SEC safety Jeff Sanchez, who had broken his arm in preseason practice. The Bulldogs' offensive line, considered the team's strength, was also banged up. Most importantly, gone was tailback Herschel Walker—the predominant reason Georgia achieved a 33–3 record and three SEC titles from 1980 to 1982 and undoubtedly the school's greatest player in history.

The Walker-less 'Dogs led the Bruins 12–8 with 33 seconds remaining in the game. UCLA was advancing toward Georgia's goal

and a possible victory, with a first down on the Bulldogs' 31-yard line. Neuheisel dropped back to throw and floated a pass to his left toward tight end Paul Bergman. Suddenly, Charlie Dean, a native Athenian and playing only because of Sanchez's season-ending injury, stepped in front of the intended receiver. The senior safety intercepted Neuheisel's pass at his 26-yard line and raced untouched down the sideline. Dean's 69-yard interception return for a touchdown secured a 19–8 victory over UCLA.

In a driving rainstorm, Georgia held a comfortable 12–0 second-quarter lead only to allow two Bruins field goals prior to halftime. The Bulldogs' offense was extremely sluggish in the second half, scoring no points. Georgia finished the game with only 59 passing yards, while four tailbacks, Walker's replacements, combined to rush for 102 yards and just 3.6 yards per carry. Scott Williams, a fullback, finished as Georgia's leading rusher.

Twice in the final half UCLA reached

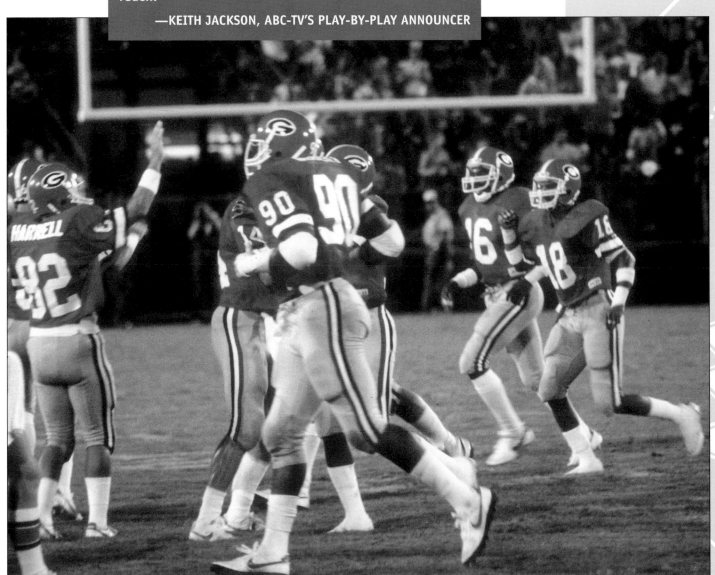

The hometown boy does it! Charlie Dean! Just ran 69 yards with a pass interception, and that puts it out of reach.

—KEITH JACKSON, ABC-TV'S PLAY-BY-PLAY ANNOUNCER

Charlie Dean (No. 18) is congratulated by teammates following his game-clinching interception return for a touchdown against UCLA in 1983. *Photo courtesy of Wingate Downs.*

THE INTERCEPTION RETURN

Rick Neuheisel took the snap from center and first looked to throw deep against the Georgia secondary. Despite the Bulldogs having only 10 men on the field, Neuheisel was forced to pass to his second option. Lined up to Neuheisel's left, tight end Paul Bergman ran a short flare pattern. Immediately prior to Neuheisel's toss reaching Bergman, Charlie Dean appeared from nowhere. The senior safety-man snared the errant pass at his own 26 and raced without interruption down the field into UCLA's end zone.

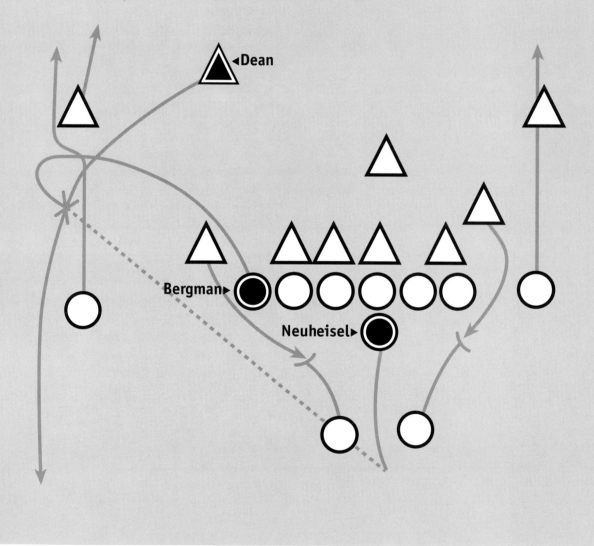

GAME DETAILS

Georgia 19 • UCLA 8

Date: September 3, 1983

Site: Sanford Stadium

Attendance: 82,122

Records: Georgia 0–0; UCLA 0–0

Rankings: Georgia: No. 15 (AP)/ No. 13 (UPI); UCLA: No. 20 (AP)/ No. 12 (UPI)

Series: Georgia 1–0 (Georgia one-game winning streak)

> **I** baited the guy [UCLA's Paul Bergman].... I hung back and waited and hoped they'd come back [pass] to him again, and they did.
>
> —CHARLIE DEAN, SAFETY

inside Georgia's 10-yard line but came away with no points. Included was a Neuheisel pass broken up by cornerback Darryl Jones in the end zone on fourth down and goal from the Bulldogs' 9-yard line with only 2:14 left in the contest.

After Jones's game-saving breakup, Georgia ran three plays and took an intentional safety instead of punting to the Bruins and likely giving them excellent field position. Trailing 12–8, UCLA returned the ensuing kickoff to its own 35-yard line.

With only 1:01 showing on the clock, the Bruins quickly ran four plays, moving the ball to Georgia's 31-yard line. On first and 10, Neuheisel first looked to throw deep, but no Bruin was open against the Dogs' straight man-on-man coverage. Incidentally, Georgia

had only 10 defenders on the field. As Bergman flared to his left, Neuheisel looked to throw to the tight end. Baiting the quarterback, Dean laid off Bergman approximately five to six yards. Just as the pass was thrown, Dean closed in on the tight end and intercepted Neuheisel.

"It was really a relief to see Charlie Dean take the ball and run down the field," said Coach Vince Dooley following the game. And run down the field Dean did, lifting his left hand in the air around UCLA's 25-yard line with his index finger pointed upward, proclaiming, "We're number one," as he crossed the Bruins' goal line for a score. The post–Herschel Walker era had officially begun in fine fashion, due in large part to a magnificent interception return by a little-known hometown hero.

RICK NEUHEISEL

Rick Neuheisel's first intention was to attend Princeton University instead of UCLA. In fact, he had already bought a plane ticket to New Jersey before changing his mind. Similar to Charlie Dean, Neuheisel played infrequently prior to his senior season, attempting just 24 passes from 1979 to 1982. He beat out Steve Bono, an eventual 14-year NFL veteran, for UCLA's top quarterback spot in 1983 and would remarkably complete more than 69 percent of his passes for 2,245 yards for the season. Neuheisel capped his fifth-year senior season by throwing four touchdowns and for nearly 300 yards, to be named the 1984 Rose Bowl's MVP in a dominant 45–9 victory over favored Illinois.

Neuheisel was the starting quarterback for the San Antonio Gunslingers in 1984 and 1985 of the now defunct United States Football League. During the 1987 NFL strike, Neuheisel quarterbacked the San Diego Chargers' scab team to a 3–0 record before the strike ended.

Recently, Neuheisel coached Colorado (1995–1998) and Washington (1999–2002) to a 61–35 combined overall record (includes five victories forfeited in 1997). Of his eight teams, seven participated in bowl games and three finished ranked in the nation's top eight. Prior to the 2008 season, Neuheisel was named UCLA's head coach after serving as an assistant of the NFL's Baltimore Ravens for three years.

Only 31 yards away from victory, quarterback Rick Neuheisel begins his throwing motion but is on the verge of being intercepted by Dean.
Photo courtesy of AP Images.

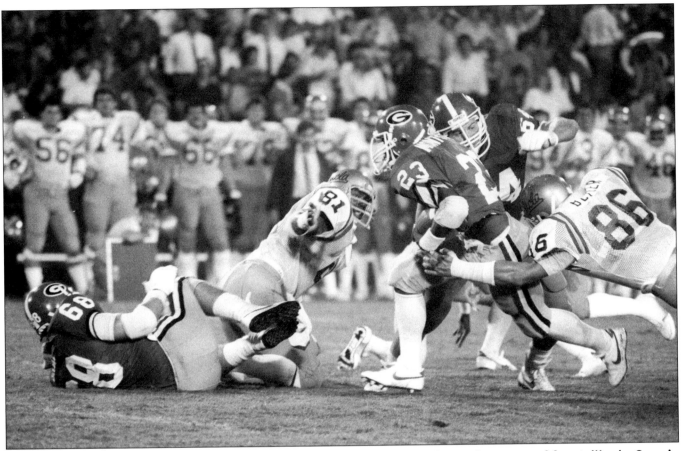

With Herschel Walker no longer in the Bulldogs lineup, Keith Montgomery (No. 23) was one of four tailbacks Georgia tried against the Bruins. *Photo courtesy of Wingate Downs.*

CHARLIE DEAN

Charlie Dean was a member of Georgia's junior varsity as a freshman in 1980 and saw limited playing time as a reserve varsity defensive back in 1981 and 1982. He was considered a backup again for his senior year until Jeff Sanchez was lost for the season to an injury. Dean made the most of his starting safety assignment by tying for the team lead in interceptions with three, despite missing two full games with injuries. The most notable of Dean's five career interceptions, the 69-yard scoring return against UCLA, is perhaps the greatest interception return for a touchdown in Georgia football history.

Along with 13 others, including Georgia football dignitaries Dan Magill and Richard Appleby, Dean was inducted into the Athens Athletic Hall of Fame in 2001. His induction is mostly because Dean quarterbacked Clarke Central High School to a state championship in 1979 and because of his game-clinching touchdown return in 1983 against the Bruins.

January 1, 1982

31 BULLDOGS' SUGAR TURNS SOUR

Dan Marino throws a 33-yard score on fourth down in the final minute to defeat Georgia in '82 Sugar Bowl

Coached by new defensive coordinator Bill Lewis, the successor to the highly esteemed Erk Russell, Georgia's defense of 1981 was one of the best in school history. During the regular season, the 262.1 yards per game it yielded was a team low for 35 years from 1972 until 2006. The 8.9 points per game it allowed has been the lowest at Georgia for the past 41 seasons. The '81 defense's blitzing style registered 52 sacks—a Bulldogs record since sacks began being recorded in 1979. Nevertheless, Georgia's defense had a formidable task at hand when it met Pittsburgh in the season-ending Sugar Bowl. A win by second-ranked Georgia, coupled with a loss that same night by No. 1 Clemson to Nebraska in the Orange Bowl, and the Bulldogs would capture their second consecutive national title.

The Panthers had one of the most prolific passing games in college football and had three first-team All-Americans on their offense alone: quarterback Dan Marino, receiver Julius Dawkins, and tackle Jimbo Covert.

Pittsburgh would easily move the football against Georgia's renowned defenders; however, because of five turnovers, the Panthers had scored only 17 points and trailed by three late in the contest. With only 42 seconds remaining, Pittsburgh faced fourth down and five on the Bulldogs' 33-yard line. The game came down to one final snap.

Georgia, believing Pittsburgh would throw a quick pass to only gain the short yardage necessary for a first down, decided to blitz. The play was designed for Marino to throw to one of his two running backs crossing short over the middle. However, Marino picked up the Bulldogs' blitz, as did the two running backs, who both stayed in and blocked for their quarterback. Unfortunately for Georgia, Pittsburgh's Johnny Brown also recognized its blitzing scheme, and the tight end broke his route and began running straight down the middle of the field. Marino lofted a perfect pass just out of the reach of Georgia safety Steve Kelly, and Brown made a falling catch in the end zone for a touchdown.

Pittsburgh led 24–20 with only 35 seconds left in the game. Georgia's Buck Belue proceeded to throw an interception, and the Bulldogs' final effort on offense failed, as did their chances for another national championship.

Georgia took a 20–17 lead with 8:31 remaining in the contest following a touchdown pass from Belue to Clarence Kay on third and goal from Pittsburgh's 6-yard line. A few minutes later, the Panthers elected to fake a punt instead of attempting a game-tying field goal. "We were not here to tie," said Pittsburgh's head coach Jackie Sherrill after the game. "We were here to win." The coach's gamble failed, and a victory for the Bulldogs seemed likely.

Georgia was soon forced to punt, and the Panthers had the ball on their own 20-yard line with 2:33 left on the clock and down by three points. In seven plays, Marino directed the offense to the Bulldogs' 46-yard line, where it encountered fourth down and four to go. On the next play, the junior quarterback picked up eight yards on a scramble and a pivotal first down to the 38-yard line. Pittsburgh netted five yards in three plays and was faced with another fourth down on the 33. Again, Sherrill refused to settle for an attempt at a tie game.

The Bulldogs decided to blitz Marino despite playing in a three-man rush and placing five men in pass coverage for most of the game. In addition, Pittsburgh was nearly unsackable; in two seasons and 750 pass attempts, Panthers quarterbacks had been sacked just 16 times and only once in 40 pass attempts by Georgia leading up to the winning touchdown.

A play that initially was intended "to mix

As Georgia is blitzing in the 1982 Sugar Bowl, Pittsburgh's Dan Marino drops back to pass on fourth down, trailing by three points and with only 42 seconds remaining. *Photo courtesy of Wingate Downs.*

up their [Georgia's] linebackers," according to Marino, suddenly changed when the Bulldogs decided to blitz and "mixed up" Georgia's secondary instead. Brown ran past Georgia cornerback Ronnie Harris and cut outside toward the sideline. Georgia's blitz left safety-man Kelly completely alone, covering Brown. Like the entire Bulldogs defense, Kelly expected a short pass from Marino. Instead, Brown broke toward the inside of the field and, in so doing, turned Kelly completely around on the play. Brown was suddenly left all alone and wide open, breaking toward Georgia's end zone while awaiting Marino's pass.

Danny [Marino] just threw it out there and let me run under it. It was right there.

—JOHNNY BROWN, PITTSBURGH TIGHT END

Pittsburgh's John Brown (left) and Dan Marino celebrate inside New Orleans' Superdome after defeating Georgia on a 33-yard touchdown pass. *Photo courtesy of the University of Pittsburgh Athletics Department.*

DAN MARINO

Dan Marino is recognized as perhaps the greatest quarterback in professional football history. The 27th selection of the 1983 NFL draft, Marino surpassed Georgia alumnus Fran Tarkenton in fewer than 13 seasons as the NFL's all-time leader in both career passing yardage and career touchdown passes as the quarterback of the Miami Dolphins. Marino's records would not be broken for 12 years until Green Bay's Brett Favre broke them in 2007.

At Pittsburgh, Marino broke the school's freshman passing record in 1979 only when Rick Trocano, the starting quarterback, was injured in the seventh game. In 1980, it was Marino who was injured halfway through the season and, ironically, replaced by Trocano.

In his final two seasons of 1981 and 1982, Marino flourished, combining to pass for 5,308 yards and 54 touchdowns, while finishing fourth as a junior and ninth as a senior in the Heisman Trophy voting. There is little doubt that Marino's greatest collegiate moment was the win over Georgia in the '82 Sugar Bowl. He was named the game's MVP, passing for 261 yards and three touchdowns in "one of the most dramatic finishes in Pitt football history."

GAME DETAILS

Pittsburgh 24 • Georgia 20

Date: January 1, 1982

Site: Superdome

Attendance: 77,224

Records: Georgia 10–1; Pittsburgh 10–1

Rankings: Georgia: No. 2 (AP)/ No. 2 (UPI); Pittsburgh: No. 10 (AP)/ No. 8 (UPI)

Series: Pittsburgh 2–0–1 (Pittsburgh two-game winning streak)

> It was fourth and five, and I thought they'd [Pittsburgh] just be going for the first down.
>
> —BILL LEWIS,
> GEORGIA DEFENSIVE COORDINATOR

BILL LEWIS

Prior to arriving at Georgia in 1980 as its defensive backs coach, Bill Lewis was the head coach at Wyoming from 1977 to 1979. When Erk Russell accepted the head coach position at Georgia Southern University, Lewis was promoted to the Bulldogs' defensive coordinating position. Lewis's defenses from 1981 to 1983 were as dominating as Russell's editions. However, as Georgia's success on the gridiron began to diminish following the 1983 season, its defense, in particular, started becoming less effective. For three seasons from 1986 to 1988, with Lewis personally coaching the defensive secondary, the Bulldogs finished last in the SEC in pass defense each season.

A few days after the Bulldogs ended the '88 regular season, Lewis was named head coach at East Carolina University. In three years, Lewis's once-lowly Pirates ended the '91 campaign with an 11–1 record and a No. 9 national ranking. The American Football Coaches Association, United Press International, and Scripps-Howard's 1991 National Coach of the Year, Lewis became Georgia Tech's head coach in 1992. However, after consecutive 5–6 seasons and a 1–7 start in 1994, he stepped down.

An assistant with Miami in the NFL for nine seasons (1996–2004), Lewis returned to the collegiate level in 2005, where he continues to coach defensive backs at the University of Notre Dame. Through 2007 he has coached in college football alone for a staggering 35 years.

October 28, 1978

"YEAH! YEAH! YEAH!"

Rex Robinson's field goal lifts '78 Wonderdogs over upset-minded Wildcats

Bulletin-board postings in the Georgia dressing room prior to the Kentucky game included a newspaper article with "33–0" displayed in its headline, reminding the Bulldogs what had transpired the year before just in case anyone had forgotten.

In 1977 Georgia was embarrassed at home, 33–0, by the Wildcats in a game witnessed by a sold-out crowd and England's Prince Charles. The loss still ranks as the second-worst defeat of the Bulldogs in Athens over the past 45 seasons. Georgia finished the year 5–6—coach Vince Dooley's lone losing campaign in 25 years. However, the nationally ranked Bulldogs of '78 were vastly improved and nicknamed the Wonderdogs because prognosticators had predicted they would follow up the 1977 season with similarly poor results.

Against the Wildcats, the Wonderdogs were playing like the underdogs from the season before, as they were losing 16–0 in the third quarter. However, Georgia quickly posted three scores, including a last-second field goal. With eight seconds remaining in the game, place-kicker Rex Robinson, who

had missed two field-goal attempts in the first half, barely made a 29-yarder to defeat Kentucky by a single point.

Down 16–0, Georgia drove to a three-yard scoring run by Willie McClendon with 6:49 remaining in the third quarter. McClendon, who entered the game as the Southeastern Conference's leading rusher, would finish the contest with 146 rushing yards on 29 carries.

A six-yard touchdown pass from Jeff Pyburn to Ulysses Norris with 10:09 left in the game and Robinson's successful point-after kick cut Georgia's deficit to two points, 16–14.

With a little more than four minutes remaining, Kentucky kicker Tommy Griggs, who had missed a point-after attempt earlier in the game, failed on a 42-yard field goal. A successful field goal would have given the 'Cats a five-point lead. Instead, the Georgia offense and quarterback Pyburn took over.

Aided by McClendon's running and key pass completions from Pyburn to Amp Arnold and Lindsay Scott, the Bulldogs drove down the field in 12 plays to Kentucky's 12-yard line. Georgia called

GAME DETAILS

Georgia 17 • Kentucky 16

Date: October 28, 1978

Site: Commonwealth Stadium

Attendance: 56,918

Records: Georgia 5–1; Kentucky 2–3–1

Rankings: Georgia: No. 16 (AP)/ No. 13 (UPI)

Series: Georgia 22–7–2 (Kentucky one-game winning streak)

> **N**obody really said anything to me [as I prepared to attempt the last-second field goal], and I was glad because it gave me a chance to say a little prayer.
>
> —REX ROBINSON, PLACE-KICKER

its final timeout. Just as Robinson lined up to try the game-winning kick, the Wildcats attempted to ice him by calling a timeout of their own. Fortunately for the Dogs, the timeout worked in their favor as they only had 10 men on the field.

"We were thinking field goal all the way," said Dooley after the game. "I knew there was no way Rex Robinson was going to miss three in a row."

Robinson almost did miss, however, as his game-winning field goal just edged inside the left upright. Nevertheless, the kick was good, and Georgia held a 17–16 advantage with three seconds left. Kentucky's final play was a bomb thrown by quarterback Larry McCrimmon, which went into the Georgia sidelines.

The '78 Wonderdogs had done it again. Led by McClendon's running, Pyburn's passing, and Robinson's toe, Georgia had defeated a superior team and had rallied in the final moments for victory. It was sweet revenge on the Wildcats for the Bulldogs' embarrassment the year before.

> **H**e puts it up. It looks good. Watch it. Watch it. Yeah! Yeah! Yeah! Yeah! Three seconds left. Rex Robinson put 'em ahead, 17–16. The bench is unconscious. He kicked the whatchamacallit out of it!
>
> —GEORGIA ANNOUNCER LARRY MUNSON'S CALL
> OF REX ROBINSON'S WINNING KICK

JEFF PYBURN

In 1976 running back Jeff Pyburn came to Georgia, where his father, Jim, had been a defensive assistant since Vince Dooley's arrival in 1964. Pyburn was switched to quarterback in '77 and, along with Fran Tarkenton, Paul Gilbert, and Andy Johnson, became the fourth starting Bulldogs signal caller in the modern era from Athens, Georgia.

Pyburn, and the entire Georgia squad of 1978, surprised most of the pundits with his play on the gridiron. He quarterbacked the Bulldogs to a 9–1–1 regular-season record, giving Georgia a 14–3–1 mark through the '78 regular season when Pyburn started. His best game likely was against tKentucky, when Pyburn completed 11 of 15 passes for 140 yards and a touchdown. Most importantly, he rallied the Bulldogs from a 16-point deficit for one of the greatest comebacks in Georgia football history.

REX ROBINSON

Rex Robinson missed his first point-after attempt at Georgia versus Oregon in 1977. He would not miss again as a Bulldog, converting 101 points after touchdowns in a row through his senior season of 1980—the second-longest streak in NCAA history at the time.

Robinson, the first of a long line of exemplary place-kickers at Georgia, was more efficient at his role than most other teams' kickers were at kicking field goals during his collegiate career. From 1977 to 1980, 55.8 percent of field-goal attempts were kicked successfully in college football. In comparison, Robinson made 56 of 84 career field goals, or 66.7 percent.

He was most accurate during his sophomore season of '78, when he converted all 29 extra-point attempts and 15 of 17 field goals. Ironically, both of Robinson's missed field goals occurred in the first half against Kentucky—a 32-yarder in the opening quarter and from 48 yards just before halftime. After the misses, Robinson would successfully kick seven consecutive field goals through the end of the regular season, beginning with the 29-yard game winner over the Wildcats.

UGA

During its initial 60-plus years of playing football, the University of Georgia had a variety of mascots. The team used a goat during its first campaign of 1892, which was followed by Trilby, a bull terrier, a couple seasons later. In the mid-1940s Georgia began using bulldogs as its mascot. Mr. Angel was first and was succeeded by Butch, Tuffy, and Mike, who died in 1955.

Uga, a solid-white English bulldog, first appeared at Sanford Stadium on September 29, 1956, during Georgia's opening home game against Florida State. Interestingly, owner Sonny Seiler initially had no intention of bringing his bulldog to the stadium until members of Seiler's fraternity insisted that he do so.

Mascot Uga VI looks on inside the New Orleans Superdome during Georgia's win over Hawaii in the 2008 Sugar Bowl. The 2007 season marked the 52nd year that an Uga was present on the Bulldogs' sideline. *Photo courtesy of AP Images.*

October 11, 2003

MOMENTUM CHANGER IN KNOXVILLE

Sean Jones returns Tennessee fumble 92 yards as first half expires

During the coaching careers of Ray Goff and Jim Donnan at Georgia, the Bulldogs were essentially a second-rate team compared to Tennessee and Florida in the Southeastern Conference East. Whereas the Volunteers and Gators annually battled for the divisional title, the Bulldogs always seemed to be hoping to land a respectable bowl bid while fighting for third place in the East.

Running back Jabari Davis of Stone Mountain, Georgia, said that he chose to attend school and play football at Tennessee because "Georgia was always talking about getting to the Peach Bowl." According to Davis, Tennessee, on the other hand, had loftier goals like the Rose Bowl.

In 2000 the Bulldogs defeated the Volunteers for the first time since 1988, ending a nine-game winning streak for Tennessee. Head coach Mark Richt arrived in 2001 and upset the Volunteers on the road. The following season, Georgia defeated Tennessee 18–13 en route to the Bulldogs' first SEC title in 20 years. Despite the fact that the Bulldogs had overtaken Tennessee and Florida as the preeminent team in the

division, Georgia apparently still received little respect from some of its opposition.

Tennessee quarterback Casey Clausen missed the 2002 Georgia game with a fractured collarbone. Following his team's loss, Clausen commented that if he had played, the Volunteers would have won by a "couple of touchdowns," and he could have beaten Georgia with one arm tied behind his back. In 2003 both Clausen and Davis would have their final chance together to face the Bulldogs to see if their actions could speak as loud as their words.

Tennessee trailed Georgia 13–7 with only seven seconds remaining until halftime but had the ball inches from the Bulldogs' goal line. On third down and goal, Clausen took the snap and turned to his right to hand the ball to Davis. Fullback Troy Fleming, in attempting to run through the line to block, accidentally bumped Clausen's hand, and the ball was fumbled around the 5-yard line. Clausen and Georgia free safety Thomas Davis dove for the football but crashed into one another. The bobbled ball rolled right into the path of roverback Sean Jones. Jones scooped up the fumble at the 8-yard line and

All-American Sean Jones, pictured during the 2003 SEC Championship Game, made several big plays during his three-season tenure at Georgia. None, however, were greater than his 92-yard fumble return against Tennessee in 2003. *Photo courtesy of Getty Images.*

started down his left sideline. With a convoy of blockers, Jones streaked 92 yards into the end zone as time expired in the first half.

What should have been a one-point advantage for Tennessee at halftime was instead a 20–7 comfortable lead for Georgia. The Bulldogs kept their momentum through the half and into the third quarter, scoring three rushing touchdowns in a span of only 2:35 and eventually winning, 41–14. For the

THE FUMBLE RETURN

In an attempt to block for his teammate, Tennessee fullback Troy Fleming inadvertently bumped quarterback Casey Clausen's hand before the quarterback's handoff was received by Jabari Davis. The ball was fumbled and trickled toward the right of the offense. At the 6 Georgia's Thomas Davis attempted to pick up the fumble, but a diving Clausen knocked the ball loose. However, the fumble rolled directly in front of roverback Sean Jones, who picked up the football at the 8. Aided by a host of Bulldogs blockers as time ran out in the first half, Jones sprinted for pay dirt with no Volunteers remotely near him.

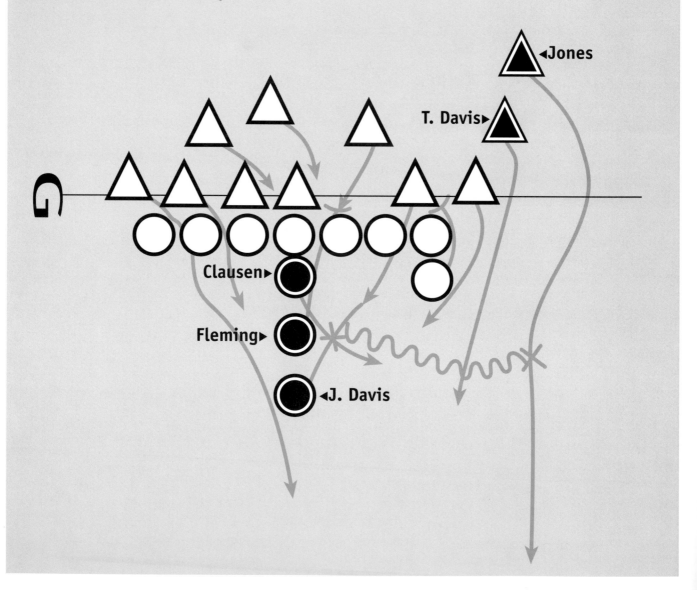

GAME DETAILS

Georgia 41 • Tennessee 14

Date: October 11, 2003

Site: Neyland Stadium

Attendance: 107,517

Records: Georgia 4–1; Tennessee 4–1

Rankings: Georgia: No. 8 (AP)/ No. 10 (ESPN); Tennessee: No. 13 (AP)/ No. 14 (ESPN)

Series: Tennessee 17–13–2 (Georgia three-game winning streak)

> **I** saw the [fumbled] ball, and I saw all green in front of me.
> —SEAN JONES, GEORGIA ROVERBACK

first time in history, Georgia defeated the Volunteers four consecutive seasons.

The Bulldogs had a 10–0 second-quarter lead until Clausen connected with Mark Jones for a 90-yard touchdown—a Tennessee record for longest pass play. Georgia's Billy Bennett kicked a field goal with 3:27 left in the quarter and gave the Bulldogs a six-point lead. In the final minutes, the Volunteers moved 87 yards in 11 plays. During the drive, Georgia committed two personal foul penalties by defenders Odell Thurman and Sean Jones within four plays of one another. The latter penalty moved Tennessee to the Bulldogs' 14-yard line with approximately 1:30 left on the clock. Three plays later, Cedric Houston rushed for two yards on first down to Georgia's 1-yard line. On second down, coach Phillip Fulmer called for Clausen to spike the ball to stop the clock. Instead, the quarterback sneaked for no gain. Because of the miscommunication, Tennessee was forced to call its final timeout of the first half with seven seconds remaining.

Only inches from tying the contest, the Volunteers lined up in their "jumbo package"—three tight ends and their two big backs: Davis (225 pounds) and Fleming (230). In hindsight, Tennessee should have selected a different package, as its special formation lost a game-changing fumble and yielded Sean Jones's magnificent 92-yard return.

During their careers at Tennessee, Clausen and Davis never defeated Georgia when seeing significant playing time in meetings between the rivals. Clausen, who always played with both arms against the Bulldogs, relieved A.J. Suggs in 2000 in a losing effort, and he started against Georgia and lost in 2001 and 2003. Davis saw action against the 'Dogs in 2002 and 2003. In those same seasons, he participated in the only two bowl games he experienced as a Volunteer—both losses in the Peach Bowl.

BRIAN VANGORDER

Brian VanGorder arrived at Georgia in 2001, along with a newly hired Mark Richt. After Georgia's defenses had been above average at best for most of the previous several years, VanGorder's defensive unit instantly began making its presence known. After ranking fourth in the country in scoring defense in 2002, the Bulldogs finished in the nation's top 10 in both total and scoring defense in 2003 and 2004. VanGorder coached six Bulldogs defenders, including Sean Jones, selected in the first two rounds of the NFL draft. In 2003 VanGorder was honored as the nation's top assistant coach.

Following the 2004 season VanGorder left Georgia and made a seemingly lateral move to coach linebackers for the Jacksonville Jaguars. Since 2005 VanGorder has held five different positions in both the NFL and college football and is currently the Atlanta Falcons' defensive coordinator.

The fiery, well-respected, and well-liked VanGorder was unfortunately a Bulldog for only four seasons. Nevertheless, he may be the best of the eight defensive coordinators Georgia has had since Erk Russell departed in 1980.

> **T**hat [Jones's return] was probably the biggest momentum changer I've ever seen in a big game.
>
> —MARK RICHT, GEORGIA HEAD COACH

SEAN JONES

During the University of Tennessee's last drive before halftime of the 2003 game, Sean Jones committed one of Georgia's two costly personal fouls. The penalty by Jones infuriated defensive coordinator Brian VanGorder to the point where the coach stepped from the sideline and literally slapped Jones upside his helmet. VanGorder must have slapped some sense into Jones as, moments later, the roverback was aware enough to recover a Tennessee fumble and race 92 yards for a score.

Jones culminated three seasons at Georgia by being selected consensus All-SEC and first-team All-American in 2003 by the American Football Coaches Association. In his collegiate career, Jones recorded 250 tackles, 10 tackles for loss, 10 passes broken up, seven interceptions, and four blocked kicks. His 16.0 career punt return average (160 yards on 10 returns—all in 2002) ranks second in school history among players with at least 10 career returns.

Jones came out of college early following his junior campaign to enter the NFL draft. A second-round selection by Cleveland, he sat out the 2004 season with a knee injury. By his third season, he was starting at strong safety for the Browns. For the past two years, Jones has recorded five interceptions each season for Cleveland.

An injured Casey Clausen looks on in disgust as Tennessee is beaten by Georgia in 2002. The Volunteers never defeated the Bulldogs with Clausen at quarterback, including a devastating 41–14 loss in 2003. *Photo courtesy of AP Images.*

November 13, 1982

THE DOGS BROKE IT UP!

Jeff Sanchez and Ronnie Harris break up Auburn's pass in end zone as Georgia wins third consecutive SEC title

The undefeated Bulldogs entered their game at Auburn in 1982 having just been ranked No. 1 in both major polls only a few days before. The conference championship and a possible national title were at stake for Georgia, whereas a win by the Tigers could propel them to a first-place tie with the 'Dogs in the SEC.

Auburn had one of the most extraordinary running games in college football. Quarterback Randy Campbell, fullback Ron O'Neal, and tailbacks Lionel James and Bo Jackson formed the Tigers' wishbone formation—an offense not normally associated with passing. Despite running the wishbone, however, Auburn's passing attack could be dangerous and was actually much more prolific than Georgia's.

Down 19–14 with 49 seconds remaining in the game, Auburn was on Georgia's 21-yard line but faced a fourth down and 17 for a first down. Campbell, who had some success throwing against an outstanding Georgia secondary, dropped back to throw. He floated a lofty pass in the end zone for split end Mike Edwards. Georgia's safety Jeff Sanchez, cornerback Ronnie Harris, and Edwards all jumped for the ball, but none of them came down with it. The football dropped harmlessly to the turf, and the Bulldogs, taking over on downs, were only 42 seconds away from their third consecutive conference title.

Early in the fourth quarter, with the Tigers trailing by six points, the 5'7", 165-pound James scored on an 87-yard run—at the time, the second-longest rushing or passing play in Auburn history. Losing 14–13, Georgia began its possession from its 20-yard line. Thirteen plays and 80 yards later, Herschel Walker scored on a three-yard run, and the Bulldogs regained the lead. On the drive, Walker rushed for 37 yards on eight carries, and quarterback John Lastinger completed a key third-down-and-six pass to Herman Archie for 17 yards; Georgia completed only three passes for the entire game for 26 yards. Walker finished the contest with 177 rushing yards on 31 carries and two touchdowns en route to eventually capturing the Heisman Trophy.

With a little less than nine minutes left in the game, Auburn began a drive from its own 20-yard line and soon reached Bulldogs territory; an O'Neal run carried the ball to Georgia's 14-yard line with 3:04 remaining.

A penalty on Auburn moved the ball back five yards, and Georgia's Tony Flack followed by tackling Jackson two yards behind the line of scrimmage. From the 21-yard line, Georgia defensive end Dale Carver made one of the most significant plays of the year for the Bulldogs by sacking Campbell for a nine-yard loss with a little more than a minute left on the clock. On third and 26, from the 30-yard line, Campbell completed a nine-yard pass to tight end Ed West.

On Campbell's fourth-down pass into the end zone, Edwards, the intended target, later claimed all he saw were two Bulldogs defenders leaping in front of him. Edwards

Auburn's fourth-down pass attempt intended for Mike Edwards (No. 89) is broken up in the end zone by Georgia's Jeff Sanchez (center) and Ronnie Harris (No. 27), clinching a 19–14 Bulldogs victory. *Photo courtesy of Wingate Downs.*

Vince Dooley receives a victory ride at Auburn, having won his sixth SEC championship (and third in a row) in 19 seasons as Georgia's head coach. *Photo courtesy of Wingate Downs.*

THE BREAKUP

As four receivers ran toward Georgia's end zone, Auburn quarterback Randy Campbell dropped back to pass. As a Bulldogs defender rushed up the middle and another blitzed from his left, Campbell was forced to throw earlier than desired. He barely got off a high, wobbly pass from his 29. The desperation heave descended left of intended receiver Mike Edwards and fell incomplete between Georgia's Jeff Sanchez and Ronnie Harris.

> **I** left my man and went for the ball. We [Sanchez and Harris] both caught the ball and dropped it.
>
> —JEFF SANCHEZ, GEORGIA SAFETY

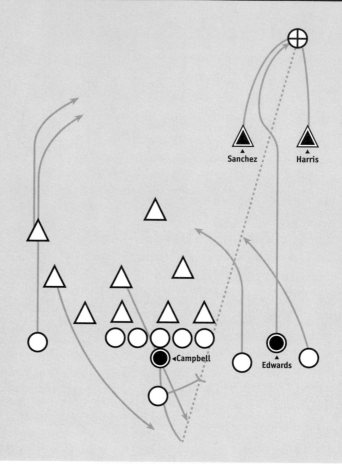

JEFF SANCHEZ

Born in Georgia, Jeff Sanchez attended Fullerton Junior College in California out of high school. In 1982 he returned to Georgia and started at safety for the Bulldogs. For the season, he finished runner-up in the nation with nine interceptions, second to teammate Terry Hoage's 12. Against Auburn, Sanchez recorded 10 tackles and intercepted a pass. The Tigers entered the game having thrown only one interception in 146 attempts for the season. The junior safety was responsible for both of Auburn's turnovers as he also recovered a Tigers fumble.

After breaking his arm, Sanchez was redshirted for the 1983 season. He returned the following year to make 113 tackles and lead the team with four interceptions. Sanchez was a first-team All-American in '84 and is one of only a few Bulldogs players in history to be named first-team all-conference in every season he played at Georgia. Despite playing for only two seasons, Sanchez's 13 career interceptions are tied for fourth all time at the school.

Sanchez was a 12th-round selection of the NFL's Pittsburgh Steelers.

GAME DETAILS

Georgia 19 • Auburn 14

Date: November 13, 1982

Site: Jordan-Hare Stadium

Attendance: 74,800

Records: Georgia 9–0; Auburn 7–2

Rankings: Georgia: No. 1 (AP)/ No. 1 (UPI)

Series: Georgia 40–38–7 (Georgia two-game winning streak)

> **W**e [Georgia's defense] had our backs to the wall, and we had to stand up and fight.
>
> —RONNIE HARRIS, GEORGIA CORNERBACK

had been lined up on the outside with Georgia's Harris while Sanchez was positioned on the inside with a different receiver. As Campbell threw toward Edwards, Sanchez abandoned his man and went for the ball. Both Sanchez and Harris leapt for the ball in front of Edwards and broke up the potential winning pass.

From its 21-yard line, Georgia ran out the remaining seconds on the clock and seized a 19–14 victory. Soon afterward, coach Vince Dooley was carried off Auburn's field on the shoulders of his players, celebrating his 150th career victory and his sixth Southeastern Conference championship.

RONNIE HARRIS

Like Jeff Sanchez, Ronnie Harris also attended a California junior college, came to Georgia, and was instantly starting in the Bulldogs' defensive backfield. Harris, from San Diego, earned recognition in his second game at Georgia by intercepting two passes against a team from his home state, the California Golden Bears. From his left cornerback position, Harris led the Bulldogs in '81 with four interceptions, not including the two he corralled against Pittsburgh's Dan Marino in the Sugar Bowl. Harris's two interceptions against the Panthers are tied for a school record for most interceptions in a bowl game.

As a senior in '82, Harris's late interception of Brigham Young University's Steve Young sealed a three-point Georgia victory. Three games later, he would pick off two passes against Ole Miss. Harris finished his final season as a Bulldog with four interceptions and was chosen to play in the 1983 Japan Bowl, a college all-star game.

Following college, Harris made the roster of the 1985 Chicago Blitz of the United States Football League. He currently is a social studies teacher and secondary coach at Oglethorpe County High School, located in Lexington, Georgia.

27

THE DROUGHT-BREAKER

Theron Sapp's one-yard touchdown plunge ends Georgia's eight-game losing streak to the Yellow Jackets

It had seemed like forever and a day since Georgia had defeated its foremost rival, Georgia Tech. Not since 1948 had the Yellow Jackets been beaten, when John Rauch quarterbacked the Bulldogs. Rauch was now Georgia's backfield coach, nine years removed since throwing his last pass in Athens. The Bulldogs had experienced a disappointing era since their last victory over their intrastate rival: only three winning campaigns in nine seasons, just one bowl game, and a 40–49–6 overall record. However, none of the many losses were as difficult to endure as the eight in a row suffered at the hands of Georgia's hated neighbors to the southwest.

In 1957, on Georgia's ninth attempt to defeat the Jackets, the Bulldogs found themselves in a scoreless tie late in the third quarter. Georgia Tech had lost a critical fumble at midfield, and behind the running of fullback Theron Sapp, Georgia had driven to the opponent's 1-yard line. The Bulldogs were faced with fourth down and goal. Georgia had ridden the standout Sapp down the field, so there was no reason not to give him the ball in this crucial situation.

Quarterback Charley Britt gave the 196-pound junior from Macon, Georgia, the ball for the ninth time on the drive. Sapp started to his right and, aided by blocks from halfback Jimmy Orr and end Ken Cooper, found an accommodating gap and spilled over Tech's defensive line. Sapp literally fell on his face in the end zone for a touchdown. "If I hadn't stumbled on the touchdown run, I would have probably run right out the back of the end zone," Sapp said a half-century after his score.

The Bulldogs' points were their first following consecutive shutouts by Florida and Auburn and their first touchdown against Georgia Tech in four years. Most importantly, with only 2:17 remaining in the third stanza, Georgia was only a little more than a quarter away from breaking its eight-game drought to the Jackets.

The game had started in 35-degree weather, and both teams seemed to feel the near-freezing effects, missing a number of scoring opportunities in the first half. On the first possession of the third quarter, Georgia Tech reached the Bulldogs' 47-yard line before losing three yards and a fumble recovered by Sapp at the midfield stripe.

From the 50-yard line, Sapp gained one yard, and halfback George Guisler followed

Game Details

Georgia 7 • Georgia Tech 0

Date: November 30, 1957

Site: Grant Field

Attendance: 40,000

Records: Georgia 2–7; Georgia Tech 4–3–2

Series: Georgia Tech 24–22–5 (Georgia Tech eight-game winning streak)

> Eight years is a long time. All streaks always end.
>
> —BOBBY DODD, GEORGIA TECH HEAD COACH

with a five-yard rush. On third and four, Sapp bulled to the 37-yard line for a first down. Guisler rushed for only two, and Britt lost four on second down back to the Jackets' 39-yard line. Faced with an improbable conversion on third down and 12 (Georgia completed only 41 passes the entire 1957 season), Britt passed to Orr for 13 yards—the only Bulldogs completion during the entire game.

On first down, Sapp rushed for seven yards. He followed that run from the 26-yard line with consecutive rushes of three yards, seven, four, three, and one to the 1-yard line. Britt, who called every play of the game as no plays were sent in from the sideline, decided to try for the end zone himself on third down and goal but was stopped for no gain.

On fourth down, Britt elected to run a play where the fullback was to slant off tackle. The Bulldogs had attempted the same play the game before against Auburn from the 3-yard line, but they'd fumbled in the 6–0 loss. The Bulldogs would not fumble this time, however, as Sapp tumbled into the end zone for a touchdown and immortality.

With approximately five minutes remaining in the game, the Yellow Jackets reached Georgia's 16-yard line before turning the ball over on downs. On the ensuing possession, Britt fumbled on his own 27-yard line, but the hero Sapp was there to recover his quarterback's blunder. The Bulldogs held on to their slim 7–0 advantage and finally defeated their arch nemesis due in large part to the effort of Sapp, forever known as "the Drought-Breaker."

> There was no way I could have not scored on fourth down and walked back to the sidelines to face my teammates.
>
> —THERON SAPP, FORMER GEORGIA FULLBACK
> 50 YEARS AFTER HIS MEMORABLE TOUCHDOWN

CHARLEY BRITT

Charley Britt is one of the most undervalued players in Georgia football history and one of the last outstanding two-way performers. He was the Bulldogs' starting quarterback for three seasons (1957–1959), including the '59 Southeastern Conference championship squad, passing for 1,281 career yards and 11 touchdowns. A standout also on defense and returning punts, Britt tallied eight career interceptions, most notably his 100-yard return for a touchdown against Florida in 1959. Britt's commendable 11.8 career punt return average includes the 39-yard touchdown return he had to help defeat Auburn for the SEC title his senior year. In 1959 Britt was selected third-team All-SEC by the United Press International.

The 25th selection of the 1960 NFL draft, Britt played defensive back for Los Angeles, Minnesota, and San Francisco from 1960 to 1964. He made 14 career interceptions, including five in each of his first two seasons (1960 and 1961) with the Rams.

THERON SAPP

Theron Sapp led the Bulldogs in rushing in both the 1957 and 1958 seasons. His 599 yards as a junior, including a "drought-breaking" 91 on 23 carries against Georgia Tech, were a team best since 1950. As a senior, he bettered his previous total by rushing for 635 yards and finished with 1,265 in three seasons (1956–1958) on Georgia's varsity. This total was tied for fifth-best in school history upon Sapp's graduation, and 50 years later, it still ranks tied for 30th at Georgia entering the 2008 season. As a junior, Sapp was chosen third-team Associated Press All–Southeastern Conference and, a year later, second-team AP and first-team United Press International All-SEC (Georgia's only first-team all-conference selection from 1954 to 1958).

Sapp's No. 40 jersey was retired at Georgia in 1959, joining Frank Sinkwich, Charley Trippi, and 26 years later, Herschel Walker as the only four Bulldogs to be bestowed that honor. Whereas Sinkwich, Trippi, and Walker are three of the greatest college football players of all time, Sapp, who had a fine career at Georgia and in seven seasons in the NFL, was mostly honored because of a single play he made to break the Bulldogs' longstanding drought against their despised state rival.

THE GEORGIA–GEORGIA TECH RIVALRY

Only 70 miles separate the two schools whose intrastate rivalry is referred to as "clean, old-fashioned hate." Georgia and Georgia Tech have met 100 times (102 according to Tech) since 1893—the Bulldogs' second-most-played rivalry in their history. In 1919 a dispute erupted between the two schools at a baseball game followed by additional controversy during a senior parade. As a result there were no scheduled regular-season games between the teams in any sport for six years.

The two bitter rivals cannot even agree on their series record. Georgia claims to have a 59–36–5 advantage through 2007, while Georgia Tech claims two additional victories (59–38–5). Georgia discredits two losses to Tech during World War II.

The Bulldogs argue that losses in 1943 and 1944 were not to "true" Georgia Tech teams. During these seasons, the Yellow Jackets' football squad was supplemented by the V-12 Navy College Training Program, which provided former or future players from other schools.

An interesting aspect concerning the football rivalry is that the yearly winner is usually amidst a series winning streak. Georgia's victory in 2007 was its seventh consecutive win over Georgia Tech, a string that followed a Yellow Jackets three-game winning streak from 1998 to 2000, which came after seven Bulldogs wins in a row from 1991 to 1997. In fact, not since 1977 has the result of the annual game not been part of at least a two-game streak in the rivalry. The longest series winning streak was when Georgia Tech was victorious for eight consecutive contests starting in 1949. The long drought was finally broken in 1957 with a 7–0 win by Theron Sapp and his fellow Bulldogs.

In the 2007 meeting of the Georgia–Georgia Tech rivalry, Yellow Jackets quarterback Taylor Bennett (No. 13) is swarmed by Georgia's Dannell Ellerbe (No. 33) and Geno Atkins during the 31–17 Bulldogs victory. The win was Georgia's seventh consecutive triumph over Georgia Tech. *Photo courtesy of AP Images.*

26 BOBO-TO-ALLEN II

Mike Bobo's touchdown pass to Corey Allen in final seconds defeats Georgia Tech for seventh consecutive season

Corey Allen told his mother not to miss the upcoming Georgia–Georgia Tech game of 1997. The Bulldogs flanker wanted to make sure that she and all their friends would be watching. The senior Allen, from Riverdale, would be returning home to Atlanta to play in his last regular-season college football game. He had played sparingly in his freshman and sophomore seasons as a Bulldog and made three starts in 1996. It was against Auburn as a junior that Allen made his unforgettable, game-tying, 30-yard touchdown reception on the final play of regulation. In his last season of 1997, Allen had finally become a starting wide receiver, and he promised his mother that he would put on a show against the Yellow Jackets.

Georgia Tech led Georgia 24–21, but the Bulldogs had moved the ball to the Jackets' 8-yard line. With only 14 seconds remaining in the game, quarterback Mike Bobo took the snap from the shotgun formation and dropped back a few steps. He lofted a fade pass toward the left corner of Tech's end zone. Bobo's pass was perfect, lobbed over Tech defensive back Travares Tillman

into the waiting arms of Allen for a Georgia touchdown.

The Bulldogs now had a 27–24 advantage with only eight seconds left on the clock. The Yellow Jackets had time to run only one play. Quarterback Joe Hamilton's desperation pass fell harmlessly incomplete to the ground, and Georgia had defeated Georgia Tech for the seventh consecutive season.

Georgia had led 14–10 at halftime and sat comfortably at 21–10 following a touchdown pass from Bobo to Hines Ward late in the third quarter. However, the Yellow Jackets scored 14 consecutive points, including a three-yard touchdown run by Charles Wiley on fourth down and one and a successful two-point conversion with 48 seconds remaining in the contest.

After the Yellow Jackets' final score, giving them a three-point lead, Tech linebacker Keith Brooking warned his teammates on the sideline, "It's not over. A lot can happen in 48 ticks." It was far from over, and a lot did happen.

For the third consecutive Jackets kickoff, Dave Frakes's kick went out of bounds,

Corey Allen's touchdown catch from Mike Bobo against Georgia Tech in 1997 with only eight seconds remaining was his second scoring reception in just over a year that directly led to a Georgia victory. *Photo courtesy of Getty Images.*

allowing Georgia to start its drive on the 35-yard line. On the first play, Bobo threw a slant pass to Champ Bailey, who ran all the way to Georgia Tech's 37-yard line. Bobo connected with Bailey again for seven yards and then passed to Robert Edwards for a nine-yard gain to the Jackets' 21-yard line. On first down with 21 seconds remaining, Bobo's toss over the middle was intercepted by Tillman, and

the Bulldogs' chances for victory seemingly had been dashed. However, Tech's Brian Wilkins had been draped all over Ward, and fortunately for Georgia, the free safety was called for interference. The ball was placed at the 8-yard line, and the 'Dogs' rally was kept alive. On the next play, Bobo found Allen in the back corner of the end zone for the winning score.

CHAMP BAILEY

It was soon realized that Roland "Champ" Bailey was a special football player in 1996 as he made the Southeastern Conference's all-freshman team; however, yet to be discovered was his versatility. Prior to his sophomore season, coach Jim Donnan announced that Bailey would play at wideout on offense in addition to cornerback on defense. Bailey made 12 catches in 1997, including five against Auburn. His two consecutive receptions versus Georgia Tech occurred on Georgia's game-winning drive; the first of 28 yards began the scoring possession. In Bailey's final season at Georgia in 1998, he was a star on both sides of the ball and on special teams. Champ recorded 52 tackles, three interceptions, and a team-high 744 receiving yards on 47 catches, and he appeared in a remarkable average of 87 plays per game (almost 50 on defense and slightly more than 27 on offense, and nearly 10 on special teams). The versatile, three-way standout finished seventh in the Heisman Trophy voting, the last Bulldog to appear in the top 10 of the award's balloting through 2007.

Bailey's versatility is evident in the career statistical categories in which he remains ranked at Georgia: second in all-time career passes broken up, 21st in kickoff return average, 23rd in interceptions, and 30th in receiving.

Bailey has played nine seasons in the NFL, five in Washington and four with Denver. Through 2007, he had recorded 42 career interceptions and 320 kick-/punt-return yards, made four receptions, and rushed for a touchdown in 2000.

One month after helping Georgia win a stunning victory over Florida in 1997 (right), Champ Bailey caught two critical passes on the Bulldogs' game-winning drive against Georgia Tech. *Photo courtesy of Getty Images.*

Game Details

Georgia 27 • Georgia Tech 24

Date: November 29, 1997

Site: Bobby Dodd Stadium

Attendance: 46,015

Records: Georgia 8–2; Georgia Tech 6–4

Rankings: Georgia: No. 16 (AP)/ No. 21 (ESPN)

Series: Georgia 51–33–5 (Georgia six-game winning streak)

> The Lord shined on us today and gave us another chance.
>
> —MIKE BOBO, GEORGIA QUARTERBACK

Earlier, when it had appeared that Georgia Tech won the game after Wiley's touchdown with less than a minute left, Georgia center Brad Stafford reminded his teammates not to give up and "remember Auburn from last year." He was referring to the Bulldogs' come-from-behind 56–49 victory in four overtimes over Auburn the previous season after being behind 28–7 at one point. Allen certainly remembered Auburn from 1996 as he put on another show a year later against Georgia Tech for his mother, friends, and everyone else who witnessed his second game-changing, unforgettable catch.

Corey Allen

After seeing limited playing time in 1994 and 1995, Corey Allen was third at Georgia in receiving as a junior with 29 catches. The Bulldogs' starting flanker in '97, Allen was second on the team behind Hines Ward with 32 catches for 510 yards. The little-known receiver played in the shadow of Ward, a childhood friend. In fact, after catching the game-winning pass against Georgia Tech, Georgia announcer Larry Munson said that it was surprising that it was Allen "not Hines Ward...in the corner." Allen caught only five touchdowns as a Bulldog, but two of them, his grab against Auburn in '96 and his second score against Tech in '97, rank among the most memorable in Georgia football history.

> Bobo threw it high enough, and I was able to jump over the defensive back.
>
> —COREY ALLEN, GEORGIA WIDE RECEIVER

After college, Allen signed with the Atlanta Falcons as an undrafted free agent but did not make the squad. He did appear in some NFL exhibition games a couple of years later but never made a team's regular-season roster. In 2001 Allen caught 12 passes with the Scottish Claymores of NFL Europe.

THE FADE

In shotgun formation Mike Bobo received the snap and drifted back to the 11. Receiver Corey Allen, lined up to the left of Bobo, ran by cornerback Travares Tillman, straight into the end zone. Bobo threw a fade pass just beyond the reach of Tillman that hit Allen squarely between the numbers approximately eight yards behind the goal line for the game-winning score.

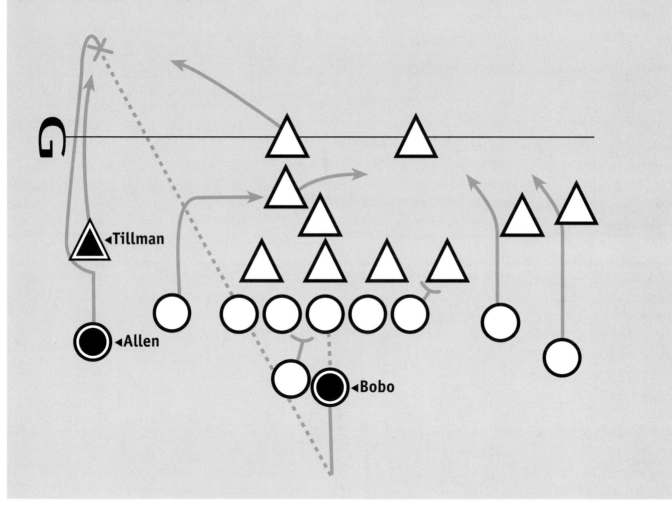

Hines Ward scores a first-quarter touchdown on a 54-yard reception from Mike Bobo for the initial points of the game. The versatile receiver scored again on another pass from Bobo in the third quarter. *Photo courtesy of AP Images.*

November 7, 1964

25 SETTLING FOR SIX

Kicker Bobby Etter defeats Gators with his feet instead of his toe in 1964

By early November of Vince Dooley's first season as Georgia's head coach, the Bulldogs had already surpassed most expectations. While many felt that Georgia would win no more than two games in the 1964 season, the Bulldogs had suffered only two defeats in seven contests entering the Florida game.

However, Georgia was facing a top-10-ranked Gators team and one that had defeated the Bulldogs in four consecutive meetings. Despite Georgia being a 10-point underdog, Coach Dooley felt his squad had an "outside chance" to defeat Florida. Indeed, Georgia used an outside chance run off a botched field goal by the most unlikely of runners to upset the Gators.

With 9:25 left in a tied, 7–7 game, Georgia sophomore Bob Etter lined up to attempt a field goal snapped from Florida's 5-yard line and placed at the 12. The snap floated "like a knuckleball" and slipped off the fingertips of holder Barry Wilson. An alert Etter scooped up the ball and, without hesitation, raced laterally to his left. After faking a screen pass, Etter dove for the goal line flag and scored what would be the game-winning touchdown.

Led by sophomore sensation quarterback Steve Spurrier, Florida, as expected, jumped out to a 7–0 second-quarter lead. Early in the fourth quarter, however, Georgia tied the Gators following a two-yard scoring run off tackle by Fred Barber.

After the ensuing kickoff, Florida lost its fourth fumble of the game (it had only lost three in six games entering the contest) recovered by Georgia cornerback Doug McFalls on the Gators' 21-yard line. Three plays netted the Bulldogs 10 yards to Florida's 11-yard line. Georgia would soon face fourth down and four on the Gators' 5.

The snap of the field goal was slightly low and outside. Wilson bobbled it toward his left, but the football just happen to roll to an unexpected but alert Etter. Redeeming himself for his misplayed snap, Wilson made a fine block on a Gator enclosing on Etter. As the kicker began to run toward the goal line, end Frank Richter took out Florida tackle Dennis Murphy, who had pulled off the line to guard against Etter's potential screen pass.

After Etter had scored the five-yard touchdown, he got up in a daze and asked, "What happened?" After being told he had

A 32-year-old Vince Dooley was seemingly not much older than the young boy he is shown holding when he coached Georgia to a 14–7 upset win over Florida in 1964—only the third victory for the Bulldogs in 30 tries against a ranked opponent since 1951. *Photo courtesy of AP Images.*

VINCE DOOLEY

When a 31-year-old Vince Dooley was hired as Georgia's head coach in 1964, it amazed just about everyone. Quarterback and later All-American safety Lynn Hughes said years later, "We were sitting on the steps at Stegeman [Hall] wondering, 'Who the hell is Vince Dooley?'"

Dooley's celebrated coaching career includes many accolades, namely 201 victories, six Southeastern Conference titles, and a national championship in 1980. Equally impressive is one little-known fact:

From 1951 until the 1964 Florida game, Georgia was a dreadful 2–27–1 against ranked opponents—both victories occurring during the 1959 SEC championship campaign. From the win over ninth-ranked Florida in '64 through the 1968 regular season, Dooley's Dogs were a remarkable 8–0–2 against ranked opposition.

The coach in his early thirties, who nearly no one gave a chance to succeed in coaching the Bulldogs, quickly turned around a Georgia football program that had been steadily deteriorating since the late 1940s.

> So, we had to "settle" for a touchdown instead of kicking the winning field goal.
>
> —DAN MAGILL, GEORGIA FOOTBALL HISTORIAN

scored a touchdown, Etter responded, "What do we do now?" Upon being told that he now had to attempt the extra point, Etter stated, "Can't…. Can't find my kicking tee."

After finding his tee, a rattled Etter missed the point after wide to his left. He had been perfect on 12 point-after attempts for the season before his miss. However, Florida was offsides, giving Etter a second chance. Etter's successful extra point gave Georgia a 14–7 lead.

The Bulldogs defense was stellar in the second half, allowing Florida to gain just 40 total yards and two

first downs. On the game's final possession, the Gators reached Georgia's 45-yard line in time for one final play, but Spurrier's last-second desperation heave into the Bulldogs' end zone was intercepted by McFalls.

Entering the Florida game of his first year on Georgia's varsity, the diminutive Bob Etter, weighing approximately 145 pounds, had never run an offensive play in football since the start of his high school playing days. He finally got his chance against the Gators and scored an improbable six-pointer when only three points were intended.

GAME DETAILS

Georgia 14 • Florida 7

Date: November 7, 1964

Site: Gator Bowl

Attendance: 48,000

Records: Georgia 4–2–1; Florida 5–1

Rankings: Florida: No. 9 (AP)/ No. 10 (UPI)

Series: Georgia 26–15–1 (Florida four-game winning streak)

> **I** thought I was dreaming [during the botched field goal].... I didn't have time to think.... I was just running.
>
> —BOB ETTER, PLACE-KICKER

BOB ETTER

Following the Florida game in 1964, Bob Etter went on to a distinguished kicking career at Georgia, where he was "one of the most valuable players in Bulldog football history," according to Georgia's 1967 football media guide.

Although Etter would not score another touchdown, he would become one of the most accurate kickers in college football during his time. He was perfect kicking points after touchdowns in 1964, and during the 1965–1966 seasons he kicked a then-school-record 24 in a row. In 1965 he led the Southeastern Conference in field goals made (10), and in '66 he became the first player in conference history to lead the SEC in scoring (57 points) strictly by place-kicking. Despite playing more than three decades ago and kicking for just three seasons, Etter still remains in Georgia's top 25 in all-time scoring with 134 career points.

Etter followed up his successful collegiate stint with two years in the NFL as the Atlanta Falcons' place-kicker in 1968 and 1969.

October 15, 1983

24 TERRY TIPS AWAY TOUCHDOWN

Terry Hoage tips a sure Vanderbilt touchdown in 1983 to help secure victory

Entering the 44th meeting between Georgia and Vanderbilt, the Bulldogs had defeated the Commodores nine straight times and had lost just once since 1961. However, the '83 Vandy squad was not necessarily the Commodores of old. It had won eight games the year before, and although Vanderbilt had a 2–3 record, all three of the losses were to nationally ranked opponents. The Commodores exhibited a high-powered passing attack, averaging more than 300 yards per game, ranking fourth in the nation. Undefeated Georgia hoped to become Vandy's fourth loss to a ranked opponent, but a victory would not be easy for the Bulldogs.

Georgia's Terry Hoage emerged in 1982 as one of the most outstanding defensive players in school history. He led the nation in interceptions with 12, including a school-record three against Vanderbilt. By 1983 the senior roverback was touted as arguably college football's greatest defensive back. A week prior to the Vandy game, Hoage missed the Ole Miss contest

with an injury and practiced only one day the following week. Against the Commodores, the consensus All-American would play out of position at safety, filling in for an injured Charlie Dean. Hoage and the rest of Georgia's pass defenders had their hands full against the Commodores' feared passing game.

Trailing the Bulldogs by only seven points with approximately 30 seconds left in the game, Vanderbilt was within striking distance to possibly hand Georgia its first loss of the season. Deep in Georgia territory, quarterback Kurt Page was chased out of the pocket and rolled to his right. He lofted a pass to split end Joe Kelly, who was wide open in the far right corner of the end zone. Just as Kelly opened his arms to make the catch, Hoage appeared out of nowhere, and leaping as high as he could, tipped the ball. Falling backward in the end zone in front of Kelly, Hoage had succeeded in breaking up a touchdown.

Earlier in the first half, Georgia's Keith Montgomery scored two touchdowns;

After his pass deflection broke up a potential game-winning touchdown pass against Vanderbilt in 1983, Terry Hoage (No. 14) celebrates with cornerback Darryl Jones (No. 17). *Photo courtesy of Wingate Downs.*

KURT PAGE

Kurt Page, Vanderbilt's record-breaking passer, threw for 6,233 career yards from 1981 to 1984, of which nearly 5,600 were in his junior and senior seasons. Page is profiled because he was the epitome of Commodores quarterbacks during the 1980s who piled up big yardage against the Bulldogs although in a losing effort. Other Vandy quarterback victims included Whit Taylor, John Gromos, Mark Wracher, and Eric Jones. Page against Georgia in '83 was no exception, when in defeat he threw for 303 yards on 33 completions—a school record until 2005.

Against Georgia as a senior, Page and backup Wracher combined to pass for 320 yards, and each threw two touchdowns. However, the Commodores fell victim 62–35.

Page has also experienced success in football since his college days. He was recently called "one of the most sought-after [high school] athletic directors in the country." Page serves as athletics director and head football coach at St. Thomas High School, an all-boys Catholic school in Houston, Texas.

Against the Bulldogs, Vanderbilt's Kurt Page threw 303 yards on a school-record 33 completions; however, he could not direct the Commodores to an offensive touchdown in a 20–13 loss.
Photo courtesy of Wingate Downs.

GAME DETAILS

Georgia 20 • Vanderbilt 13

Date: October 15, 1983

Site: Vanderbilt Stadium

Attendance: 41,223

Records: Georgia 4–0–1; Vanderbilt 2–3

Rankings: Georgia: No. 8 (AP)/ No. 6 (UPI)

Series: Georgia 27–15–1 (Georgia nine-game winning streak)

> **I** don't know if I'd made it if the quarterback hadn't floated the ball just a little bit.
>
> —TERRY HOAGE, DEFENSIVE BACK

however, two turnovers by backup quarterback Todd Williams led to 10 Vanderbilt points, and the Commodores trailed by only four at halftime.

Vanderbilt kicked a third-quarter field goal and pulled within a point. Kevin Butler countered with two field goals, the second giving Georgia a 20–13 lead with 1:41 remaining in the contest.

Despite the Bulldogs often placing eight defenders in pass coverage, they could not stop Page's passing prowess. In the game, the junior quarterback threw for more than 300 yards on 33 of 56 passes. Commodore Keith Edwards finished with 17 receptions—a Southeastern Conference record that stood for 18 years. Prior to Vandy's final drive, Page had thrown three interceptions, including one corralled by Hoage in the second quarter on the Bulldogs' 16-yard line.

In the final two minutes of play and trailing by a touchdown, Page drove the Commodores to Georgia's 24-yard line. On second down and 10 to go, Page threw what appeared to be the perfect pass. Kelly, running a post route to the corner of the end zone, was also in the apparent perfect place. Attempting to cover the intended receiver, Hoage first slipped and fell on the artificial turf. Picking himself up, he ran toward Kelly and arrived at the very last moment to tip away Page's pass. Two plays later, Andre Holmes intercepted Page on the goal line, conserving the Bulldogs' seven-point lead.

Following Georgia's 20–13 victory, coach Vince Dooley said the leaping pass breakup was the greatest play he had ever seen and that Hoage was the best defensive player he had coached in his 20 years at Georgia.

> **W**here did he come from? I thought it was a touchdown all the way.
>
> —KURT PAGE, VANDERBILT QUARTERBACK

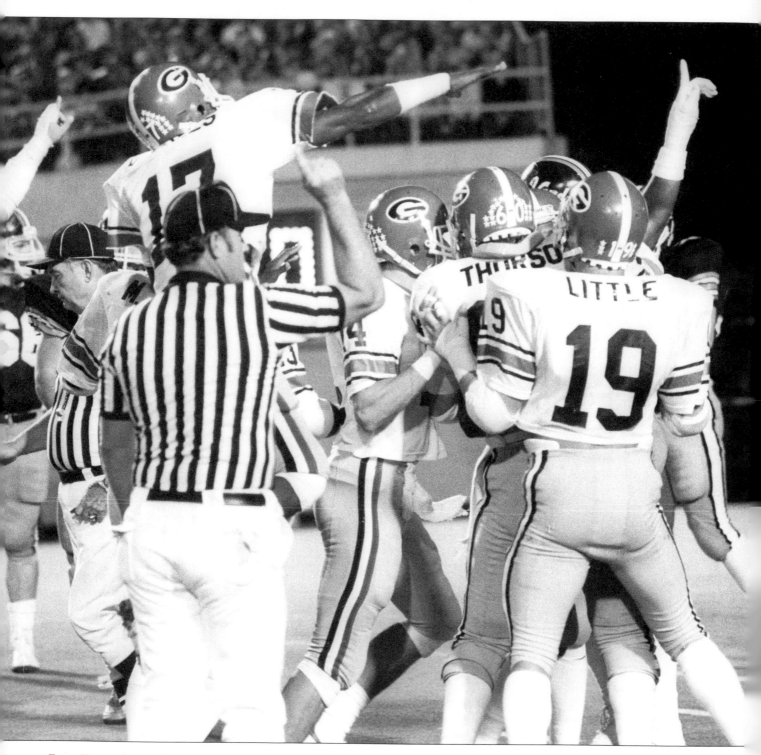

Terry Hoage (center) is mobbed by several Georgia defenders, celebrating his breakup of the Commodores' pass into the end zone. *Photo courtesy of Wingate Downs.*

TERRY HOAGE

Terry Hoage played most of his senior year in 1983 with tendinitis or injuries to his ankle or knee. He was forced to miss three entire games and only started five for the season. When he was able to participate, Hoage often played out of position because of other injuries to Georgia's secondary. After intercepting 12 passes as a junior, Hoage was limited to two in 1983.

Despite these circumstances, Hoage was selected consensus All-American for a second time and remarkably finished fifth in the Heisman Trophy voting. These accolades are a tribute to how valuable Hoage was to the Bulldogs despite his injuries. Whether it was making 16 tackles and two sacks in the season opener against UCLA, blocking two field goals against Clemson to help preserve a tie, or breaking up Vanderbilt's potential game-tying touchdown, Hoage seemed to always make pivotal plays for Georgia in 1983.

After playing 12 years in the NFL, recording 21 interceptions and two touchdowns (one rushing!), Hoage was elected into the College Football Hall of Fame in 2000 and the CoSIDA Academic All-American Hall of Fame in 2004 (Georgia's only member). He currently owns and operates Terry Hoage Vineyards in Paso Robles, California.

All-American Terry Hoage (No. 14) pursues Penn State's Curt Warner (No. 25) during the 1983 Sugar Bowl. By the end of the 1982 season, Hoage, who intercepted 12 passes during the year, was considered one of the greatest defenders in college football. In his senior campaign of 1983, Hoage finished fifth in the Heisman Trophy voting, despite missing three games and only starting in five during the season. *Photo courtesy of AP Images.*

23 THE PERFECT BOUNCE

Fumble bounces off turf to quarterback Andy Johnson, who scoots into end zone to topple Tennessee

Underachievement and misfortune had plagued the Bulldogs during the first two months of the 1973 season. They had suffered upset losses to Vanderbilt and Kentucky and had been tied by Pittsburgh; all three teams had been 13-point underdogs or more to Georgia. Whether it was blowing a huge lead, losing a critical fumble, or throwing an interception when driving for the game-winning score, the '73 Bulldogs had experienced more than their share of bad breaks.

Entering the Tennessee game in Knoxville, Georgia had only a 3–3–1 record. With a highly probable loss pending against the Volunteers, who were a double-digit favorite, the Bulldogs were expected to have their worst start to a season after eight games since two years prior to coach Vince Dooley's arrival at Georgia.

The Bulldogs surprisingly kept the entire game close with Tennessee and were down only 31–28 late in the fourth quarter. On second down from the Volunteers' 8-yard line with a little more than one minute remaining, quarterback Andy Johnson took the snap from center. He turned and faked a handoff to fullback Bob Burns and then attempted to hand the ball to reserve tailback Glynn Harrison. Excluding participation on special teams, it was Harrison's first play of the game. In the exchange between Johnson and Harrison, the ball was dropped to Tennessee's artificial turf. Fortunately for the Bulldogs, the fumbled ball took a perfect bounce from the turf back into Johnson's hands. The alert quarterback, without hesitation, took the football on a hop and ran around his left end into the end zone for a touchdown. Georgia held off the Volunteers on their final drive and won, 35–31.

All season, the Bulldogs had struggled on offense, averaging just 259 total yards and scoring only 13 offensive touchdowns

> **I**t was my only play on offense [for the game].... Andy stuck the ball in, but he saw something and he pulled it out.
>
> —GLYNN HARRISON, GEORGIA TAILBACK

GAME DETAILS

Georgia 35 • Tennessee 31

Date: November 3, 1973

Site: Neyland Stadium

Attendance: 70,812

Records: Georgia 3–3–1; Tennessee 6–1

Rankings: Tennessee: No. 11 (AP)/ No. 11 (UPI)

Series: Tennessee 8–6–2 (Tennessee two-game winning streak)

> **W**hen the ball bounced back to Andy, well, that's the way it's been bouncing [this season] for the other team.
>
> —JIMMY POULOS, GEORGIA TAILBACK

in seven games. However, against the Volunteers, Georgia seemingly ran the ball at will and matched them score-for-score early in the contest. Trailing 21–14 at halftime, Tennessee scored 17 consecutive points and led by 10 entering the final quarter. The Bulldogs narrowed the gap to 31–28 following a Johnson touchdown pass with 4:27 left in the game.

The Volunteers ran three plays and were forced to punt on fourth down and two from their 28-yard line. With Tennessee's Neil Clabo set to kick, the Vols inexplicably ran a fake, snapping the ball to upback Steve Chancey. Georgia read the fake perfectly as Ric Reider and Bubba Wilson smothered Chancey for a two-yard loss.

With approximately three minutes remaining, Johnson ran for four yards on first down to Tennessee's 22-yard line. Tailback Jimmy Poulos carried twice to the 12 and picked up a first down. Burns followed with a four-yard run, and Georgia was faced with second and six on the Volunteers' 8-yard line.

The winning play was designed to have Harrison run up the middle, but at the last moment, Johnson pulled the football from the tailback in an attempt to keep it. The result was a fumble—a blunder that just happened to take a lucky bounce back to Johnson. If the game had been played six years earlier on Neyland Stadium's grass instead of artificial turf, the football would likely have bounced away from instead of directly to Johnson. Tennessee's Tartan Turf, the very same controversial playing surface that angered Georgia when it was installed prior to the 1968 season, had conceivably helped the Bulldogs defeat the Volunteers.

As he ran untouched toward the corner of the end zone for the game-winning touchdown, the normally emotionless Johnson branded a huge grin on his face. He and thousands of other exuberant Bulldogs could celebrate at last in 1973. Georgia had finally caught a break that had bounced from Tennessee's turf.

THE BOUNCE

Andy Johnson faked to fullback Bob Burns and tried to hand off to halfback Glynn Harrison at the 9, but the football was fumbled in the exchange. Fortunately for Georgia, the ball took a single bounce from the turf directly to Johnson. Johnson, who began running to his left after attempting his handoff, kept his momentum and, with ball in tow, ran around the left end into Tennessee's end zone for a touchdown.

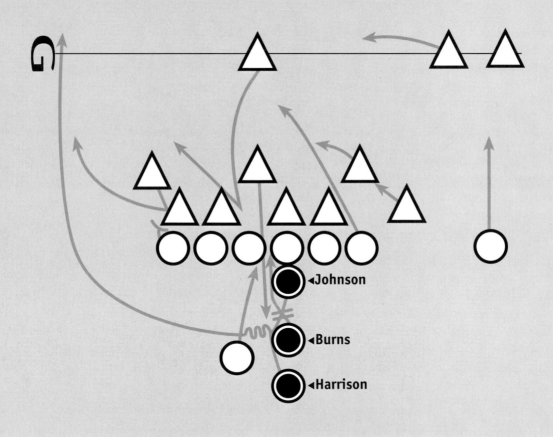

ANDY JOHNSON

Known more as a running quarterback at Georgia than as a passer, Andy Johnson rushed for 1,799 yards and passed for 1,518 from 1971 to 1973. He is the only Bulldogs quarterback in history with at least 1,000 yards passing to have more rushing yardage than passing.

Johnson appropriately did not play quarterback in the NFL but was a running back and receiver for New England from 1974 to 1981. He rushed for 2,017 career yards, caught 161 passes, and had 604 kick/punt return yards. Johnson was responsible for 26 professional touchdowns, including passing for four touchdowns in his final season on seven of nine passes for 194 yards—the only passing touchdowns, completions, and yardage for Johnson in seven NFL seasons.

GLYNN HARRISON

After playing mostly on special teams in 1972 and 1973, "Glidin'" Glynn Harrison rushed for a combined 1,853 yards in his junior and senior seasons to become one of the best running backs in school history. But Harrison's outstanding career at Georgia, according to author Clyde Bolton, almost did not materialize.

Harrison hardly played as a freshman, appearing in just two offensive plays; however, he was projected to be Georgia's primary punt returner prior to the '73 season. The night before the season opener with Pittsburgh, coaches informed Harrison that a player who had been injured was healthy and would assume the punt-return duties. An angry Harrison attempted to call his dad to see if he could transfer from Georgia and have his father pay his way to Georgia Tech—the school Harrison grew up cheering for. Fortunately for Harrison and the Bulldogs, no one answered the phone. He decided to continue playing for Georgia and appeared in the opening game against the Panthers. On his first play covering a Bulldogs punt, Harrison's head hit the knee of Pitt's returner. He was knocked out cold for five minutes and had to be carried from the field.

Of the 46 Georgia players who have rushed for 900 career yards or more in the modern era, Harrison's remarkable 6.35 career rushing average is the school's best. A ninth-round selection in the NFL draft, Harrison played for one season in the pros, rushing for 41 yards on 16 carries with Kansas City in 1976. Despite playing in only eight games, he was second on the Chiefs in kickoff returns with 278 yards on 13 returns.

22

THIRD TIME'S A CHARM

Bob McWhorter's third attempt at the goal line finally defeats Georgia Tech

In the early years of collegiate football, the Yellow Jackets, not the Red and Black, ruled the sport in the state of Georgia. While the university often struggled to finish with a winning campaign until 1910, Georgia Tech had lost only 15 of 58 games since coach John Heisman's arrival in 1904. Heisman had defeated the Red and Black five consecutive times while at Tech. He was also 6–1–1 against Georgia as Auburn and Clemson's coach (1895–1903).

With approximately two minutes remaining in their 1910 meeting, Georgia had the ball on Tech's 4-yard line in a 6–6 tied game. The marvelous Bob McWhorter was given the ball but had difficulty crossing the Yellow Jackets' goal. On second down, he came up short again. Finally, on his third attempt, McWhorter crashed the line and scored a touchdown, giving the Red and Black an 11–6 advantage (touchdowns were worth five points from 1898 to 1911). With one and a half minutes left, the game was called because of darkness, and Georgia had defeated Tech for the first time since 1903.

After unexpectedly beating its first five opponents of the 1910 season, Georgia was defeated by Sewanee and then fought a much-inferior Clemson team to a scoreless tie. As they had in the past, the Jackets fully expected another victory over their state rivals. Pregame comments included, "Tech will take the game," by Heisman, and "There will be a Tech victory today," from Georgia Tech's generally soft-spoken captain, left end Dean Hill.

There seemed to be some validity to Hill's prophecy as Tech's captain scored the game's first points on a five-yard run in the first quarter. In the second stanza, McWhorter raced for an apparent 95-yard touchdown; however, it was "ruled his elbow out of bounds" around midfield. He was credited with a 45-yard run—one of four rushes in the contest for McWhorter gaining 25 yards or more. Nonetheless, the Georgia offense soon stalled and Tech held a 6–0 halftime lead.

Following a 30-yard punt return by George Woodruff in the final quarter, McWhorter ran around end for a 20-yard

The 1910 Georgia squad was the school's best in its first 19 seasons of playing football. The year was highlighted with an 11–6 victory over Georgia Tech. Against the Red and Black's intrastate rival, newcomer Bob McWhorter (standing, fourth from left) broke a fourth-quarter tie with a goal-line plunge late in the game. *Photo courtesy of Hargrett Rare Book & Manuscript Library/University of Georgia Libraries.*

HAFFORD HAY

Along with McWhorter, coach Alex Cunningham, and John Henderson, Hafford Hay left the Gordon Institute and came to the University of Georgia in time for the 1910 football season. Hay, the Red and Black's starting quarterback in eight of the team's nine games, was considered "heady" under center and a standout on defense. Although a neophyte, it was said he ran the squad like a veteran. Despite Hay's small stature, he was also recognized as a dangerous broken-field runner.

In addition, Hay served as Georgia's sole kicker, converting 33 point-after touchdowns. Against Mercer, he kicked a field goal—an extremely rare occurrence for Georgia until the 1960s. Hay also tallied four touchdowns on the season, scoring a total of 56 points—second best on the squad behind McWhorter's 100.

Nothing is known regarding Hafford Hay following the Red and Blacks' successful season. He lettered only in 1910 and did not return the following year. After quarterbacking one of Georgia's greatest teams, the cool field general seemingly disappeared.

touchdown. Hafford Hay's successful conversion tied the game, and it appeared for the first time in the 13-game series that the team that scored first could lose.

On the ensuing drive, the Jackets were forced to punt despite a 40-yard penalty committed by Georgia tackle Omar Franklin for "slugging" an opposing player. Tech's defense held the Red and Black, but the Jackets' offense promptly fumbled on their own 27-yard line.

McWhorter ran for 23 yards to the 4-yard line before stepping out of bounds. From there, the star halfback bucked the line three times, barely scoring on his third try by three inches. Hay's point-after attempt missed, but it did not matter. In what was called "the greatest game ever," the Red and Black had finally defeated Georgia Tech, 11–6, on a short buck by Georgia's great back.

GAME DETAILS

Georgia 11 • Georgia Tech 6

Date: November 19, 1910

Site: Ponce de Leon Field

Attendance: 6,000

Records: Georgia 5–1–1; Georgia Tech 4–2

Series: Georgia Tech 6–5–1 (Georgia Tech five-game winning streak)

> Georgia's whole 11 fought like demons and snatched victory from apparent defeat by a brilliant finish.
>
> —*ATHENS BANNER*

> When McWhorter shot through the line to the touchdown that broke the tie, they [Georgia fans] went wild, swarming down on the field.
>
> —DICK JEMISON, *ATLANTA CONSTITUTION*

BOB MCWHORTER

Bob McWhorter came to Georgia from the Gordon Institute (a preparatory school). He instantly made an impact by scoring 12 touchdowns in the first two games of 1910. By the Georgia Tech contest, the "Gordon phenom" was already considered one of the best players in the South. McWhorter's long runs were a feature of every game, and he had a peculiar hip motion that made it difficult to tackle him after he began running.

McWhorter finished his freshman season at Georgia with 20 touchdowns. His 61 career touchdowns are unofficially a school record, while McWhorter's 331 points rank third (Georgia began keeping official statistics in the 1940s).

If not for insufficient documentation prior to the '40s, McWhorter would hold numerous records. In his senior season of 1913, against Alabama Presbyterian, it was reported the All-American halfback had six rushes of 50 yards or more—these runs by themselves would be sufficient for a single-game school rushing record.

Following his playing days, McWhorter, as he had been at Georgia, continued to be an authoritative figure. He earned a law degree from the University of Virginia, refereed college football games, practiced law in Athens, and served as the mayor of Athens for four terms from 1939 to 1947.

January 1, 1981

"ONSIDE KICK" ULTIMATELY WINS CHAMPIONSHIP

Misplayed kickoff in 1981 Sugar Bowl is the difference in a win over Notre Dame

At the conclusion of the 1980 regular season, never before in college football had there been so many questions regarding which team deserved to be ranked No. 1. Georgia ended its regular season ranked first in both major polls and with a perfect record, the only major college football team to finish unscathed. Nevertheless, there was some question as to whether or not Georgia was entitled to play for the national championship. The Bulldogs were receiving little respect from those in the media or their opponent in the upcoming Sugar Bowl, the University of Notre Dame. Georgia's schedule was perceived as having been weak, and the Bulldogs were one-point underdogs to the Fighting Irish. Many felt Georgia would need the luck of the Irish to defeat Notre Dame.

Georgia's Rex Robinson kicked off late in the opening quarter of a 3–3 tie game. Robinson's high kick drifted down around the 5-yard line. Notre Dame's Jim Stone

and Ty Barber did not field the ball, which bounced between the two return men. Stone, realizing their mistake, attempted to recover the bouncing and free ball. As Georgia's Steve Kelly blocked Stone away from the play, his brother Bob Kelly recovered the ball on Notre Dame's 1-yard line. After the change of possession, Georgia's Herschel Walker dove into the end zone for a touchdown two plays later. The Bulldogs had capitalized on a critical Notre Dame mistake by recovering, in essence, a 59-yard onside kick, which led to a 10–3 lead.

On the first possession of the game, the Fighting Irish passed their way down the field to a field goal by Harry Oliver. Georgia's initial offensive drive resulted in Walker separating his shoulder on the second play and the Bulldogs losing yardage and being forced to punt. Notre Dame came right down the field again and set up for another Oliver field goal. Seldom-used freshman Terry Hoage blocked Oliver's kick, and instead of trailing 6–0, the Bulldogs had the ball in Fighting Irish territory down by only three points.

Georgia reached Notre Dame's 18-yard line, but an 11-yard sack of quarterback Buck Belue forced the Bulldogs to attempt a field goal on fourth down. Robinson's 46-yard field goal was successful, and the game was tied.

The ensuing kickoff has been called "one of the strangest plays in the history of college football." For Georgia, however, it was one of the greatest. Fortunately, Stone and Barber were fielding the kick near a loud and raucous Bulldogs crowd. Stone, the "call-man," called for Barber to field Robinson's kick, but Barber could not hear him over the crowd noise. The two had also misplayed the bowl's opening kickoff because of the noise, although Stone was able to recover and down the kick in the end zone. This time, however, there was no recovery for Notre Dame as the older Kelly brother gladly accepted the Irish's gift just outside the goal line.

After the recovered kick, Belue was stopped for no gain, but Walker, fully recovered from his injury, scored on second down and Georgia took a lead it would never relinquish.

The Hoage-blocked field goal and the recovered kickoff were just two of several mistakes made by Notre Dame in losing the Sugar Bowl. On the Fighting Irish's first possession of the second quarter, they fumbled deep in their own territory, and Georgia recovered on the 22-yard line. Three plays later, Walker scored again, and the Bulldogs led 17–3.

At the bottom of this pile, with the football, is Georgia's Bob Kelly. His recovery of a misplayed kickoff against Notre Dame in the 1981 Sugar Bowl was the key play in winning the game and ensuring the Bulldogs' eventual capturing of the national title. *Photo courtesy of Wingate Downs.*

In Georgia's 17–10 win over Notre Dame, the Bulldogs were outperformed in every statistical facet of the game, except the number of miscues. The Fighting Irish's consequential errors included three interceptions, one fumble, a blocked field goal, and two missed field goals. However, none was bigger than the Bulldogs' first-quarter "onside kick"—the difference in the University of Georgia capturing its first undisputed national title in any sport.

THE KELLY BROTHERS

Bob and Steve Kelly were both stars at Benedictine High School in Savannah, Georgia. Bob, two years older, played for Furman University in 1976 but transferred to Georgia after one year. In 1978 he was the Bulldogs' starting safety as only a sophomore and recorded 57 tackles and one interception on Georgia's nine-win squad. However, in his final two years, Bob was relegated to playing reserve defensive back and on special teams.

Georgia's third tailback as a true freshman in 1978, Steve finished his sophomore season as the Bulldogs' starting tailback. In 1979 he averaged 5.6 yards per carry with 459 yards rushing, including 117 yards on 13 attempts in a 16–3 win over Georgia Tech in the season finale. However, as the 1980 season began, Georgia had a number of quality players at the tailback position, including freshman Herschel Walker. Steve was moved to cornerback and played sparingly as a third-string junior.

How deserving it was when Catholic brothers Bob and Steve, both demoted during their times at Georgia, teamed up to make a spectacular play against Notre Dame with the national championship at stake. Bob, whom Vince Dooley has called the ultimate team player, commented following Georgia's win over the Fighting Irish that the Bulldogs in 1980, as a team, never overpowered anyone, "but we always just seem to be there to make the play."

Steve with the block on the kick returner and Bob with the recovered kick, the Kelly brothers certainly were there to make an unforgettable play in the 1981 Sugar Bowl.

After starting for Georgia at safety as a sophomore in 1978, Bob Kelly (No. 29) played only a reserve role in his final two seasons. Nevertheless, in his final game as a Bulldog, Kelly made one of the greatest plays in school history. *Photo courtesy of Wingate Downs.*

GAME DETAILS

Georgia 17 • Notre Dame 10

Date: January 1, 1981

Site: Superdome

Attendance: 77,895

Records: Georgia 11–0; Notre Dame 9–1–1

Rankings: Georgia: No. 1 (AP)/ No. 1 (UPI); Notre Dame: No. 7 (AP)/ No. 8 (UPI)

Series: First meeting

> **T**y just didn't hear me.... It was the crowd; it was pretty loud.
>
> —JIM STONE, NOTRE DAME KICK RETURNER

> **T**hose guys [Stone and Barber] have been fielding kickoffs for three years and haven't had any confusion.
>
> —DAN DEVINE, NOTRE DAME HEAD COACH

Two plays after Kelly's recovery, freshman Herschel Walker dives into the end zone for the Sugar Bowl's first touchdown. Slightly more than two minutes later, Walker would score again, and Georgia would eventually win 17–10. *Photo courtesy of AP Images.*

January 1, 1946

LEFT, RIGHT, LEFT, TOUCHDOWN

Charley Trippi zigzags through Tulsa for a startling 68-yard punt return

Halfback Charley Trippi had returned from military service during the 1945 season just in time to lead the Bulldogs to devastating defeats of Chattanooga, Florida, Auburn, and Georgia Tech by a combined 136–7 score. Georgia was rewarded with a trip to the first annual Oil Bowl in Houston against No. 17 Tulsa. Rumors had persisted leading up to the game that Charley Trippi possibly was going to sign a professional contract after the bowl game and bypass his senior year. With 27,000 in attendance, a near-sellout crowd at Rice Stadium, the game was considered a toss-up, with hopes for a Georgia victory being pinned on the performance of the great and perhaps departing Trippi.

In the final quarter, with Georgia leading 14–6, Tulsa was forced to punt. Hardy Brown punted to Trippi, who had averaged 20 yards on 11 punt returns during the regular season. From his own 32-yard line, Trippi ran diagonally from one sideline to the other, zigzagging as far back as his own 20-yard line. Trying to pick up blocking, Trippi began heading back to the sideline where he first started his return. Finally, Georgia blockers began opening a running lane for Trippi. He first ran past some would-be tacklers, faked one Tulsa defender off balance, and then proceeded to head down the side. Trippi reached Tulsa's 10-yard line, where it appeared he would be tackled; two Golden Hurricane players were waiting to knock him out of bounds. Trippi lowered his head and attempted to run right through them. As the junior wonder rammed into the two Tulsa players, both crashed off Trippi's shoulders. Trippi continued on into the end zone for a heart-stirring, 68-yard touchdown.

In Georgia's first bowl game in three years, the Bulldogs scored first on a four-yard run by Charles "Rabbit" Smith. Georgia reached inside Tulsa's 18-yard line on two other occasions in the opening period but came away empty-handed.

Tulsa outplayed the Bulldogs in both the second and third quarters. Camp Wilson scored for the Golden Hurricane, pulling Tulsa within one point. Leading 7–6 in the fourth quarter, Trippi connected with John

Blockers, including J.P. Miller (No. 53), clear a path for Charley Trippi (No. 62) as he returns a Tulsa punt 68 yards for a touchdown in the 1946 Oil Bowl. *Photo courtesy of AP Images.*

Donaldson for a 65-yard touchdown pass. On Tulsa's next possession, Brown punted to Trippi, and the result is still proclaimed by many as the greatest punt return in the history of football.

There are several reasons why Trippi's return was so spectacular. First, he ran from sideline to sideline, then returned to his original sideline, all the while losing ground as he waited for blocking to develop. In the process, he lost more than 10 yards from where he first began his return. Second, in reversing his field and zigzagging through Tulsa players, Trippi covered much more than 68 yards on the ground. Some onlookers estimated that he easily ran for at least twice the yardage he got credit for and might

have covered as many as 200 yards in total. Lastly, after all the reversing and running, Trippi somehow had the strength to bowl over the two remaining would-be tacklers standing in his way of a touchdown.

After his awe-inspiring performance in the 20–6 win over Tulsa, Trippi, for the sake of the Georgia football program and its faithful following, dispelled the rumor of him turning professional early. Reportedly, the Bulldogs had entered the Oil Bowl counting on Trippi's rushing, passing, and punting to lead them to victory. From the all-everything back, Georgia got in return the aforementioned, plus a brilliant, 68-yard exhibition into the end zone and a promise to return for the 1946 season.

CHARLEY TRIPPI

Charley Trippi, son of a coal miner from Pittston, Pennsylvania, wanted to attend Fordham University in New York City out of high school. That is where most of the kids from his area went to college. Harold "War Eagle" Ketron, captain of the Red and Black's 1903 squad, approached Trippi and recruited him to play at Georgia. Ketron lived in nearby Wilkes-Barre, Pennsylvania, and was the manager of a Coca-Cola plant. He promised Trippi that as long as he went to Georgia, he would have a job at his plant. As Trippi recalls, he graduated from high school on a Friday. The following Monday, he was driving a Coca-Cola truck for Ketron.

There was much more in store for Trippi than driving a truck in Wilkes-Barre. At Georgia, as he displayed in the '46 Oil Bowl, he was a star rusher, passer, receiver, punter, and returner—the entire package. According to author Loran Smith, Georgia quarterback John Rauch (1945–1948) compares Trippi to Michael Jordan. They are the only players Rauch has seen in his life that could dominate a sport as they did.

Some still declare that Trippi's unbelievable return against Tulsa is the greatest punt return in the history of football. *Photo courtesy of AP Images.*

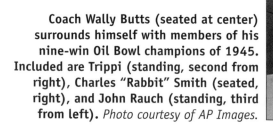

Coach Wally Butts (seated at center) surrounds himself with members of his nine-win Oil Bowl champions of 1945. Included are Trippi (standing, second from right), Charles "Rabbit" Smith (seated, right), and John Rauch (standing, third from left). *Photo courtesy of AP Images.*

Game Details

Georgia 20 • Tulsa 6

Date: January 1, 1946

Site: Oil Bowl

Attendance: 27,000

Records: Georgia 8–2; Tulsa 8–2

Rankings: Georgia: No. 18 (AP); Tulsa: No. 17 (AP)

Series: First meeting

> I started to the left then went to the right then back to the left and picked up my blocking.
>
> —CHARLEY TRIPPI, HALFBACK

> They will be talking about Charlie [sic] Trippi as long as there is a cow in Texas.
>
> —GUY TILLER, *ATLANTA JOURNAL* STAFF WRITER

Charles "Rabbit" Smith

Charles "Rabbit" Smith came to Georgia at a most opportune time. In 1943 Frank Sinkwich had graduated, and Charley Trippi had been summoned by the military. This resulted in playing opportunities for Smith and other 17-year-olds too young for the World War II draft.

As Sinkwich and Trippi had in '42, Smith and teammate Johnny Cook starred in Georgia's backfield on its war-torn teams of 1943 and 1944. Smith was small but quick, weighing approximately 155 pounds. Against Kentucky in 1945, the game prior to Trippi's return to the team, Rabbit rushed for 212 yards—the first unofficial 200-yard rushing performance in Georgia football history. As Trippi led the Bulldogs' ground attack in the last half of the 1945 and 1946 seasons, Smith was relegated to second-string status. Nevertheless, he finished his collegiate career with 133 career points; his 22 touchdowns remain tied for 13th of all time in school history.

Like Trippi, Smith played for the 1947 NFL champions Chicago Cardinals. While his teammate led the Cardinals in receiving and kick returns and was second in rushing, Smith played a minor role, rushing for 23 yards and intercepting a pass in seven games. Too small to play professional football, Smith's NFL career lasted just one season, and he would eventually enter coaching.

19

JASPER SANKS'S PHANTOM FUMBLE

An erroneous ruling arises as Georgia drives for winning score against Tech in '99

Georgia and Georgia Tech entered their gridiron contest in 1999 with identical but somewhat disappointing 7–3 records. Led by high-powered offenses, both teams had lofty expectations only to have their defenses falter in upset losses. The Bulldogs sought revenge as the Yellow Jackets had won the previous year, following a controversial call on a fumble. Georgia had held a 19–7 fourth-quarter lead, but Georgia Tech, behind quarterback Joe Hamilton, cut its deficit to a single point. On the game's winning drive, Hamilton fumbled, and the Bulldogs recovered the ball. However, officials called it otherwise, and Georgia Tech maintained possession. Soon afterward, Tech's Brad Chambers kicked a 35-yard field goal with two seconds remaining, snapping Tech's seven-game losing streak to Georgia. A year later, the Dogs would experience déjà vu, losing a fumble on a questionable call and then losing the game on a field goal.

In a tied 48–48 contest, Georgia had a first down and goal on Georgia Tech's 2-yard line with 13 seconds remaining. Instead of attempting a field goal, Bulldogs coach Jim Donnan elected to run one more play. Sophomore Jasper Sanks ran a drive at left guard, falling just short of the 1-yard line. After being tackled and clearly down, Sanks lost the football. Tech safety Chris Young, hoping the ball was still in play, picked up the apparently dead ball just outside the end zone, ran behind his goal line, and curiously ran to the sideline to hand the ball to coach George O'Leary. As Georgia ran its field-goal unit onto the field, Georgia Tech was awarded possession by the officials.

> **I** was already on the ground. They [Georgia Tech] just came and took the ball out of my hand.
>
> —JASPER SANKS, GEORGIA RUNNING BACK

In 1999 Georgia Tech fans and players celebrate after handing Georgia a 51–48 overtime defeat, likely the Bulldogs' most heartbreaking loss in years. *Photo courtesy of Georgia Tech Athletic Association.*

JASPER SANKS

Perhaps the most-hyped Georgia football recruit since Herschel Walker besides Matthew Stafford was running back Jasper Sanks. Sanks was a *USA Today* and *Parade* magazine first-team All-American at Carver-Columbus High School. When he signed with Georgia prior to the 1997 season, the Bulldogs faithful instantly envisioned him as the school's next great back. However, Sanks's career is generally recognized more as five years of disappointment than anything else.

Sanks's lackluster football career at Georgia began with his failing to make the qualifying entrance exam scores. After a year at Fork Union Military Academy, Sanks carried the ball only 10 times as a freshman in '98. As a sophomore, he led the Bulldogs with nearly 900 yards rushing but lost two critical fumbles that season: one versus Florida, which ended momentum Georgia had gained in the game, and the other the aforementioned "nonfumble" against Georgia Tech. Sanks's final two seasons were characterized by fluctuating weight, diminished quickness, and injuries as he combined for only 690 rushing yards in 2000 and 2001. Against Auburn in 2001, Sanks was stopped short of the goal line on Georgia's final play in a seven-point loss. By the end of the year, he was dismissed from the team for rules violations, and with that, his football career came to an end.

Jasper Sanks's playing days at Georgia were not a complete disappointment. His three consecutive 130-yard rushing performances toward the beginning of his sophomore season have been achieved by few at the school. Sanks's 1,651 career rushing yards rank 18th in school history, ahead of such notables as Keith Henderson, Ronnie Jenkins, Horace King, and Theron Sapp. Most admirably, the 21-year-old showed courage after his fumble and Georgia's loss to Georgia Tech in 1999. While some prominent teammates refused to answer questions after the defeat, namely a dejected Quincy Carter, Sanks bravely stood tall and faced the media. Among his comments, the young running back said it was a "bizarre" game and echoed what everyone else witnessed that day—he was undoubtedly down on the ground when the football popped out of his grasp.

Although he had a respectable playing career at Georgia, Jasper Sanks was unfortunately better known for his off-the-field troubles and his two prominent lost fumbles in 1999—the first coming against Florida followed by the "phantom" fumble at Georgia Tech. *Photo courtesy of Getty Images.*

GAME DETAILS

Georgia Tech 51 • Georgia 48

Date: November 27, 1999

Site: Bobby Dodd Stadium

Attendance: 46,450

Records: Georgia 7–3; Georgia Tech 7–3

Rankings: Georgia: No. 16 (AP)/ No. 21 (ESPN); Georgia Tech: No. 20 (AP)/ No. 16 (ESPN)

Series: Georgia 52–34–5 (Georgia Tech one-game winning streak)

> **I**t looks like they [the game's officials] had a miss.... It certainly appears...that [Sanks] was down.
>
> —BOBBY GASTON, THE SEC'S SUPERVISOR OF FOOTBALL OFFICIALS

Georgia was forced to play in overtime. In the extra period's first drive, quarterback Quincy Carter threw an interception. From Georgia's 25-yard line, Georgia Tech ran two plays for four yards and elected to kick a field goal on third down. Luke Manget's kick was blocked by Kendrell Bell. Nonetheless, holder George Godsey recovered the block behind the line of scrimmage, ran for five yards, and the Yellow Jackets had regained possession on Georgia's 21-yard line. After he had headed off the field, dejected because his kick was blocked, Manget was given another chance at victory on fourth down. His second 38-yard attempt was successful, and Georgia Tech prevailed in overtime, 51–48.

As they had done for most of the season, both squads displayed exceptional offenses but exhibited subpar defenses. The teams combined for 1,102 total yards and nearly 100 points. Hamilton threw for 341 yards and four touchdowns and led all rushers with 94 yards on 15 carries. Carter passed for 345 yards on 29 of 55 passing and was responsible for three touchdowns.

Georgia trailed by 17 points on two occasions in the third quarter, including once with only 17 minutes to play in the game. The Bulldogs scored 24 consecutive points and led 48–41, but Georgia Tech rallied and tied the contest with 2:37 remaining. In the final minutes, Georgia drove 62 yards in nine plays. Sanks carried twice for 25 yards to reach the Yellow Jackets' 2-yard line.

On Jasper Sanks's "nonfumble," side judge Ron Leatherwood correctly signaled Georgia's ball; however, he was overruled by umpire Bud Williams. Three of the four officials initially said there was no fumble, although head referee Al Ford would later comment that two of his officials saw the ball pop out before the play was dead. They were incorrect in their assessment, as television replays undeniably showed that Sanks was down prior to fumbling the football.

The game's officials, regarded as the best in the Southeastern Conference, were scheduled to officiate the following week's SEC Championship Game until their blunder; they were suspended by the conference for their mistake. Several seasons later, instant replay was established in college football to prohibit similar errors from occurring. This action by the NCAA came just a few years too late for Georgia's "phantom fumble" of 1999.

November 7, 1931

18 Buster Busts Loose

Buster Mott returns kickoff 97 yards for a touchdown to defeat New York University

Georgia, regarded as the most publicized non-Eastern college football team to ever play in New York City, visited the Violets of New York University at Yankee Stadium in 1931. The Bulldogs were undefeated, seeking a national championship, and considered the school's best team ever and one of the greatest in southern football history. Georgia had defeated New York University the season before by one point; a wider scoring margin was predicted for the Bulldogs this time.

Surprisingly leading 6–0 at halftime, NYU's Jim Tanguay kicked off to begin the second half. Shielding his eyes from the glaring sun, junior Buster Mott received the kick at the 3-yard line in the left corner of the field. Mott quickly moved behind a wedge formed by a number of Bulldogs blockers. Around the 35-yard line, an accumulation of both teams' players seemed jumbled around the ball. Suddenly, Mott broke out of the mass escorted by four teammates. At midfield he sped through his blocking and left the chasing Violets behind, headed toward the sideline, and ran into the end zone for a thrilling 97-yard kickoff return.

From the outset, NYU dominated Georgia, becoming the first team during the season to easily run on the Bulldogs' stout defense. The Violets would finish the game with 193 rushing yards and a total of 253. However, NYU would cross Georgia's goal line on just one occasion. Bob McNamara scored on a four-yard run in the second quarter, but Tanguay's extra-point attempt was blocked by Georgia's Red Maddox.

The Bulldogs' powerful running game was shockingly held in check by the Violets. After averaging more than 305 rushing yards and nearly 15 first downs through the first five games of the year, Georgia struggled to gain 110 yards and six first downs. In fact, things were going so badly for Georgia that substitute tackle Carter Townsend suggested the team pray together at halftime. Led by Townsend, the Bulldogs asked for divine intervention in the second half against the Violets.

Their prayer was answered, as Tanguay's kickoff was on a direct line. Mott instantly got behind the protection of the flying wedge until midfield. It was reported that a few opposing hands brushed Mott

Pictured are members of Georgia's 1931 backfield. From left to right: halfbacks Homer Key, Buster Mott, and Spurgeon Chandler, and quarterback Austin Downes. Mott's 97-yard kickoff return for a touchdown against New York University led to a 7–6 Bulldogs victory and is the greatest kick or punt return in school history. *Photo courtesy of Hargrett Rare Book & Manuscript Library/University of Georgia Libraries.*

SPURGEON CHANDLER

Spurgeon "Spud" Chandler is one of the greatest athletes ever at the University of Georgia. Besides enjoying a successful football career, in which he was responsible for 19 touchdowns rushing, receiving, and passing, Chandler was a star pitcher for the baseball team. As a senior in 1932, the right-hander had a 6–2 record for the 11–4 Bulldogs, captained by Vernon "Catfish" Smith.

Following Georgia's 7–6 win over NYU in 1931, Chandler prophesized his professional baseball future. He reportedly told a newspaper writer that before long he would be pitching "in this lot [Yankee Stadium]."

Chandler was correct in his bold prediction. After five seasons in the Yankees' minor league system, he first appeared in the major leagues in 1937 at 29 years of age. In 11 seasons, he won 109 games, had a .717 winning percentage, and had a 2.84 career ERA. Chandler was also a four-time All-Star, American League MVP and Major League Player of the Year in 1943, and a member of six World Series champion teams. In the rich history of the New York Yankees, he is the only pitcher to be selected Most Valuable Player. Chandler is also undoubtedly the most outstanding major leaguer to have played baseball at Georgia.

---

during his scoring run, but none could grasp a hold of him. Mott's 97-yard dash remains the third-longest kickoff return for a touchdown in school history. With quarterback Austin Downes holding, Vernon "Catfish" Smith successfully kicked the point after touchdown, and Georgia led by a single point.

As it had done repeatedly during the first half, NYU threatened to score several times in the third and fourth quarters. Spurgeon Chandler, who intercepted a pass on the goal line in the first quarter, recovered a late Violets fumble and twice punted Georgia out from near its own goal line. With fewer than five minutes remaining in the game, Smith tackled NYU's Bill Abee just short of the goal on a fourth-down run. On the Violets' final possession, Downes intercepted a pass in Bulldogs territory. Georgia ran out the clock for a victory over NYU by a score of 7–6 for the second consecutive season.

During Mott's game-winning return, it was said that Steadman Sanford, likely the most influential individual in Bulldogs football, "leaped up...his face glowing with happiness and a smile that was easy to see." What the eminent Sanford saw, along with 63,000 other witnesses, was the greatest kickoff return in Georgia football history.

GAME DETAILS

Georgia 7 • New York 6

Date: November 7, 1931

Site: Yankee Stadium

Attendance: 63,000

Records: Georgia 5–0; NYU 5–1

Series: Tied 1–1 (Georgia one-game winning streak)

> Buster Mott, the bustin' halfback from Atlanta, gave sophisticated New Yorkers a thrill the first play of the second half.
>
> —*THE RED AND BLACK*

> It was a beautiful, dramatic run, pulsing with all the great thrilling elements that make the game great.
>
> —RALPH McGILL, *ATLANTA CONSTITUTION* SPORTS EDITOR

BUSTER MOTT

In his first game at Georgia versus Oglethorpe University in 1930, the first two times he touched the football, Buster Mott remarkably scored touchdowns: a 60-yard run and a 51-yard interception return. Mott's fantastic feat would later be featured in *Ripley's Believe It or Not!* The Georgia newcomer would score three more touchdowns in 1930. In the Bulldogs' memorable season of 1931, besides the 97-yard kickoff return, Mott scored four additional touchdowns. He finished the season ranked second on the team in touchdowns scored (five) and third in rushing (358 yards). In his final season, Mott scored two touchdowns, including his second as a Bulldog on a kickoff return.

After college, the 5'8", 193-pound fullback/halfback/quarterback played two seasons in the NFL for Green Bay, Cincinnati, St. Louis, and Pittsburgh. Mott played sparingly in the professional ranks, seeing action in five games, starting one, rushing for 37 career yards, and catching one pass.

September 14, 2002

17 POLLACK'S MIDAIR SCORING STRIP

David Pollack amazingly seizes football from Gamecocks quarterback throwing from out of his own end zone

Led by quarterback David Greene, running back Musa Smith, five senior offensive linemen, and several excellent receivers, Georgia's offense in 2002 was one of the best in recent memory. However, when the Bulldogs encountered South Carolina on the road in Columbia, the Gamecocks' pesky defense and the effects of Tropical Storm Hanna slowed the Georgia offense to a crawl. The Bulldogs ended their game still not having scored an offensive touchdown against South Carolina since the first quarter two meetings prior in 2000. Nonetheless, Georgia was victorious, requiring something other than its offense: a defensive play that defies comprehension.

In a defensive standoff, Georgia led South Carolina 3–0 early in the final quarter. Facing second down from his own 7-yard line, South Carolina quarterback Corey Jenkins rolled to his right, looking downfield to pass. Standing in his own end zone, Jenkins began his throwing motion; Georgia defensive end David Pollack raced

toward the Gamecocks quarterback. Pollack jumped in the air as Jenkins threw the football, somehow grabbed and cradled the ball as it was released, and fell to the ground in the end zone still clutching the football—a mind-boggling touchdown that one needs to observe several times before believing it actually occurred.

Pollack, who earlier had recovered a Gamecocks fumble on Georgia's 2-yard line, had energized the team all by himself and had given the Bulldogs a two-score advantage.

A South Carolina touchdown was answered by a Billy Bennett field goal with 2:54 left in the game, and Georgia held a 13–7 lead. The Gamecocks promptly began marching for the game-winning touchdown, moving 71 yards in nine plays to the Bulldogs' 2-yard line. On fourth down and one with 20 seconds left in the contest, Jenkins's pitch hit running back Andrew Pinnock in the chest. Pinnock's fumble and South Carolina's fourth turnover of the game was recovered by Georgia's Thomas Davis.

I'm just trying to make a play, to get back there [to the quarterback] as fast as I could.
—DAVID POLLACK, GEORGIA DEFENSIVE END, PRIOR TO SCORING THE TOUCHDOWN

David Pollack celebrates after scoring his miraculous touchdown against South Carolina in 2002 where he stripped the opposing quarterback of the football in the end zone. *Photo courtesy of AP Images.*

The Bulldogs ran the remaining 12 seconds off the clock and escaped Williams-Brice Stadium with a win.

Prior to the fourth quarter, the lone highlights of a drudging game were a Bennett field goal early in the opening quarter and a 52-minute delay brought on by the tropical storm—the only time in Georgia football's modern history that a game has been interrupted by the weather.

On the touchdown play, Pollack got around Gamecocks tackle Watts Sanderson and was only trying to get a hand on the ball as he lunged toward the quarterback. He leaped just as Jenkins threw and somehow, some way, was soon clutching the football in South Carolina's end zone. Everyone witnessing this chain of events was beyond bewildered.

Jenkins later commented that after attempting to pass, he assumed that Pollack only knocked the ball to the ground incomplete. Only when he heard someone shout "touchdown" did he realize what had occurred.

Writer Tim Tucker reported that Coach Richt, at that instant, "quietly and wrongly assumed that the refs must have blown the call"; the stripped ball surely hit the ground before Pollack could seize it. The coach would later realize that his star defensive end, in fact, had executed something that Richt would call the greatest defensive play he had ever seen.

DAVID POLLACK

David Pollack arrived at Georgia as a little-known fullback prospect in 2001. By the second game of his sophomore season of 2002 against South Carolina, he had quickly established himself as one of the best and most relentless defensive linemen in college football. Against the Gamecocks, Pollack recorded 14 tackles, recovered a fumble, and made one of the most incredible touchdowns in recent memory in all of football. He was named CBS Player of the Game and Southeastern Conference Defensive Player of the Week for his performance. Those honors would be just two of many. Pollack would eventually become the most decorated player, besides Herschel Walker, in Georgia football history.

Pollack was a three-time first-team All-American (2002–2004), was a two-time SEC Defensive Player of the Year (2002, 2004), twice won the Ted Hendricks Award as the nation's top defensive end (2003–2004), received the Rotary Lombardi Award as the nation's top lineman, and received the Chuck Bednarik Award as the nation's top defensive player in 2004.

Pollack's 36 school-record sack total is seven more than the second most in Georgia history (Richard Tardits, 29). He also ranks first at Georgia in career total tackles for loss and quarterback hurries. Pollack is 16th in career tackles and even recorded 18 career passes broken up from his defensive lineman position, ranking tied for 15th at the school.

Perhaps more than pure athletic ability, Pollack demonstrated an intense and unfaltering demeanor that enabled him to succeed on the gridiron at Georgia for four seasons. He was known to "give it his all" on every single play, his "motor" constantly running in games, and even during practices.

Pollack was the 17th overall selection in the 2005 NFL draft, chosen by the Cincinnati Bengals. In his rookie season he played in 14 games and started five, making 35 tackles and four and a half sacks. During his second game of the following season, Pollack unfortunately suffered a neck fracture that ended his season and likely his professional football career. Nearly two years later, he has yet to reappear on a football field and recently announced his retirement from the NFL. More important than football, Pollack, among other things, is involved with the David Pollack's Empower Foundation, providing a wide range of services to children.

GAME DETAILS

Georgia 13 • South Carolina 7

Date: September 14, 2002

Site: Williams-Brice Stadium

Attendance: 84,227

Records: Georgia 1–0; South Carolina 1–1

Rankings: Georgia: No. 9 (AP)/ No. 10 (ESPN)

Series: Georgia 39–13–2 (South Carolina two-game winning streak)

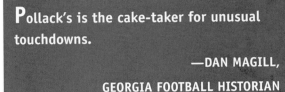

Pollack's is the cake-taker for unusual touchdowns.

—DAN MAGILL,
GEORGIA FOOTBALL HISTORIAN

Pollack rests on the sideline following his remarkable touchdown. As only a sophomore, he would eventually be selected the SEC's Most Valuable Player in 2002—the first Bulldog to earn the honor since Garrison Hearst in 1992 and the first defender in 14 years (after Tracy Rocker of Auburn in 1988). *Photo courtesy of Getty Images.*

November 5, 1910

16 A HEADGEAR HOAX

Sewanee is fooled by a George Woodruff pass as Hafford Hay scores a touchdown

Georgia entered the 1910 season as it had for most of its first 18 campaigns—with hopes for success but with moderate expectations. Besides the undefeated and Southern Intercollegiate Athletic Association championship squad of 1896, there had been little achievement in Georgia's first two decades of football. In fact, for their first 18 seasons, the Red and Black finished with a winning year on just seven occasions.

However, the 1910 season began like none before, led by a particular player and coach like none previously at Georgia. In just five games, newcomer halfback Bob McWhorter and head coach Alex Cunningham had established themselves as being among the South's best at their respective positions. Along with quarterback Hafford Hay, halfback George Woodruff, and fullback W.F. McClelland, the group guided the Red and Black to an undefeated record, outscoring the opposition by a combined 258–5 score.

Georgia's next opponent, Sewanee, had been relishing its success since it began playing football in 1891. The Purple Tigers

were regarded as one of the best teams in the entire country, having been defeated only 14 times in 104 games since the start of the 1898 season. This included Sewanee's acclaimed team of 1899, which recorded a perfect 12–0 record, including five wins in a six-day period—all by shutouts and on the road. The Purple Tigers were also amidst a 55-game home unbeaten streak that would not come to an end until 1914.

As expected, Georgia trailed 15–6 late in the game but had the ball on Sewanee's 30-yard line. Darkness and a thick fog had settled in, and the contest was expected to be called by officials at any moment. The Red and Black needed a quick score, and the innovative Cunningham was just the coach to call a play appropriate for the occasion.

Woodruff dropped back to pass and lofted the "ball" downfield. Barely able to see through the fog, Sewanee desperately tried to defend the Georgia receivers as it tried to spot the thrown ball. Much to their chagrin, what was thrown was not a football but Woodruff's headgear. When they realized they were victims of chicanery, the

The great 1910 Georgia team may have lost to Sewanee, but in the process, players George Woodruff (top center) and Hafford Hay (top right) executed one of the most unusual trick plays in sports history. *Photo courtesy of Hargrett Rare Book & Manuscript Library/University of Georgia Libraries.*

Purple Tigers watched as Hay, with the actual ball in tow, raced untouched for a touchdown.

The Red and Black had left Athens by train for Sewanee the night before. The all-night trek endured several delays, and the Georgia squad did not reach its destination until immediately prior to game time. The tired team arrived to a waterlogged field and an encompassing dense fog at the home of a team that had not been beaten on its own turf in more than 17 years.

GEORGE WOODRUFF

George "Kid" Woodruff came to Georgia in 1907. Despite his small stature, he was the Red and Black's starting quarterback by the end of the year. Considered a star by 1908, the 140-pound Woodruff scored the only points in a 2–0 victory over Davidson College, recording a safety. After sitting out 1909, Woodruff teamed with Hafford Hay, Bob McWhorter, and W.F. McClelland to constitute one of the most feared backfields in football. Besides Woodruff's running and passing, he was considered the best defender on the team. In addition, one newspaper recognized him as the best blocker ever in the South.

During his playing career, Woodruff suffered several injuries, in part because of his small size. Nevertheless, "Kid" was a standout in most games and viewed as the "hardest" player in southern football, always playing despite any pain he was experiencing.

In 1910 Woodruff's future in coaching was apparent when it was written that the halfback "has constantly infested [sic] ginger into the [Georgia] 11 when needed." Becoming Georgia's head coach in 1923, Woodruff compiled a 30–16–1 five-season record, including 9–1 in 1927. His '27 Dream and Wonder Team was selected national champions by the Boand and Poling systems.

George "Kid" Woodruff was an integral part of Georgia's backfield from 1907 to 1911. Pictured here much later as the Bulldogs' head coach, Woodruff coached Georgia to a national championship in 1927. *Photo courtesy of AP Images.*

GAME DETAILS

Sewanee 15 • Georgia 12

Date: November 5, 1910

Site: McGee Field

Records: Georgia 5–0; Sewanee 6–1

Series: Sewanee 6–2 (Sewanee five-game winning streak)

> The great Kid [Woodruff], feigning a pass, hurled his headgear far down the field.
>
> —FUZZY WOODRUFF, AUTHOR AND WRITER

The Purple Tigers' 15–0 fourth-quarter advantage was highlighted by an 85-yard run by All-Southern Alvin "Chigger" Browne in the opening stanza. With seven minutes remaining in the game and the fog at its thickest, McWhorter returned a Sewanee punt 80 yards for a score. On the ensuing kickoff, the Purple Tigers fumbled, and Georgia was given a scoring opportunity in Sewanee territory. On the very next play is when Cunningham caught the Purple Tigers defense off guard with Woodruff's thrown headgear rather than the football.

Shortly after Hay strolled over Sewanee's goal line, the game was called because of fog and darkness. After dominating most opponents for decades, it was reported that Sewanee was "glad to grope its way off the field" with a 15–12 victory. Georgia had shocked the stunned Sewanee team just as it had surprised all of college football in 1910. And although the Red and Black might have suffered its first loss of the season, they executed the greatest trick play in Georgia football history.

ALEX CUNNINGHAM

Coach Cunningham brought instant success to the Georgia football program in 1910. He was unlike any of the 14 Red and Black coaches who predated him. Cunningham held preseason practices a full two weeks earlier than any other Georgia team had done. The training the team withstood was like none ever implemented before and was a major reason why Cunningham's starting 11, unlike previous editions, would finish games strong. Cunningham was also the first Georgia coach to successfully implement player substitution; the Red and Black rarely lost a standout player to an injury.

Cunningham's coaching prowess resulted in productive offenses. Whereas the 1909 Georgia squad averaged a paltry two points per game, Cunningham's first team was averaging 45 through six games after the Sewanee loss—tops in all of college football. The 1910 Red and Black finished the season with a 25.4 scoring margin—third best ever at Georgia.

Besides Vince Dooley, Mark Richt, and perhaps Wally Butts, Cunningham may be the most successful Georgia head coach of all time, especially considering the state of the program that he inherited.

January 2, 1984

15 FUMBLE HOOKS 'HORNS

Texas fumbles punt to Bulldogs and loses '84 Cotton Bowl and national title

Georgia's loss to Auburn in 1983 broke the Bulldogs' consecutive streak of three Southeastern Conference titles and Sugar Bowl appearances. Georgia's consolation was a trip to the Cotton Bowl to face second-ranked Texas, the Southwest Conference champion. The Longhorns were undefeated, practically playing a home game in Dallas, and were the favorite by more than a touchdown. In addition, Texas's defense was considered perhaps the most dominant ever in college football. Texas was also aware that a defeat of Georgia, coupled with a win by Miami of Florida over top-ranked Nebraska on the same day would result in the Longhorns being named national champions. Some of the Texas players had even admitted that the Nebraska-Miami matchup later that night in the Orange Bowl was in the back of their minds leading up to their game against Georgia.

Trailing by six points and facing fourth down at their 34-yard line with 4:32 remaining in the game, the Bulldogs elected to punt to Texas, hoping their defense could hold the Longhorns for one more possession. Punter Chip Andrews hung a high, short punt over Texas's 30-yard line. Longhorn defensive back Craig Curry tried an over-the-shoulder catch of the ball just as Georgia's Melvin Simmons shouted, "Miss it, miss it!"

Curry obliged and dropped the punt. Jitter Fields, Texas's regular punt returner, could not recover his teammate's fumble as the ball squirted through his arms during a mad scramble. Special teams player Gary Moss of Georgia recovered Curry's blunder on the Longhorns' 23-yard line and gave the Bulldogs a rare scoring opportunity.

Normally accurate kickers Jeff Ward of Texas and Georgia's Kevin Butler had combined to make only four of eight field goals during the first 55-plus minutes of play as the Longhorns led 9–3. The Bulldogs would need some sort of break for a Cotton Bowl victory as their offense had struggled mightily against Texas's vaunted defense.

As Georgia lined up to punt, Texas head coach Fred Akers sensed a Bulldogs fake and left his first-team defense on the field, inserting only Fields. Akers also instructed Curry, who had never fielded a punt as a Longhorn, to not attempt to catch the ball if Georgia did indeed punt. Coach Vince Dooley said following the game a fake punt never entered his mind; there was too much time left on the clock.

Three plays after Gary Moss's game-changing fumble recovery in the 1984 Cotton Bowl, quarterback John Lastinger scores the winning touchdown on a 17-yard run. *Photo courtesy of AP Images.*

For whatever reason, Curry did not abide by his coach's demands, and his first attempt at returning a punt ended in tragedy with Moss's recovery. Georgia gained six yards in two plays to Texas's 17-yard line. On third down and four, quarterback John Lastinger forced Curry into another mistake. Lastinger ran an option to his right, and Curry decided to take the pitchman, Tron Jackson. Instead, Lastinger turned upfield and dashed into the end zone for the game-winning touchdown

with 3:22 remaining. Butler's extra point broke the tie and gave the Bulldogs a 10–9 lead.

On the ensuing possession, Texas ran three plays and was forced to punt. Georgia got the ball back and ran the clock out, converting a fourth and one on the Longhorns' 36-yard line in the process.

A sobbing Curry left the Texas dressing room only 45 minutes following the game, avoiding the media altogether. He had made two deciding mistakes; his first, the

CHIP ANDREWS

Chip Andrews was Georgia's starting punter in 1983 and 1984 after transferring from the University of Tennessee at Chattanooga in '80, redshirting in '81, and playing junior varsity in 1982. During his collegiate career, Andrews had a reputation for producing lofty and lengthy punts. Of the 23 Bulldogs who have punted at least 50 times since the mid-1940s, Andrews's 43.2 average on 109 career punts is the best of them all.

However, it was a short punt by Andrews that led to Georgia's celebrated fumble recovery against

Texas. The shortened punt surprised Texas's Fred Akers, who later admitted he thought Andrews would kick it farther. A longer punt likely would have been fielded by Jitter Fields and not Craig Curry and in turn, probably not muffed. Andrews averaged 41.2 yards on nine punts in the Cotton Bowl.

Andrews was drafted by the United States Football League's Jacksonville Bulls in the 1985 territorial draft but never saw any playing time.

Seniors John Lastinger (No. 12), Terry Hoage (No. 14), and Guy McIntyre (No. 74) crowd around the winners' trophy with Coach Vince Dooley following Georgia's 10–9 upset victory over Texas in the Cotton Bowl. *Photo courtesy of AP Images.*

GAME DETAILS

Georgia 10 • Texas 9

Date: January 2, 1984

Site: Cotton Bowl

Attendance: 67,891

Records: Georgia 9–1–1; Texas 11–0

Rankings: Georgia: No. 7 (AP)/ No. 7 (UPI); Texas: No. 2 (AP)/ No. 2 (UPI)

Series: Texas 3–0 (Texas three-game winning streak)

> **I** have no excuses [for fumbling]. I don't know why I did it.
>
> —CRAIG CURRY, TEXAS DEFENSIVE BACK

muffed punt, was the turning point in Georgia's improbable victory.

En route to a 10–1–1 record and a No. 4 national ranking, the 1983 Georgia Bulldogs, led by the program's most accomplished class of seniors in history, often had to find ways to win. It was no different in the '84 Cotton Bowl. The overconfident Longhorns, on the other hand, found a way to lose as they looked forward to a game other than their own and a national title that never materialized.

GARY MOSS

Gary Moss, who began his Georgia career as a reserve cornerback, had moved to tailback by the end of the '83 season. Ironically, the converted rusher made one of the greatest special teams plays in Georgia football history and, later, was a standout defensive back in his final two seasons.

As a sophomore in 1983, Moss intercepted one pass (before moving to tailback) and led the team in kickoff returns with a 23.0 average on eight returns. Besides his unforgettable fumble recovery in the '84 Cotton Bowl, Moss also made a tackle on special teams and returned three punts for 57 yards.

After sitting out the 1984 season, Moss became one of Georgia's most highly regarded defensive backs

> **I** didn't think I would get it at first, but it just bounced the right way.
>
> —GARY MOSS, GEORGIA DEFENSIVE BACK

of the 1980s. He led the Bulldogs in interceptions in 1985 and 1986, finishing his career with 10, which still ranks among the school's career leaders. Moss also broke up a combined 20 passes in his junior and senior seasons.

After college Moss played for the Atlanta Falcons' scab team during the 1987 NFL strike. As he had done while at Georgia, Moss returned punts and kickoffs and also intercepted a pass in three games.

October 26, 1895

A First in Football

Albeit illegal and a fluke, Georgia allows football's first forward pass in 1895

When Georgia and North Carolina faced one another for the first time in 1895, both teams were considered the schools' best ever in their short histories of playing football. The Red and Black's starting 11 averaged 167 pounds per man, interestingly considered heavy at the time. Even more intriguing was the fact that George Butler was playing for the Tar Heels. Butler was a standout quarterback and extra-point specialist on Georgia's first three teams (1892–1894) and was captain of the '93 and '94 squads.

Nevertheless, the game would become even more compelling and noteworthy shortly after its start. What was intended as a punt turned into a George Stephens–to–Joel Whitaker touchdown toss for a North Carolina touchdown—football's first forward pass.

Prior to the forward pass being allowed by the game's rules, football was more like a rugby scrum than the sport we know of today. During the first few minutes of the Georgia–North Carolina contest, the rugby style of play, as usual, was on display in a scoreless tie.

According to author John Stegeman, some of the spectators at Athletic Park,

including Auburn head coach John Heisman, scouting for his game against Georgia a month later, were unwilling to remain on the sidelines. Instead, they situated themselves on the field behind the offensive team. Georgia fumbled on the game's first possession, and four minutes into the contest, North Carolina was forced to punt after a series of short gains. Stephens retreated to kick "only to find himself trapped between the oncharging Georgia linemen and the fans who had lined up behind the Carolina team. Coach Heisman, for one, had to duck to keep out of the way."

Instead of punting, Stephens threw a desperation forward pass downfield to teammate Whitaker. Whitaker caught the ball, ran through Red and Black defenders like "lightning," and crossed Georgia's goal line. The referee signaled a North Carolina touchdown, claiming he had not seen the illegal pass. The Red and Black faithful were incensed. A fight between players on the opposing teams might have led to a riot if not for the presence of Atlanta Chief of Police Arthur B. Connolly and his patrolmen.

Besides the fortuitous fluke, neither side scored the rest of the game, and North

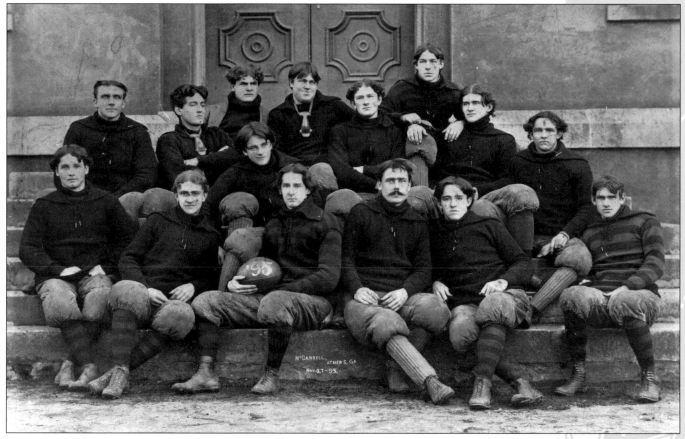

Although they finished with a losing 3–4 record, the 1895 Red and Black were considered one of the better teams in the South. Nevertheless, they may be most remembered as the team that yielded football's very first forward pass. *Photo courtesy of Hargrett Rare Book & Manuscript Library/University of Georgia Libraries.*

Carolina held on to the 6–0 victory. The next day, newspapers hardly knew how to describe football's first forward pass. The *Atlanta Journal* portrayed the play as a "fumble[d] pass" in addition to a "bad pass."

Although Georgia was on the opposing side of the successful illegal pass, the school had an impact on the play's eventual acceptance as a facet of football's offensive arsenal. In 1905, Heisman wrote to Walter Camp, head of a collegiate football rules committee and "Father of American Football," describing the forward pass he witnessed in Atlanta 10 years prior and recommending that it become a part of the sport's rules "in order to open up the game."

A year later, on September 5, 1906, St. Louis University's Bradbury Robinson threw football's first legal pass incomplete against Carroll College of Wisconsin. However, on his next attempt, Robinson completed a 20-yard pass to teammate Jack Schneider for a touchdown.

GLENN "POP" WARNER

After playing collegiate football at Cornell University and graduating from its law school, Glenn "Pop" Warner began his illustrious football coaching career at the University of Georgia at the young age of 24. He signed a 10-week contract to coach the Red and Black's 1895 squad for $34 per week.

Upon witnessing Georgia's pathetic athletic field for the first time and having only 12 players around which to build his team, Warner longed for Cornell and northeastern football. However, he quickly got over his reservations. Although Georgia finished with a losing 3–4 record in 1895, the Red and Black were considered one of the best teams in the South. Warner's 1896 team recorded a perfect 4–0 mark—one of only three undefeated and untied seasons in Georgia football history.

Warner left Georgia to coach his alma mater in 1897. For 44 uninterrupted seasons, the "Gridiron's Greatest Strategist" coached six institutions to a remarkable 319–106–32 career record. Behind Joe Paterno, Bobby Bowden, and Paul "Bear" Bryant, Warner needed the fourth fewest games (415) to reach 300 victories.

After coaching at Georgia for only two years, Glenn "Pop" Warner went on to coach five other schools for 42 additional seasons. He is still regarded as one of college football's greatest coaches. *Photo courtesy of AP Images.*

Game Details

North Carolina 6 • Georgia 0

Date: October 26, 1895

Site: Athletic Park

Attendance: 1,000

Records: Georgia 1–0; North Carolina 2–0

Series: First meeting

> This was clearly a fluke, but then they [fluke plays] count for just as much as hard-earned plays.
>
> —*ATLANTA CONSTITUTION*

> The Stevens-to-Whitaker pass became something of a cause célèbre.... The play went down in athletic history as the first of its kind in the annals of football.
>
> —JOHN STEGEMAN, AUTHOR OF *THE GHOSTS OF HERTY FIELD*

John Heisman

Coach John Heisman must have scouted Georgia well in its game against North Carolina in 1895, as his first Auburn team defeated the Red and Black 16–6 later that season.

Prior to five seasons at Auburn, Heisman coached at Oberlin College and the University of Akron for three combined years. From 1900 to 1927, he had successful stints at Clemson, Georgia Tech, University of Pennsylvania, Washington and Jefferson College, and Rice University, and captured a national title at Georgia Tech in 1917. He tied the NCAA football record for most schools as a head coach with eight and finished with an accomplished 185–70–17 record. Other accomplishments include the Heisman Trophy, annually given to college football's most outstanding player, being named in his honor.

Heisman is also characterized as an innovator of football, including bringing the forward pass to the game after first witnessing Georgia allow North Carolina's "fluke" play in 1895.

September 6, 1980

13 FRESHMAN FLOORS VOLUNTEERS

Herschel Walker runs over and through Tennessee for first touchdown as a Bulldog

Who is going to start at tailback? As Georgia approached the 1980 season, it was one of only a few questions or concerns for the Bulldogs, who were returning 18 of 22 starters from the previous year's squad that just missed winning a Southeastern Conference title and going to the Sugar Bowl. Georgia's starting tailback and leading rusher in 1979, Matt Simon, returned but was hampered with an injury. Carnie Norris had started a couple of games at tailback as a freshman in '79, and Donnie McMickens was a returning senior but had little experience. Highly recruited Herschel Walker was also vying for the starting tailback position. Although just a true freshman, even "the hostages in Iran have probably heard of Herschel Walker," wrote Billy Harper of the *Athens Banner-Herald.*

The week of Georgia's opening game it was announced that McMickens would start at tailback; Walker was the third stringer. There were concerns that Walker had played Class A high school football—the smallest classification with the smallest players.

In addition, coach Vince Dooley had said Walker did not show "enough moves" in preseason practices; he would just bull over defenders instead of eluding them. Ironically, the coach would soon witness one of the greatest displays of a player bulling over and through an opposing defense.

Late in the third quarter, Tennessee held a 15–2 advantage, but Georgia had possession on the Volunteers' 16-yard line. Quarterback Buck Belue turned and handed the ball to Walker. The freshman started to his left, broke a tackle at the 15-yard line, and then faced safety Bill Bates, who was squared up and ready to take down the tailback. The powerful Walker ran smack into Bates at the 8-yard line. Walker's legs continued to churn as he bulled over Tennessee's safetyman. Two other Volunteers defenders converged on Walker inside the 5-yard line. Herschel split the two defensemen, leaving one, lineman Mike Casteel, lying on the turf in pain. Walker strolled the last two or so yards into the end zone for his first collegiate score—a touchdown like few had seen before and, more importantly, a scoring run that had put the Bulldogs back into the game.

In the second quarter Georgia fell behind Tennessee, 9–0, as penalties, fumbles, and missed assignments afflicted the Bulldogs. Georgia needed to ignite a stagnant offense, and Walker was inserted into the game midway through the quarter in the hope that he could provide the spark. The freshman tailback looked promising the first few times he touched the football, gaining two yards on his first carry, then rushing for six more, and later catching a pass for nine yards. Nevertheless, the Bulldogs never threatened to score and went into halftime with a nine-point deficit.

Tennessee increased its lead to 15–0 on a touchdown pass with a little more than four minutes remaining in the third quarter. The 1980 season seemed to be starting like the year prior, when Georgia began the '79 campaign with three consecutive losses. The Volunteers would be unsuccessful in their try for two points, a failing attempt that eventually cost them the game. Georgia was forced to punt on the ensuing drive. Bates caught Jim Broadway's kick at his 27-yard line and fumbled after being immediately hit by Joe Happe, who was playing with a broken hand. Georgia and Tennessee players repeatedly tried to recover Bates's miscue, and the ball traveled backward nearly 40 yards through the back of the end zone for a Georgia safety.

After the safety and Tennessee's kickoff, the Bulldogs began the next drive at midfield.

Pictured as a true freshman in 1980, Herschel Walker stormed onto the college football scene by scoring two touchdowns against Tennessee in his first game. Most notable was a 16-yarder where he flattened and split the Volunteers defenders on his way into the end zone. *Photo courtesy of Getty Images.*

A Belue–to–Lindsay Scott pass completion for 24 yards moved the ball to the Volunteers' 16-yard line. On the next play, Walker scored his remarkable, unforgettable, and initial touchdown at Georgia.

HERSCHEL WALKER

A full-blown recruiting war for Herschel Walker materialized among many colleges leading up to the 1980 season. Never before had an athlete been so highly recruited by the University of Georgia. There were a number of rumors, stories, and speculations regarding his college choice and why he decided Georgia over all the other pursuers. Nevertheless, the Bulldogs landed perhaps the most-prized recruit in history and took advantage of Walker's speed and power in his first game. Walker said following the victory over Tennessee, "Georgia was the best decision I ever made."

Leading up to the season opener, coach Vince Dooley remarked that he did not see Herschel making a significant contribution to the Bulldogs in '80. Walker was far from spectacular in practices and, as mentioned, entered the season as Georgia's third tailback. Even Walker admitted that he had a lot to learn. In particular, he needed to learn "more moves." However, when Georgia's offense remained sluggish against the Volunteers, Dooley inserted the freshman on "instinct." The rest is history.

THE PHENOM'S FIRST SCORE

Buck Belue took the snap and handed it to tailback Herschel Walker. Walker started to his left and immediately broke a tackle at the 15. The freshman phenom ran through a large hole and straight into the arms of safety Bill Bates at the 8. Walker literally ran over Bates, split two other approaching defenders between the 2 and 3, and sauntered over the goal line for his first of many collegiate touchdowns. "My God, a freshman!"

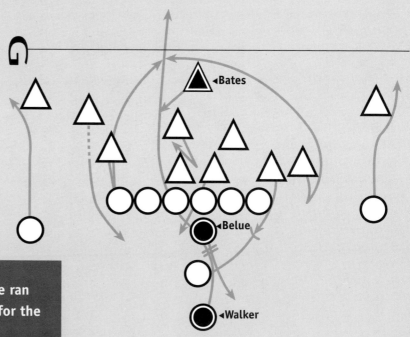

> [Herschel] gave us a lift when he ran over that safety and moved on in for the first touchdown.
>
> —BUCK BELUE, GEORGIA QUARTERBACK

Georgia 16 • Tennessee 15

Date: September 6, 1980

Site: Neyland Stadium

Attendance: 95,288

Records: Georgia 0–0; Tennessee 0–0

Rankings: Georgia: No. 16 (AP)/ No. 20 (UPI)

Series: Tennessee 8–7–2 (Georgia one-game winning streak)

> The shortest distance between two points is a straight line.
>
> —HERSCHEL WALKER, FRESHMAN TAILBACK

Walker scored again with 11:16 left in the game on a nine-yard run. His second touchdown run was a lot easier than the first as he tip-toed at left end through falling defenders and ran untouched into the end zone for the score. Rex Robinson's point-after attempt was successful, and Georgia had its first lead of the night, 16–15. The Dogs barely held on to their one-point advantage, including forcing a Tennessee fumble in the final minutes at Georgia's 5-yard line.

Georgia's win over Tennessee in 1980 is memorable in many ways. Most significantly, the game introduced freshman tailback Walker—a budding superstar who, in running over Bates and into the end zone, signaled he was destined to become one of college football's best.

BILL BATES

Bill Bates, a Knoxville, Tennessee, native, was a four-year starter at safety for the University of Tennessee (1979–1982). As a junior in 1981, he led the team with four interceptions and was named Associated Press second-team All-SEC. Bates's six career fumble recoveries still rank among the best of all time at the school.

An undrafted free agent, Bates played 15 seasons as a defensive back in the NFL (1983–1997), all with the Dallas Cowboys. He and Herschel Walker were teammates for six seasons (1986–1989, 1996–1997), and both retired the same year. During his professional career, Bates recorded 18½ sacks, 14 interceptions, and seven fumble recoveries. Recognized for exceptional play on special teams, he was chosen All-Pro and went to the Pro Bowl in 1984. Bates was also a member of three Super Bowl winning teams.

After Bates retired from playing in the NFL, he became an assistant coach for seven years in Dallas and later for the Jacksonville Jaguars. He currently is an assistant at Nease High School in Florida, runs a cattle ranch near Dallas, and is a motivational speaker.

Notwithstanding, and perhaps unfortunately for Bates, mentioning the name "Bill Bates" to most Georgia fans recalls his fumbled punt, the turning point of the '80 Georgia-Tennessee game, and worse, getting run over by a particular freshman tailback.

12 PHENOMENAL CATCH FORCES OVERTIME

Corey Allen's touchdown reception ties the Tigers in '96, initiating the first of four overtimes

In the 100th edition of the Deep South's oldest rivalry, Georgia slumped into 20th-ranked Auburn University's Jordan-Hare Stadium with perhaps its worst team in 35 years. The Bulldogs seniors had a losing 20–21–1 overall record since 1993, including a deplorable 0–12–1 mark versus rivals Florida, Tennessee, and Alabama and Auburn. Quarterback Mike Bobo and running back Robert Edwards, preseason all-conference contenders, were benched following their lackluster performances in a 47–7 loss to Florida two weeks prior to the Auburn meeting. The junior Bobo, who had promising freshman and sophomore campaigns, was completing fewer than half his passes for the season and led the Southeastern Conference in interceptions (15), including nine in the previous four games, compared to a single touchdown pass. Starting in his place was Brian Smith, a fifth-year senior who had thrown for minus-one yard for the year on two of five passing. The Bulldogs had not defeated a ranked opponent in nearly four years, and it appeared likely they would not do so in the imminent future.

Toward the end of the game, Georgia was the benefactor of a gratuitous act by Auburn, but it should have been another defeat and the final horn of the centennial meeting. Instead, the Bulldogs had the ball on the Tigers' 30-yard line with one second remaining and trailing 28–21. Bobo, who had come off the bench late in the first half, took the snap and rolled to his right as time expired. He lofted a strike to a leaping Corey Allen, who made the catch just in front of the goal line. While in the air, Allen twisted and lunged over the front right corner of the end zone for an improbable touchdown.

Georgia was losing 28–7 late in the second quarter when quarterback Smith was replaced by Bobo. The former starter aroused a stagnant offense, completing 21 of 37 passes in the game for 360 yards, two touchdowns, and no interceptions. Despite playing with a minor concussion, receiver Hines Ward totaled 251 all-purpose yards, including 67 on a scoring pass from Bobo early in the final quarter to reduce the Bulldogs' deficit to seven points.

Down 28–21, Georgia got the ball on its own 18-yard line with no timeouts and only 1:07 left in the game. Bobo, who completed only one of six passes in the Bulldogs' previous possession, threw incomplete on first down. On the next play, he connected with Ward for a 15-yard gain. Five consecutive completions later, Bobo had driven Georgia to Auburn's 21-yard line. With fewer than 10 seconds remaining, Bobo was sacked for a nine-yard loss by Marcus Washington, and the game clock was about to expire. Fortunately for Georgia, Auburn sophomore Charles Dorsey, thinking the game was over, grabbed the football after Bobo had been sacked. The officials stopped the clock with six seconds left to spot the ball. This allowed Bobo to spike the football on the next play, stopping the clock with one final second remaining.

During Allen's leaping and twisting touchdown, the junior's first points at Georgia, a flag was thrown by an official. After the miraculous score, Allen inquired about the penalty and was told he had been interfered with by Auburn's Jayson Bray. Georgia's touchdown pass stood, and the Bulldogs were only an extra point away from sending the game into the conference's first overtime period (the NCAA adopted overtime for Division I-A football at the start of the 1995 bowl season).

Hap Hines's successful point-after kick forced the beginning of what would eventually be four overtime periods. On the fourth and final extra frame, Georgia's Torin Kirtsey rushed for a one-yard touchdown,

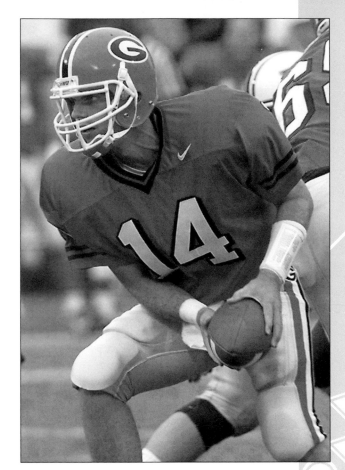

On the last regulation play against Auburn in 1996, quarterback Mike Bobo threw a 30-yard touchdown pass to Corey Allen, forcing the first overtime contest in SEC history. *Photo courtesy of AP Images.*

and Hines's conversion gave the Bulldogs a 56–49 advantage. On Auburn's ensuing possession, quarterback Dameyune Craig was stopped just short of a first down on fourth and three from Georgia's 18-yard line.

After the comeback victory, Georgia's first-year coach Jim Donnan said, "We needed this to step up respectability."

For one of the few times during a substandard, four-year period, the Bulldogs finally earned a measure of respect in defeating a superior opponent.

JIM DONNAN

What was called the "Donnan of a New Era" when Jim Donnan arrived at Georgia in 1996 from a successful six-season stint at Marshall University soon turned to despair when the Bulldogs lost their season opener to Southern Mississippi—10½-point underdogs. Donnan would soon turn the program around, recording a 10–2 mark in 1997—twice as many victories as his first campaign. Nine- and eight-win seasons followed for three years, but it was not quite good enough for Georgia administrators. Donnan's contract was terminated following the 2000 season and five years at the helm. Although he had been successful in elevating the football program to a higher level than his predecessor Ray Goff, the Bulldogs were still regarded as a second-rate program in the Southeastern Conference. Donnan's downfall was his lack of success against premier opposition, winning just 30 percent of the games against Florida, Tennessee, Auburn, and Georgia Tech, and 35 percent against ranked opponents.

Donnan, who has yet to return to coaching, currently works as a college football analyst for ESPN. Still residing in Athens, he also travels giving motivational and leadership speeches.

The 56–49 win over Auburn in four overtimes was one of Coach Jim Donnan's biggest victories during his five-year tenure at Georgia. Pictured is Donnan coaching his final game as a Bulldog—a 37–14 win over Virginia in the 2000 Oahu Bowl. *Photo courtesy of Getty Images.*

GAME DETAILS

Georgia 56 • Auburn 49 (four overtimes)

Date: November 16, 1996

Site: Jordan-Hare Stadium

Attendance: 85,214

Records: Georgia 3–5; Auburn 7–2

Rankings: Auburn: No. 20 (AP)/ No. 21 (CNN)

Series: Auburn 47–44–8 (Auburn three-game nonlosing streak)

> When I caught it, I knew it wasn't in [the end zone].... I tried to wiggle and get the ball across.
>
> —COREY ALLEN, GEORGIA WIDE RECEIVER

MIKE BOBO

Mike Bobo's play was certainly encouraging as Eric Zeier's backup in 1994 and before a fractured knee in Georgia's fourth game of 1995 forced Bobo to sit out the rest of his sophomore season. However, Bobo's early success, for whatever reason, did not continue into the following year.

Under a new coach, Bobo suffered, as did the entire team, for the first eight games of 1996. After being benched most of the first half against Auburn, Bobo responded by performing exceptionally well in Georgia's final three games and through the end of his senior season in 1997. In Bobo's final 15 games as the Bulldogs' quarterback, including the '98 Outback Bowl, he remarkably completed 65.1 percent of his passes for 3,934 yards, 26 touchdowns, and just nine interceptions as Georgia won 12 of the 15 games. Bobo's 155.8 passing rating in '97 ranked sixth highest in the nation and remains a single-season school record.

> It's been really hard. It's been frustrating, but I couldn't do anything but keep fighting.
>
> —MIKE BOBO, GEORGIA QUARTERBACK, DISCUSSING BOBO AND THE TEAM'S RECENT STRUGGLES

Bobo served as an administrative assistant and graduate assistant at Georgia in 1998 and 1999. After coaching Jacksonville State's quarterbacks in 2000, Bobo was brought back to Athens by Mark Richt in 2001. Since then, Bobo has coached the Bulldogs' quarterbacks. He began calling Georgia's offensive plays in the '06 Georgia Tech game and was promoted to offensive coordinator in 2007. Currently, Bobo is regarded as one of the best offensive young minds in college football.

October 6, 2001

11 CRUSHED BY A HOBNAILED BOOT

Georgia pulls upset over Vols as David Greene passes to Verron Haynes for winning score

The odds the Bulldogs faced when they traveled to play at the University of Tennessee in 2001 seemed insurmountable. Georgia, 11-point underdogs, had not won in Knoxville in 21 years and was facing a sixth-ranked Volunteers team that had defeated 38 consecutive unranked opponents in Neyland Stadium. Since 1974 the Dogs had beaten only one team as big a favorite as Tennessee (Florida in 1997). In addition, the Bulldogs' first-year coach, Mark Richt, and redshirt freshman quarterback David Greene were playing on the road for the first time. After a decade of being Tennessee's subordinate, Georgia was seeking a redefining moment with a newcomer coach and quarterback in its pursuit to become one of the conference's elite teams after years of absence.

That moment appeared to have come when it looked like the Bulldogs had won the game, but then victory seemed to be snatched from the Bulldogs with under a minute remaining. However, led by the direction of freshman Greene, Georgia

placed itself in a position for another opportunity to achieve a major upset.

With only 10 seconds left to play, the Bulldogs lined up in a three-receiver set, facing first down and goal on Tennessee's 6-yard line and trailing 24–20. On a play called P-44-Haynes, Greene ran a play-action pass, faking a handoff to the tailback. Meanwhile, fullback Verron Haynes feigned a block on blitzing middle linebacker Dominique Stevenson and slipped unseen into the end zone. Stevenson bit on Greene's play-action, leaving no defender within five yards of Haynes. Greene calmly floated a soft pass to the wide-open fullback for a touchdown. Georgia had retaken the lead, 26–24, and would be only five seconds from accomplishing a stunning victory.

With 5:44 left in the game, a field goal by Georgia's Billy Bennett had broken a 17–17 tie. A Bulldogs win appeared certain when Jermaine Phillips intercepted Tennessee's Casey Clausen with 1:53 remaining. Georgia's offense then ran three plays and was forced to punt. Four plays

With just seconds remaining, fullback Verron Haynes catches a six-yard touchdown pass from David Greene to defeat Tennessee in 2001. *Photo courtesy of AP Images.*

later, from his own 38-yard line, Clausen threw a short screen pass to Travis Stephens, who raced down his left sideline for a 62-yard touchdown with only 44 seconds remaining in the contest. Stephens and the Volunteers had presumably broken the Bulldogs' hearts and regained the lead, 24–20.

Tennessee's plan to not give Georgia good field position on the ensuing kickoff by squib-kicking backfired, as Randy McMichael took the squib at his own 34-yard line and returned it seven yards. As Greene huddled with his offense, the young but poised quarterback told them they "gotta believe," stay focused, and they had plenty of time to score. On first down, Greene passed short to Damien Gary, who avoided a tackle and gained 13 yards to Tennessee's 46-yard line. With 34 seconds remaining, Greene threw incomplete to Michael Johnson, but on second down, Greene threw

a 26-yard gain to McMichael, running a seam route and making a one-handed diving catch of a pass that was nearly intercepted. With 20 seconds left to play from the 20-yard line, Greene found McMichael again for 14 yards with a defensive back draped all over him. The Bulldogs called their final timeout to set up P-44-Haynes.

In four games at Georgia, Richt had almost called the play on several occasions but waited until the perfect opportunity arose. In the huddle, Haynes said he was surprised when the play was called and said a quick prayer before lining up at fullback. At the line of scrimmage, Greene's assignment was to check Tennessee's defensive alignment. If the Volunteers had one safety positioned, the quarterback was instructed to throw the ball away. If two safeties were present, the play should work to perfection. Tennessee's defensive formation included two safeties, and Haynes's prayer was answered.

LARRY MUNSON

Since 1966 Larry Munson has been the legendary voice of the Dogs as Georgia football's play-by-play announcer. Munson's broadcasting career, which exceeds six decades, began with calling University of Wyoming football games in the 1940s. Known, among other names, as "the 12th Man" of Bulldogs football, Munson's one-of-a-kind, emotion-filled, gravely voice is considered one of the very best in all of sports.

Munson is just as much a part of Georgia football lore as Herschel Walker, Vince Dooley, or mascot Uga. Of the greatest 50 plays in Bulldog football history chronicled in this book, nearly 60 percent were called by the great Munson. One of his greatest calls was against Tennessee in 2001, when, following Verron Haynes's winning score, Munson blurted, "We just stepped on their face with a hobnailed boot and broke their nose. We just crushed their face."

Prior to the start of the 2007 season, after 41 years, the 84-year-old Munson announced he would only broadcast home games because of his failing health. The members of the Bulldog Nation wish Munson a healthy and hopeful return to Georgia's broadcasting booth for 2008.

For more than four decades, Larry Munson has been the voice of Georgia Bulldogs football. Many of his calls are legendary, including his "hobnailed boot" call when David Greene connected with Verron Haynes to defeat Tennessee. *Photo courtesy of AP Images.*

GAME DETAILS

Georgia 26 • Tennessee 24

Date: October 6, 2001

Site: Neyland Stadium

Attendance: 107,592

Records: Georgia 2–1; Tennessee 3–0

Rankings: Tennessee: No. 6 (AP)/ No. 7 (ESPN)

Series: Tennessee 17–11–2 (Georgia one-game winning streak)

> By the grace of God I caught the ball. That was the longest five seconds, but the ball finally got there.
>
> —VERRON HAYNES, GEORGIA FULLBACK

> I knew when I saw two safeties it [a touchdown] would be there if Verron could slip past that linebacker. It was a great call.
>
> —DAVID GREENE, GEORGIA QUARTERBACK

VERRON HAYNES

A transfer from Western Kentucky University in 1999, Verron Haynes was a seldom-used blocking back prior to the 2001 Tennessee game. Following the win over Arkansas the week before, Haynes demanded of coach Mark Richt to "give me the ball." Richt obliged.

Against the Volunteers, Haynes caught four passes for 59 yards, including the game-winning touchdown. Two weeks later against Kentucky, he rushed for 86 yards, caught three passes for 73 yards, and scored three touchdowns. By the end of the season, with Musa Smith hampered with injuries and Jasper Sanks kicked off the team, Haynes had been switched from fullback to tailback and was Georgia's primary running threat. In the Bulldogs' final four games, including the Music City Bowl against Boston College, Haynes averaged more than 163 rushing yards on 29 carries per game and scored a total of five touchdowns. His 691 rushing yards, not including 132 in the Music City Bowl, led the team in 2001. Haynes's best rushing performance was 207 yards on 39 carries against Georgia Tech. Through the 2007 season, he is only one of eight Bulldogs (along with Charles "Rabbit" Smith, Charley Trippi, Kevin McLee, Herschel Walker, Lars Tate, Rodney Hampton, and Garrison Hearst) to rush for 200 or more yards in a single game since 1945.

In 2007 Haynes completed his sixth season with Pittsburgh in the NFL. In 61 career games, he has rushed for 738 yards, caught 58 passes, and scored five touchdowns.

10 TIME ON GEORGIA'S SIDE

Tigers run out of time on goal line, handing the Bulldogs a victory in 1992

During the Ray Goff regime (1989–1995), the Bulldogs were noticeably less lucky than usual. Such was the case in 1992, although Georgia was experiencing its best season in nearly a decade. Entering their game against probation-bound Auburn, the Bulldogs, one of the best teams in the nation, had won all seven of their victories rather easily but had suffered two heartbreaking losses. In a 34–31 defeat by Tennessee, Georgia allowed the Volunteers to drive 80 yards in the final minutes, including converting a fourth down and 14, to score the winning touchdown. In a two-point setback to Florida, the Dogs yielded a late third-and-long conversion by the Gators while miscommunication transpired between Georgia's sideline and defense. Florida gained a critical first down and eventually ran out the clock.

With games against Auburn, Georgia Tech, and a bowl likely still on the docket,

a once presumably successful season was far from guaranteed, especially if Georgia's misfortune continued. However, at Auburn, the tides would finally turn for the Bulldogs as they had Lady Luck on their side.

The Bulldogs called a timeout with only seconds remaining in the game to regroup. The Auburn Tigers had possession inside Georgia's 1-yard line, trailing 14–10, and seemed certain to hand the Bulldogs their third nail-biting loss, the second in a row. A huddle of Auburn head coach Pat Dye, quarterback Stan White, and quarterbacks coach Randy Campbell phoned offensive coordinator Tommy Bowden in the booth to discuss their plan of attack. On second and goal with 19 seconds left, even without any timeouts remaining, the Tigers had enough time to run three plays if needed, or so they thought.

White took the snap, reversed, and attempted to hand the football to tailback

> **W**e don't coach our guys to jump right up so they can line up and run another play.
>
> **—RAY GOFF, GEORGIA HEAD COACH**

Very late in this 1992 game there was mass confusion between Georgia and Auburn, including with the officials. The clock ran out, leaving the Tigers with no time to run a play, and the Bulldogs escaped with a 14–10 win. *Photo courtesy of Wingate Downs.*

James Bostic. Fullback Joe Frazier, leading into the line to block for Bostic, inadvertently bumped White's arm before a handoff could be made to the tailback. The football popped into the air and fell to the turf just shy of the goal line. Already down, Bostic recovered the ball and attempted to stretch his arms into the end zone. As the final seconds slowly began to dwindle, chaos and confusion ensued at Jordan-Hare Stadium.

Auburn players first proclaimed to the officials that Bostic had scored. The Bulldogs asserted they had recovered a fumble, while White demanded the officials to mark the

PAT DYE

Pat Dye followed brothers Wayne (1954–1956) and Nat (1956–1958) from a farm in Blythe, Georgia, to the University of Georgia to play football. Pat was involved in several great plays as a Bulldog: against Kentucky in 1958, Dye, who had quit the team for a day the prior week along with fellow sophomore Fran Tarkenton, stole a kickoff return from the arms of Calvin Bird and sped 28 yards for a touchdown. His key fumble recovery against Auburn in 1959 set up Tarkenton's winning fourth-down touchdown pass (see Number 3, Tarkenton Tames Tigers) to clinch the Southeastern Conference championship. As a senior in 1960, Dye blocked a Georgia Tech extra-point attempt and field goal in a 7–6 Bulldogs victory. As a sophomore, Dye led Georgia with two interceptions for 33 yards as a reserve guard. He started for the Bulldogs in 1959 and 1960 at left guard, earning first-team All-American honors both seasons.

After playing for a short stint in the Canadian Football League, Dye was an assistant coach under Paul "Bear" Bryant at Alabama for nine seasons. From 1974 to 1979, he was the head coach at East Carolina, compiling a remarkable 48–18–1 record. After one season at the University of Wyoming,

Dye accepted Auburn's head coaching and athletics director positions when they were turned down by Vince Dooley in December 1980. Following a 5–6 first year at Auburn, Dye directed nine consecutive Tigers teams (1982–1990) to eight or more wins and bowl appearances. It had been 26 years since Auburn's last conference championship (1957) before Dye won four SEC titles (1983, 1987–1989) in seven seasons. Part of Dye's instant success at Auburn was his ability to recruit from his native state, luring the best talent from Georgia.

In September 1991, allegations surfaced that improper benefits were given to former Auburn football players. A year later, Dye acknowledged that he knew of the illegal payments. During this time, the Tigers struggled, only achieving a combined 10–11–1 record in 1991 and 1992. Seeking his 100th win at Auburn, Dye's last home game resulted in the 14–10 controversial loss to Georgia in 1992. Not surviving the charges made by his former player Eric Ramsey, Dye resigned after the season, and Auburn football was placed on probation from 1993 until Thanksgiving of 1995.

Dye currently lives on a farm near Notasulga, Alabama. He still maintains a relationship with Auburn University, working in fundraising and public relations.

Pat Dye was an All-American defensive lineman at Georgia. Ironically, he later had great success coaching rival Auburn, where he won four SEC titles and defeated his alma mater seven times in eight tries from 1983 to 1990. *Photo courtesy of AP Images.*

GAME DETAILS

Georgia 14 • Auburn 10

Date: November 14, 1992

Site: Jordan-Hare Stadium

Attendance: 85,214

Records: Georgia 7–2; Auburn 5–3–1

Rankings: Georgia: No. 12 (AP)/ No. 12 (UPI)

Series: Auburn 45–43–7 (Georgia one-game winning streak)

The bottom line is that we lost, and I really don't know how it happened.

—JOE FRAZIER, AUBURN FULLBACK

football. As referees argued with players on both sides, time ran out on the stadium clock, and Georgia escaped with a fortuitous four-point victory.

A 64-yard touchdown pass from Georgia's Eric Zeier to Garrison Hearst had given the Bulldogs a 14–7 third-quarter lead. Auburn's Scott Etheridge kicked a field goal in the final quarter, but White would soon follow by throwing an interception in the end zone late in the game. The Tigers defense held and regained possession in Georgia territory with 2:36 left to play. White drove the offense to the Bulldogs' 5-yard line and called Auburn's final timeout. On first down, a run by Orlando Parker nearly scored before being knocked out of bounds short of the goal line.

Dye's plan of action was to run Bostic and, if he did not score, have White spike the ball on third down and goal. This would leave Auburn with one final down to cross Georgia's goal line with conceivably enough time.

On the deciding play, Georgia rushed all 11 defenders, voiding any kind of pass coverage. This defensive scheme was later referred to by Goff as a bad call because if Auburn had passed the football instead of attempting to run Bostic, a winning touchdown likely would have

been scored by the Tigers. Instead, Auburn bobbled the handoff, which Bostic did not gain complete control of until he was downed on the ground. As Bostic tried to push the football over the goal line, Georgia safety Greg Tremble began wrestling him for it. As the seconds ticked off, linebacker Mitch Davis purposely laid on top of an Auburn player so he could not get up and get into formation (a later admission). Among others, linebacker Danny Ledbetter, knowing better and purposely wasting valuable time, argued it was the Bulldogs' possession. Just as an official declared, "No, it's Auburn's ball," there was no time to run an additional play.

As Auburn players and coaches demanded that more time be placed on the clock, game officials and the Bulldogs quickly left the field. The officials had lost themselves in the chaotic final seconds and, in the process, contributed toward a bitter loss for Auburn. They soon were running for their safety, dodging bottles and half-filled cups being thrown from the stands by enraged Tigers supporters.

November 8, 1975

9 END AROUND TO APPLEBY

Tight end Richard Appleby runs from left to right, plants his feet, and throws an 80-yard bomb to defeat Florida

The Bulldogs of the mid-1970s won ball-games with a tenacious and attacking Junkyard Dogs defense and a consistent and skilled running game. In the 1975 Florida game, neither Georgia's offense nor its defense was particularly effective.

As the No. 11 Gators had done for most of the season, they were in total control against the Bulldogs but only led 7–3 with less than four minutes remaining in the contest. For any chance of victory in the final minutes, Georgia would need to resort to something other than running the football and then hope the Junkyard Dogs could hold down the second-best offense in the nation.

On a wet Gator Bowl surface late in the game, Florida drove to Georgia's 38-yard line with a four-point lead but was forced to punt. Tom Dolfi's kick went into the end zone and was brought out to Georgia's 20-yard line. On first down, quarterback Matt Robinson took the snap and faced his left. Senior Richard Appleby, as he had done several times during the season, ran an end around from his left to right and was handed the football by Robinson. From his tight end position, Appleby carried the football six times in 1975, but on this particular play, he would suddenly stop and plant his feet on the rain-soaked turf. Appleby arched back his right arm and threw a long, wobbly spiral nearly 50 yards in the air. Flanker Gene Washington, left all alone by an unsuspecting Gators secondary, caught the ball in stride around Florida's 35-yard line and easily strolled untouched into the end zone for a touchdown, waving the football in the air in celebration. Georgia had struck quickly on a trick passing play and had assumed its first lead over the Gators with 3:12 left in the game.

Nonetheless, the 54th Georgia-Florida meeting was far from over. Trailing 10–7, the Gators reached the Bulldogs' 36-yard line before quarterback Don Gaffney was sacked by defensive end Dicky Clark, resulting in a fumble recovered by corner-back David Schwak. Georgia was forced to punt, and the Gators flew down the field again and had a first and 10 on the Bulldogs' 21-yard line. Gaffney proceeded to throw three consecutive incomplete passes. With just 50 seconds remaining, Florida kicker David Posey lined up to attempt a game-tying, 38-yard field goal. His kick was unsuccessful, barely getting off the ground, and Georgia had upset the Gators.

GAME DETAILS

Georgia 10 • Florida 7

Date: November 8, 1975

Site: Gator Bowl

Attendance: 70,416

Records: Georgia 6–2; Florida 7–1

Rankings: Florida: No. 11 (AP)/ No. 10 (UPI)

Series: Georgia 32–19–2 (Georgia one-game winning streak)

> **I** had been throwing it well in practice. I saw Gino [Washington] wide open; I knew it was a TD.
>
> **—RICHARD APPLEBY, TIGHT END**

The 1975 Georgia-Florida game was far from over even when the Bulldogs scored on the Richard Appleby–to–Gene Washington 80-yard pass. The Gators had two additional possessions, and it was up to defensive coordinator Erk Russell's (pictured) Junkyard Dogs to keep Florida off the scoreboard. *Photo courtesy of Hargrett Rare Book & Manuscript Library/ University of Georgia Libraries.*

The End Around

Matt Robinson faced his left and faked a handoff to running back Glynn Harrison. Tight end Richard Appleby, who had lined up to Robinson's left, came off the line and was handed the ball by the quarterback. Appleby ran to the right, waiting for Florida's secondary to defend Georgia's apparent running play. At the 12 Appleby suddenly stopped and threw a bomb to a waiting Gene Washington. Washington caught the pass in stride at the Gators' 35 and coasted into the end zone untouched.

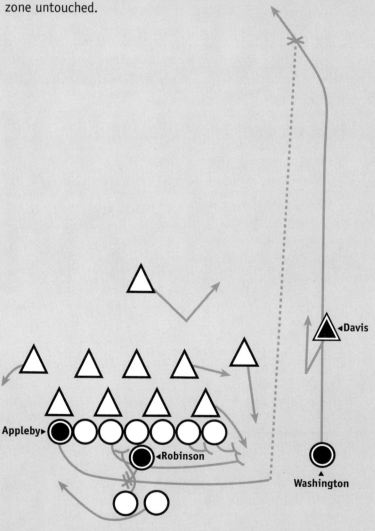

The Appleby-to-Washington end around, or wide-counter pass, had been called by offensive coordinator Bill Pace at halftime. The play was set up throughout the game as Georgia executed four end-around runs (two each by Appleby and Washington), netting 38 yards and three first downs. The Bulldogs figured another end-around play would catch Florida off guard. To throw against the Gators' excellent pass defense, Georgia would have to use trickery as Ray Goff and Robinson had combined to complete just two of nine passes for 29 yards and two interceptions in the game.

When Appleby received the handoff from Robinson, he waited patiently for Florida's secondary to pull up from pass coverage and play the run. Once they did, Appleby stopped and flung the ball to a streaking Washington, who had run by cornerback Harry Davis. As Washington ran by Davis, the Gators defender attempted to knock down the Bulldogs speedster but to no avail. Seconds later, Washington and his teammates were celebrating in the end zone, having completed the 80-yard play.

Following the 10–7 Georgia victory, Appleby commented that the end-around play was only his third pass attempt while playing organized football. This one against Florida had far better results than his previous two: an interception thrown while playing for Clarke Central High School in Athens, Georgia, and a second interception thrown only three weeks prior against Vanderbilt.

Washington, who made several big plays during his career at Georgia (see Number 33, Shoestring Sinks 'Dores), said that his end-around catch from Appleby was "the biggest. It has to be."

Matt Robinson

Georgia's second-string quarterback heading into the 1974 season, Matt Robinson quickly claimed the starting position and was one of the few Bulldogs bright spots during a 6–6 campaign. Robinson directed an offense that finished second in the conference (397.7 yards per game), while his 1,317 passing yards were a Southeastern Conference best. He also rushed for 265 yards and seven touchdowns. With the start of the 1975 season, Georgia moved to more of a run-oriented offense. Robinson split time with running quarterback Ray Goff, passing for only 978 combined yards in 1975 and 1976. Robinson, recognized as a knowledgeable and intelligent quarterback and a perfect fit in Georgia's veer offense, completed his collegiate career by directing the Bulldogs, along with Goff, to an SEC title in 1976.

Robinson was a ninth-round selection of the New York Jets in the 1977 NFL draft. Primarily a backup from 1977 to 1982 with New York, Denver, and Buffalo, Robinson left for the Jacksonville Bulls of the United States Football League in 1984 and played for Portland the following season.

After retiring from professional football, Robinson continued to work in the sport. From 1995 to the early 2000s, he was a host or cohost of the Jacksonville Jaguars' television and radio programming.

> **I** watched the ball come right into my hands.... There wasn't a single Florida defensive back around me.
>
> —GENE WASHINGTON, FLANKER

Richard Appleby

Along with Horace King, Larry West, Chuck Kinnebrew, and Clarence Pope in 1971, Richard Appleby was in the first group of African American football recruits at the University of Georgia. Because freshmen were not eligible to play until 1972 and because of academic problems, Appleby did not see varsity action until 1973. However, once he finally stepped foot on the field, Appleby was a permanent fixture for the Bulldogs, starting three seasons (1973–1975) at tight end. Appleby started the last half of the '73 season at split end, filling in for an injured Gene Washington.

Appleby was only the second Bulldog ever to lead Georgia in receiving three separate seasons. Appleby's 902 career receiving yards still ranks 31st of all time at Georgia (seventh upon his departure from the school). His 18.8 career receiving average is third best for players with 45 career catches or more. Appleby also rushed seven times for 68 yards while at Georgia and completed one pass for 80 yards—the end-around touchdown against Florida in '75.

A fourth-round selection by Tampa Bay in the 1976 NFL draft, Appleby never played a down of professional football. Today, he is a successful businessman in Hawaii.

December 2, 1978

B-E-L-U-E Spells Relief

Freshman Buck Belue comes off bench against Yellow Jackets and tosses game-winning touchdown on fourth down

The Wonderdogs of 1978, picked in the preseason to finish eighth or lower in the Southeastern Conference, continued to surprise everyone as they were instead ranked eighth in the nation with an 8–1–1 record entering the Georgia Tech game. A Sugar Bowl berth and a conference championship were still very much a possibility for the "Cardiac Kids," who had rallied for victories in five games, including deficits of 14–0 and 16–0 to Louisiana State and Kentucky, respectively.

The Dogs would need another successful comeback effort to defeat the Yellow Jackets, and they were down 20–0 midway through the second quarter. Things had gotten so bad that quarterback Jeff Pyburn was benched with 4:38 until halftime in favor of freshman Buck Belue.

Belue did rally Georgia, but Georgia Tech still held a 28–21 advantage late in the game. The Bulldogs faced fourth down and three on the Yellow Jackets' 42-yard line with fewer than three minutes remaining. Belue took the snap and rolled to his right. He thought about running for the first down until two Tech defenders grabbed a hold of him. Belue broke containment and suddenly spotted receiver Amp Arnold, who had slipped past a cornerback to become wide open. The freshman quarterback lofted a pass to a waving Arnold, who caught it near the Yellow Jackets' 20-yard line and ran easily and untouched into the end zone. Georgia would go on to win 29–28. Belue's celebrated pass would be his greatest as a Bulldog until nearly two years later in Jacksonville against the Florida Gators.

Two Willie McClendon touchdown runs cut Georgia's deficit to 20–14 in the third quarter. The Bulldogs scored their third consecutive touchdown on an electrifying punt return by Scott Woerner, and Georgia led for the first time. However, on the ensuing kickoff, Georgia Tech's Drew Hill returned the kick from behind his own goal line and went more than 100 yards for a score. The Yellow Jackets had jumped back ahead, 28–21, late in the third quarter.

Following a Georgia Tech punt, Georgia had possession on its own 16-yard line with 5:52 remaining in the game. After three plays, the Bulldogs faced fourth and two on the 24. Belue rolled out for a six-yard gain and a critical first down. On the next play, Arnold, a high school quarterback,

Perhaps the most exciting game since they kicked the first football here in 1892.

—JESSE OUTLAR, *ATLANTA JOURNAL-CONSTITUTION*

completed a 21-yard pass to tailback Matt Simon. The following three plays netted Georgia seven yards, and the Wonderdogs were faced with their second fourth-down play of the drive.

The acclaimed touchdown pass was only supposed to be a quick-out reception for a five- to six-yard gain. Belue could not throw the quick-out because Arnold was covered, so he decided to run upfield. As soon as Belue began to run, Arnold's defender decided to run toward the quarterback to assist with the tackling, leaving Arnold wide open. After Belue avoided being tackled, he spotted Arnold all alone, threw him the ball, and Arnold scored with 2:24 left on the clock.

Two weeks earlier, Georgia had decided to kick a point-after touchdown late in its game to tie Auburn, 22–22. The tie would

eventually cost the Bulldogs an SEC title. Down 28–27 to Georgia Tech, they decided to try for the two-point conversion and the win. Belue first threw incomplete, but pass interference was ruled on the Yellow Jackets. Given a second chance, Belue faked to McClendon, kept to his left, and pitched the ball to Arnold, who strolled across the goal line for the two-point score.

On their final drive, the Yellow Jackets moved from their 9-yard line to Georgia's 37. However, Tech's Mike Kelley was intercepted by David Archer, another Bulldogs star freshman of the game. The interception preserved Georgia's 29–28 victory. Nonetheless, the comeback victory is most remembered for the fourth-down scoring pass thrown by an unproven newcomer in rallying Georgia past its state rival.

Freshman quarterback Buck Belue sits on the sideline after his fourth-down touchdown pass to Amp Arnold and subsequent two-point conversion defeated Georgia Tech in 1978. *Photo courtesy of Hargrett Rare Book & Manuscript Library/University of Georgia Libraries.*

BUCK BELUE

A highly recruited football and baseball player from Valdosta, Georgia, Belue's distinguished collegiate football career first garnered attention when he rallied the Bulldogs past Georgia Tech in '78. As he had against the Yellow Jackets, Belue supplanted Jeff Pyburn as the starting quarterback in 1979 and rallied Georgia to a 6–5 record and nearly an SEC title and Sugar Bowl birth after an 0–3 start. Belue is the only Georgia quarterback to lead the Bulldogs to successive conference titles (1980–1981) and an undisputed national championship (1980). His 90.0 winning percentage (27–3 record) as a starting quarterback is a school record and upon graduation ranked second-best of all time in college football behind Nebraska's Jerry Tagge's, who achieved 94.2 percent (24–1–1).

Belue participated in both professional baseball and football. He played three years in the Montreal Expos' farm system and was the third-leading passer of the United States Football League's Jacksonville Bulls in 1985. He later was a coach at Valdosta State University and a TV sports anchor in Savannah, Georgia. Belue currently cohosts an afternoon radio sports talk show in Atlanta.

THE FOURTH-DOWN FORTUNE

Freshman Buck Belue took the snap and immediately began sprinting to his right, looking to throw. For an instant, he decided to turn upfield and run for a first down. Unexpectedly Belue spotted a wide-open Amp Arnold. Arnold had initially executed a quick-out route, but as soon as Belue began to run, the receiver continued his pass pattern downfield. As he was being grabbed, and just before getting brought down, Belue decided against running and instead tossed a pass to Arnold. Arnold caught the football on the 23 and sprinted across the Yellow Jackets' goal line.

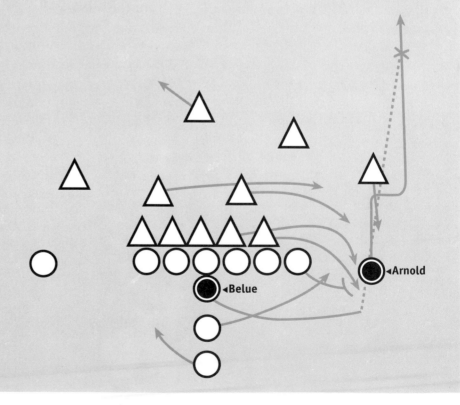

GAME DETAILS

Georgia 29 • Georgia Tech 28

Date: December 2, 1978

Site: Sanford Stadium

Attendance: 59,700

Records: Georgia 8–1–1; Georgia Tech 7–3

Rankings: Georgia: No. 11 (AP)/ No. 8 (UPI)

Series: Georgia 36–29–5 (Georgia Tech one-game winning streak)

> I didn't see him [Arnold] catch it, but I jumped off the ground to see him score.
>
> —BUCK BELUE, QUARTERBACK

WILLIE McCLENDON

Despite being Georgia's primary running back for only one season, Willie McClendon finished his career as the school's third all-time leading rusher with 2,228 yards and still remains ranked eighth after nearly 30 years. Playing behind Kevin McLee, McClendon combined to rush for more than 900 yards in 1976 and 1977. As a senior in 1978 and getting the majority of the carries at Georgia's tailback position, McClendon rushed for 1,312 yards, including 100 or more in each of the Bulldogs' first eight games of the season.

A third-round NFL selection in 1979 by Chicago, McClendon spent four years with the Bears (1979–1982), backing up the great Walter Payton. Following a three-year playing career in the United States Football League, McClendon was an assistant coach at Valdosta State College for three seasons. He returned to Athens in 1989 to become Georgia's running backs coach for the first five years of the

Ray Goff regime (1989–1993), coaching the likes of Rodney Hampton, Larry Ware, Garrison Hearst, Mack Strong, and Terrell Davis.

Willie's son Bryan was a receiver at Georgia from 2002 to 2005, catching 56 career passes for 830 yards. Bryan currently serves as a UGA graduate assistant.

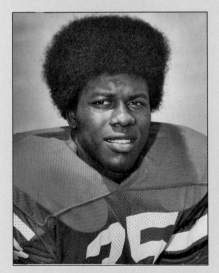

Losing 20–0 in the second quarter against the Yellow Jackets, Willie McClendon's two touchdown runs put the Bulldogs back into the game. The All-SEC tailback began the 1978 season with eight consecutive 100-yard rushing performances. *Photo courtesy of Hargrett Rare Book & Manuscript Library/University of Georgia Libraries.*

September 18, 1965

7 GEORGIA'S FAMOUS FLEA-FLICKER

Moore-to-Hodgson-to-Taylor covers 73 yards and shocks national champion Alabama

The Bulldogs faced the daunting task of opening the 1965 season against Bear Bryant's Alabama Crimson Tide. Alabama, college football's winningest team of the 1960s, was in the seventh season of nine consecutive in which it would finish in the final Associated Press top-10 rankings. The Crimson Tide was declared the national champion in 1964 by the two major polls, the AP and United Press International, and had defeated Georgia five straight seasons by an average scoring margin of nearly four touchdowns per victory.

Georgia, on the other hand, was just starting to turn its football program around. After 15 years of mostly inadequate play, the Bulldogs began a new era in 1964 under the leadership of newly hired coach Vince Dooley. Dooley guided his first Georgia team to seven wins and a Sun Bowl victory—only the Bulldogs' second bowl appearance in 14 seasons. Although the 51st meeting between the schools was being played in Athens, a Georgia win appeared highly unlikely. It seemed a miracle would need to occur for

the Bulldogs to claim a victory over the Tide—a miracle that indeed transpired.

After leading 10–0 in the second quarter, Georgia allowed Alabama to score 17 consecutive points, including a short scoring run by quarterback Steve Sloan with only 3:14 left in the game. On the ensuing possession, Georgia had the ball on its own 27-yard line, trailing by seven points. Dating back to the previous season, the Bulldogs had scored only three offensive touchdowns in their last four games, and there was no reason to believe they could mount a scoring drive against Alabama's mighty defense. It would likely take some sort of freakish play for any success, so Dooley reached into his bag of tricks.

Kirby Moore took the snap from center Ken Davis and rolled slightly to his left. As Alabama's Tom Somerville closed in on the quarterback, Moore threw and completed a short pass to end Pat Hodgson at the 37-yard line. Just as Hodgson began to drop to a knee, he smoothly lateraled the ball to the left of Alabama's Frank Canterbury

Preston Ridlehuber (No. 12) helps an exhausted Pat Hodgson (No. 87) off the field following Georgia's flea-flicker play in 1965 against Alabama. Hodgson began the 73-yard play by first catching a short pass from Kirby Moore. *Photo courtesy of Hargrett Rare Book & Manuscript Library/University of Georgia Libraries.*

KIRBY MOORE

Kirby Moore was Georgia's number one quarterback on its 1963 freshman team. While playing on the Bulldogs' B-team the following season, Moore nearly quit the squad to play baseball exclusively. However, when he realized how well he performed against Georgia's varsity defense in practice, Moore decided to continue playing football. In Georgia's '65 season opener against Alabama, the sophomore came off the bench to relieve senior starter Preston Ridlehuber, who was injured with pulled muscles. Moore rushed for 43 yards and passed for 99, including 73 yards on the winning flea-flicker play.

Because of Moore's presence, Ridlehuber was eventually moved to halfback. Moore would be Georgia's chief signal-caller from 1965 to 1967. He was only the fourth Bulldog, joining John Rauch, Zeke Bratkowski, and Larry Rakestraw, to lead Georgia in passing for three seasons since 1940. A fantastic running-passing combination quarterback, Moore is second of all Georgia quarterbacks in career passing yardage (1,710), who have in addition rushed for 1,000 or more yards, trailing only James Jackson (1984–1987). Statistics aside, the highlight of Moore's career at Georgia was leading the Bulldogs to a 10–1 record and Southeastern Conference title as a junior in 1966.

Currently, Moore heads the law firm Kirby R. Moore, LLC, in Macon, Georgia.

Following the flea-flicker play and down 17–16 to the Crimson Tide, Georgia elected to try a two-point conversion as quarterback Kirby Moore (bottom left, No. 14) rolls out to his right looking for a receiver. *Photo courtesy of Hargrett Rare Book & Manuscript Library/University of Georgia Libraries.*

GAME DETAILS

Georgia 18 • Alabama 17

Date: September 18, 1965

Site: Sanford Stadium

Attendance: 41,500

Records: Georgia 0–0; Alabama 0–0

Rankings: Alabama: No. 5 (AP)

Series: Alabama 28–18–4 (Alabama five-game winning streak)

> The Bulldogs executed a blackboard dandy just like coach Vince Dooley diagrammed it.
>
> —HARRY MEHRE, FORMER GEORGIA HEAD COACH (1928–1937)

into the hands of trailing teammate Bob Taylor. Taylor outsped linebacker Paul Crane to the sideline and took off down the left side, completing a 73-yard flea-flicker touchdown play with 2:08 remaining in the ballgame and Georgia trailing by a single point.

What many Bulldogs fans are unaware of is that more drama unfolded in the contest's final two minutes—drama that is the reason why Georgia's famous flea-flicker play is ranked seventh of all time instead of in the top three.

After the touchdown, Dooley called back kicker Bob Etter to return to the sideline; Georgia was going for two points and the lead instead of kicking the extra point for a tie. Moore completed his second short pass to Hodgson in two plays, and the Bulldogs took an 18–17 advantage.

Following the kickoff, Alabama had great field position on its own 41-yard line. Quickly, the Crimson Tide moved to Georgia's 26 with 14 seconds left on the clock. In a bid to reclaim the lead and a victory that seemed lost, Alabama kicker David Ray lined up to attempt a 42-yard, game-winning field goal. Ray's kick fell short and wide left, and Georgia regained possession. Moore needed to only run a quarterback sneak to finish off the highly favored Crimson Tide and give Coach Dooley one of the most significant victories in Georgia football history.

The flea-flicker play had been put in Georgia's practice regimen the week of the Alabama game after Dooley, a former Auburn assistant coach, remembered it was previously used by Georgia Tech against the Tigers. Dooley called the play at the perfect time, following Sloan's apparent game-clinching touchdown and as many Bulldogs fans were leaving Sanford Stadium, conceding a loss. And although people even today question whether Hodgson had control of the football before he lateraled to Taylor, which would have negated Taylor's touchdown, the flea-flicker ultimately defeated the seemingly invincible Crimson Tide.

THE FLEA-FLICKER

Kirby Moore rolled out, and just before Alabama's Tom Somerville reached him, fired a short pass to end Pat Hodgson at the 37. Dropping to a knee and surrounded by defenders, Hodgson lateraled the ball backward to Bob Taylor, who had been trailing Moore's pass. Catching the lateral at the 33, Taylor ran toward the left sideline and was soon in the clear, easily outdistancing the Crimson Tide defenders for a long touchdown.

> **R**egardless of the situation when time is running out, you're always in the game if you never quit.
>
> —VINCE DOOLEY, GEORGIA HEAD COACH,
> TO THE TEAM FOLLOWING THE VICTORY

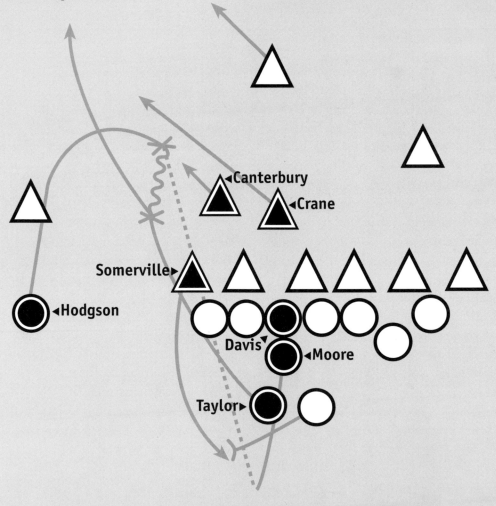

BOB TAYLOR

"Bullet" Bob Taylor came to Georgia in 1962 without a scholarship but departed in 1965 as the school's 11th all-time leading rusher. He finished his sophomore season as the Bulldogs' first-team left halfback and was second on the team in both rushing and scoring. On Vince Dooley's first Georgia team in 1964, Taylor was second on the team in rushing and kickoff returns and was considered an all-SEC contender for his upcoming senior year.

In 1965 he was recognized as "one of the greatest runners in Georgia history" as he tallied 321 rushing yards and a 4.9 average (for the season, the team, as a whole, averaged 3.2 yards per carry) in just five games. In the Bulldogs' fifth contest of the year, Taylor had rushed for 69 yards on 12 carries against Florida State. With three minutes remaining in the third quarter, Georgia had a 3–0 lead when Taylor exited the game with a broken leg. The Bulldogs would eventually lose 10–3, and Taylor would never play football again.

Taylor practiced law in LaGrange, Georgia, before retiring from the profession.

Coaches Paul "Bear" Bryant (left) and Vince Dooley (right) meet at midfield following Georgia's shocking 18–17 win over Alabama. *Photo courtesy of Hargrett Rare Book & Manuscript Library/University of Georgia Libraries.*

September 22, 1984

6 Butler's Booming Game-Winner

With only seconds remaining, Kevin Butler stuns second-ranked Clemson with a 60-yard, game-winning field goal

During the late 1970s and for most of the '80s, perhaps there was no bigger and more hated rival for the Bulldogs—including Florida, Auburn, and Georgia Tech—than the Clemson Tigers. Georgia and Clemson had begun the decade of the 1980s by each winning a national championship. Entering the 1984 encounter, both teams had won three games and played to a tie in their previous seven meetings. The Bulldogs were tackling no paper tiger in '84; Clemson was ranked No. 2 in the Associated Press Poll and was considered likely the best Tigers team ever at the school, including the 1981 national title squad. Despite having won 25 of its previous 26 games at Sanford Stadium, Georgia, a three-and-a-half-point underdog, was not favored at home for the first time since hosting Louisiana State in 1979.

The underdog Bulldogs had rallied and were tied with the Tigers, 23–23, in the final quarter. Georgia faced fourth down from Clemson's 44-yard line with 17 seconds remaining. The Bulldogs had only one option: Coach Vince Dooley raised his hand

in the air and ordered, "Field goal!" The field goal attempt would be for more than 60 yards. Although none longer had been made in the history of the Southeastern Conference, Dooley had confidence in his place-kicker, Kevin Butler, who had kicked a 70-yarder earlier that week in practice.

From Georgia's own 49½-yard line, Butler took his accustomed three steps back and two steps to the side from the kicking tee. Holder Jimmy Harrell took the snap, and Butler boomed a perfect 60-yard kick through the uprights as Sanford Stadium became absolutely unhinged. Actually, the senior place-kicker's field goal would have been good from 65 yards out and perhaps even 70.

With 11 seconds left to play, Clemson's Ray Williams caught Butler's ensuing kickoff on his own 20-yard line and ran 10 yards. Suddenly, Williams threw the ball across the field to teammate Terrance Roulhac, who began streaking down his left sideline. He ran out of bounds at Georgia's 35-yard line, hoping to set up a game-tying field goal by Clemson's accomplished kicker, Donald

Kevin Butler (center) trots off the field with lineman Mike Weaver (No. 63) after making his 60-yard winning field goal against Clemson in 1984. Butler's kick broke a 23–23 tie with 11 seconds remaining and tied an SEC record for the longest field goal. *Photo courtesy of Wingate Downs.*

Igwebuike. Fortunately for Georgia, it was ruled that Roulhac went out of bounds with no time remaining. The game was over, and the Bulldogs had won 26–23 against their bitter rival.

Taking advantage of four interceptions thrown by Georgia's Todd Williams in the first half, the Tigers held a comfortable 20–6 halftime advantage. Perhaps catching an overconfident Clemson squad off guard, the Bulldogs finally began to generate some offense in the third quarter. Georgia scored a touchdown on a pass from Williams to Herman Archie, and later in the quarter, key completions by Williams to Andre

"Pulpwood" Smith and Archie led to a one-yard touchdown run by Cleveland Gary. A fourth-quarter field goal by Butler gave Georgia a short-lived lead as an Igwebuike field goal tied the game 23–23 late in the contest.

The Bulldogs began their final possession on their 20-yard line with 2:10 remaining on the clock. Two consecutive short completions from Williams to Fred Lane and Tron Jackson earned a first down to the 31-yard line. After an incomplete pass, Jackson ripped off a 24-yard gain to Clemson's 45. With 1:19 left, Williams completed a pass for only one yard and followed

TODD WILLIAMS

Todd Williams's father, Dale, was a reserve quarterback at Georgia from 1959 to 1961. In 1981, Todd was chosen State Back of the Year, guiding Waycross High School to Georgia's AAA state championship coached by his father. Todd backed up John Lastinger at quarterback in 1982 and 1983. After rallying the Bulldogs to tie Clemson in '83, Williams was giving the starting nod over Lastinger the following week against South Carolina before being injured in the third quarter.

As a junior in 1984, Williams directed an inexperienced Bulldogs offense; only two starters returned from the year prior. After an outstanding performance in the season opener against Southern Mississippi, when he completed 12 of 16 passes for 123 yards, with no interceptions, and rushed for 38 yards, Williams was dreadful versus Clemson before reviving the Bulldogs' young offense in the second half. The five interceptions he threw against the Tigers, four in the first half alone, were as many as he had his entire senior year in high school. Williams later said he was praying just prior to Kevin Butler's game-winning field-goal attempt against Clemson, hoping the place-kicker would get the quarterback "off the hook."

Hampered by injuries, Williams missed three regular-season games during his junior campaign, most of the '84 Citrus Bowl, and was redshirted in 1985. Williams returned in 1986 as a backup to James Jackson and Wayne Johnson, attempting just one pass the entire season.

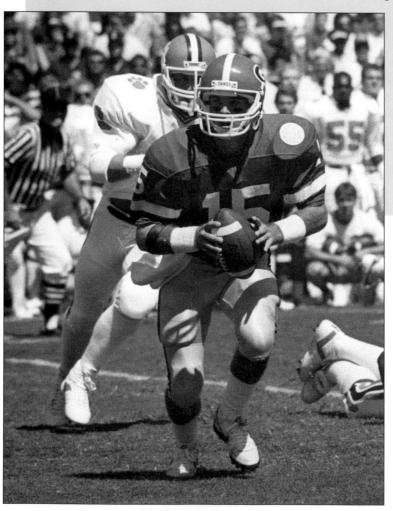

Quarterback Todd Williams struggled in the first half against the Tigers, completing just three of 11 passes and throwing four interceptions. However, in the second half he rallied the Bulldogs to an eventual upset victory over the No. 2–ranked team in the country. *Photo courtesy of Wingate Downs.*

GAME DETAILS

Georgia 26 • Clemson 23

Date: September 22, 1984

Site: Sanford Stadium

Attendance: 82,122

Records: Georgia 1–0; Clemson 2–0

Rankings: Georgia: No. 20 (AP)/ No. 17 (UPI);
Clemson: No. 2 (AP)/ Not ranked by UPI because of probation

Series: Georgia 34–14–4 (16–16 tie in 1983)

> **I**t was one of the sweetest kicks I've had. It's the best feeling I've ever had.
>
> —KEVIN BUTLER, PLACE-KICKER

with back-to-back incompletions, setting up fourth and nine at the 44-yard line.

Butler had shockingly missed a 26-yard field goal earlier in the game, his first failed kick of fewer than 30 yards since his freshman campaign. However, he had already made seven field goals in less than two games for the season. In addition, he was aided with a 10-mile-per-hour wind at his back.

As he jogged onto the field to attempt his game-winning try, Butler recalled that no one said a word to him except his holder, Harrell, who told him only to keep his head down and kick the ball hard. Butler obliged, knocking through the longest and maybe the most celebrated field goal in conference history.

> **H**e [Butler] flat busted it. He kicked the fool out of it.
>
> —DANNY FORD, CLEMSON HEAD COACH

KEVIN BUTLER

Following Georgia's 1980 national championship season, one of the biggest concerns of Coach Vince Dooley was replacing two-time All-American place-kicker Rex Robinson. As it would turn out, Kevin Butler was more than sufficient in succeeding Robinson and became arguably the greatest kicker in the history of college football.

Butler rewrote Georgia and the Southeastern Conference's record book for kicking. He finished in the top 10 nationally each of his four seasons in successful field goals per game, and upon graduation, his 77 career field goals ranked second in the history of college football. Butler was a four-time All-SEC performer and was chosen first-team All-American in 1983 and 1984, including consensus All-American as a senior. After nearly a quarter of a century, his 27 times kicking two or more field goals in a game remains an NCAA record, tied with fellow Bulldog Billy Bennett (2000–2003). Of the more than 800 players in the College Football Hall of Fame as of 2007, Butler, inducted in 2001, is the sole place-kicker.

In 13 seasons (1985–1997) in the NFL, Butler kicked 265 field goals and scored 1,208 points with Chicago and Arizona. He is still close to Georgia's football program, and his son Drew is a punter on the Bulldogs squad.

November 16, 2002

70-X-Takeoff Snatches Eastern Title

David Greene's fourth-down pass to Michael Johnson upends Auburn and takes SEC East in '02

Entering the 2002 season, Georgia was in the same predicament as South Carolina, Kentucky, and Vanderbilt, having never won an SEC East title since the conference split into divisions in 1992. During the Bulldogs' 10-season absence from the SEC title game, Tennessee made the trip to the championship three times, while Florida did it on seven occasions. However, Georgia won its first eight games of the '02 campaign and was in prime position to take its initial divisional title before a 20–13 loss to Florida put the Bulldogs' quest on hold. After a win over Ole Miss, Georgia needed to defeat Auburn to capture the SEC East. The nationally ranked Tigers were playing at home and would be benefiting from the Bulldogs having lost two of their top three wide receivers: split end Terrence Edwards and flanker Damien Gary. Georgia's injuries would force a little-known receiver into action and involve him in one of the greatest plays in school history.

The Bulldogs trailed the Tigers 21–17 with only 1:31 remaining in the game.

Georgia was on Auburn's 19-yard line but had no timeouts and was confronted by a fourth down and 15; a victory and a divisional title appeared highly doubtful.

With Michael Johnson to his left and Mario Raley and Fred Gibson on the right, quarterback David Greene took the snap from a shotgun formation. After a short drop, he pump-faked a pass toward Gibson, hoping to draw Auburn's free safety to Georgia's talented flanker. Greene suddenly shifted and lofted a pass in the back left corner of the end zone toward Johnson. The 6'3", 215-pound split end turned and leaped over Auburn cornerback Horace Willis. Johnson caught Greene's pass with both hands and pulled it away from the defender, outfighting Willis for the ball. The Bulldogs had scored an inconceivable touchdown by the reserve receiver and had taken their first lead of the game with 1:25 to play.

Georgia was behind, 14–3, at halftime, but the deficit would have been greater were it not for free safety Sean Jones's two interceptions and a fumble recovery in the first half. Late in the third quarter, a Georgia touchdown cut Auburn's lead to four points. Nevertheless, the Bulldogs' chances at a possible victory seemed to disappear when they lost the ball on downs with 2:33 remaining in the fourth quarter; however, the Tigers, for their sixth consecutive possession, ran three plays and were forced to punt.

Georgia began its final drive on its own 41-yard line. On second down and six from the 45, Greene connected with Gibson for a 41-yard gain with 1:46 left on the clock. From Auburn's 14-yard line, Greene threw three consecutive incomplete passes while the team committed a five-yard false start penalty.

Facing fourth down and long, the play was brought in from the sideline—70-X-Takeoff—and Greene added in the huddle, "Let's go get it." The play was designed for both Johnson and Gibson to run straight into the end zone. Gibson was designated the decoy while Johnson, or the *X*, would be the primary receiver. Coach Mark Richt said later he felt that of the

Michael Johnson leaps over Auburn's Horace Willis to catch David Greene's fourth-down pass in 2002. Johnson's scoring reception with 1:25 remaining to play gave the Bulldogs a lead they maintained until the end of the game, clinching their first SEC East title. *Photo courtesy of Getty Images.*

DAVID GREENE

Interestingly, several of David Greene's family members, including his father, attended Auburn University. Prior to his senior year in high school, Greene visited Auburn on a recruiting trip but was largely ignored by assistant coaches. Auburn's disregard would eventually come back to haunt the Tigers.

Greene first made a name for himself in only his fourth game as a redshirt freshman, guiding Georgia on its game-winning drive in an upset over Tennessee on the road. He was eventually chosen Southeastern Conference Freshman of the Year in 2001 and followed

> **One big play for history. Either make it and win the SEC East, or go home and watch somebody else play in the conference championship game.**
>
> **—DAVID GREENE, QUARTERBACK**

as the conference's Offensive Player of the Year as only a sophomore. In addition to Auburn in 2002, Greene directed two other fourth-quarter comebacks (Clemson and Alabama) as Georgia won 13 games, its first SEC title in 20 years, and was Sugar Bowl champion. Two years later, Greene finished an unprecedented and brilliant collegiate career. The three-time All-SEC performer holds many school records, including a conference-record 11,528 career passing yards. Greene is the winningest Division I-A quarterback in history with a 42–10 career record as a starter and may be the greatest quarterback ever at Georgia.

Greene has been with Seattle (2005–2006) and Kansas City (2007) in the NFL since being a third-round selection in the 2005 draft.

Late in the fourth quarter, David Greene and Coach Mark Richt discuss strategy just prior to Greene's winning touchdown toss against Auburn. *Photo courtesy of AP Images.*

GAME DETAILS

Georgia 24 • Auburn 21

Date: November 16, 2002

Site: Jordan-Hare Stadium

Attendance: 86,063

Records: Georgia 9–1; Auburn 7–3

Rankings: Georgia: No. 7 (AP)/ No. 7 (ESPN); Auburn: No. 24 (AP)

Series: Auburn 51–46–8 (Auburn three-game winning streak)

> **I** wasn't even open, but I had to make the play.
>
> —MICHAEL JOHNSON, WIDE RECEIVER

receivers, Johnson had the better chance of catching a thrown jump ball. Gibson, considered one of the best receivers in the conference, would certainly be covered thoroughly by the Tigers' secondary. Furthermore, Gibson had a cast on the base of his left hand.

As he broke the huddle and lined up opposite Willis, who was a former Bulldogs signee from Mableton, Georgia, Johnson later recalled he did not want to let the Bulldog Nation down. A minute and a half later, the Bulldogs had defeated the Tigers on "the Plains," 24–21. The substitute receiver had accomplished the exact opposite of what he wanted to avoid, securing a title for the Bulldogs and their Nation.

MICHAEL JOHNSON

A big, strong, and physical receiver, Michael Johnson did not see playing time as a Bulldog until the season opener of his third season at Georgia. Entering the '02 Auburn game, the junior receiver had made only six career starts and 18 catches in nearly two entire seasons. Injuries to Terrence Edwards and Damien Gary propelled Johnson as the Bulldogs' starting split end and David Greene's primary target against the Tigers. In recording one of the best receiving performances in school history, Johnson caught 13 passes for 141 yards, including his fourth-down touchdown grab. Only minutes prior to his game-winning reception,

Johnson had fumbled following a 10-yard gain, halting a Georgia drive in Auburn territory with the Bulldogs trailing 21–17. Three Georgia possessions later, he more than made up for his earlier blunder.

As a senior in 2003, Johnson finished fourth on the team in receiving, catching 27 passes for 361 yards. Despite playing in only three seasons and making 12 career starts, Johnson's 62 receptions for 847 yards rank 26th of all time at Georgia. Few catches, however, were as significant as his 19-yarder for a touchdown that toppled the Tigers in 2002 and gave the Bulldogs their first SEC East title.

November 20, 1920

BUCK'S HISTORIC RETURNED BLOCK

Buck Cheves returns Puss Whelchel's blocked field goal for a touchdown to defeat Alabama

In the Georgia-Alabama game of 1919, kicker Talty O'Connor of the "Thin Red Line" was the difference in a Crimson Tide victory. His two field goals drop-kicked from Georgia's 45- and 17-yard lines were the only points scored in a hard-fought affair. The loss by the Red and Black would be only their second of nine games during the season. It was also the final setback suffered by Georgia coach Alex Cunningham, who after eight seasons would leave the university to eventually become a general in the U.S. Army.

By the 1920 football season, Herman Stegeman was appointed as Georgia's new head football coach. Stegeman had already guided three Georgia baseball and basketball teams to winning campaigns. Cunningham's assistant in 1919, Stegeman was a standout football player at the University of Chicago and a member of its 1913 national championship squad; however, he had never been a head football coach. The young and inexperienced Stegeman, surprising almost everyone, coached the Bulldogs (Georgia was nicknamed the

"Wildcats" until the fifth game of the 1920 season) to an undefeated record heading into their game against 'Bama.

Late in the fourth quarter of a 14–14 tie game, hundreds of spectators began leaving Ponce de Leon Park. As O'Connor lined up to attempt a field goal from Georgia's 20-yard line, the dispersing crowd assumed the obvious: O'Connor, who rarely missed field goals, would certainly boot the ball successfully through the goal posts and, as he had the previous year, defeat Georgia with his toe.

The football was snapped to O'Connor. As he calmly dropped the ball to the ground, Georgia guard and kick-blocking extraordinaire "Puss" Whelchel broke through the line and leaped high in the air. O'Connor's drop kick caromed off Whelchel's hands. Georgia's James "Buck" Cheves grabbed the blocked ball on the 18-yard line and raced 82 yards for a miraculous Bulldogs score. It was Georgia's third touchdown scored unconventionally against Alabama, and it proved to be the source of the game-winning points in a 21–14 win.

Georgia and Alabama battle on the gridiron at Atlanta's Ponce de Leon Park. In 1919 the Red and Black were defeated by two Crimson Tide field goals at "Poncey." However, Georgia retaliated a year later by beating Alabama on a blocked field-goal return for a touchdown. *Photo courtesy of Hargrett Rare Book & Manuscript Library/University of Georgia Libraries.*

The Bulldogs offense struggled the entire game against the Thin Red Line. Fortunately for Georgia, its offense was not needed in the contest. On the second play of the game, Alabama's Mully Lenoir lost a fumble recovered by Georgia's Paige Bennett, who ran 45 yards for a touchdown.

On the ensuing drive, the Tide was forced to punt after three plays. Whelchel blocked 'Bama's kick, and Artie Pew scooped up the block and raced 10 yards for a score. In the game's first five downs and without Georgia's offense running a single play, the Bulldogs held an early 14–0 lead.

HERMAN STEGEMAN

Herman Stegeman coached the Bulldogs in football for only three seasons, compiling a 20–6–3 record. Of the 15 Georgia football coaches in history who coached for at least 10 games, besides Mark Richt, Stegeman has the highest career winning percentage (.741). Notwithstanding, Stegeman is recognized for being so much more at Georgia than just a successful football coach for a short three-year stint.

While being affiliated with the university from 1919 to 1937, Coach Stegeman won four championships in four different sports. As mentioned, his 1919 baseball club was the Southern Champion, the 1920 football Bulldogs captured the Southern Intercollegiate Athletic Association championship, and Stegeman's

1930–1931 basketball squad lost only two games on its way to winning the Southern Conference title. In addition, in 1937 Stegeman guided the Bulldogs' track team to an SEC title—the only track and field team conference championship in school history.

Although Stegeman was often coaching more than one team while at Georgia, along with serving in various other positions at the university, he was committed to not overusing the athletes he coached. For example, Buck Cheves desperately wanted to play baseball, in addition to football and basketball, but Stegeman refused, citing Cheves's small, 145-pound stature as reason.

The 1920 Georgia squad finished the year with an 8–0–1 record, highlighted by a 21–14 victory over Alabama. To date, the 1920 team is one of only four Georgia teams to finish a season without a loss. *Photo courtesy of Hargrett Rare Book & Manuscript Library/University of Georgia Libraries.*

GAME DETAILS

Georgia 21 • Alabama 14

Date: November 20, 1920

Site: Ponce de Leon Park

Attendance: 11,000

Records: Georgia 6–0–1; Alabama 8–0

Series: Georgia 7–4–3 (Alabama one-game winning streak)

> **B**uck Cheves was the whole show in Georgia's backfield.
>
> —*BIRMINGHAM NEWS*

Lenoir redeemed himself for his earlier fumble by scoring a touchdown in the second quarter. During the next stanza, Alabama scored on a long-pass play, and the Crimson Tide had tied the game, 14–14.

Midway through the final quarter, Alabama had a first down on Georgia's 18-yard line, but the defense forced the Tide to lose two yards in three plays. On fourth down from the Bulldogs' 20-yard line, O'Conner entered the game to attempt the game-winning field goal with approximately five minutes remaining.

Whelchel's second blocked kick of the game took a single bounce from the field into Cheves's hands. With the entire Alabama special teams unit in pursuit, the Georgia quarterback streaked across the Tide's goal line in, according to author Charles E. Martin, "probably the weirdest game ever played by a Georgia team."

BUCK CHEVES

During the 1919 season, "Buck" Cheves, along with teammate Artie Pew, would curiously not wear headgear during games despite the disapproval of the Georgia coaches. Cheves informed author Clyde Bolton that he would first take the field with his headgear on; however, he would quickly remove it, throwing the headgear to the sideline. At the time, substitutions could not be made until halftime or unless a player was injured. So, if Cheves or Pew took the field at the beginning of a game and took their headgear off, there was not much the Georgia coaches could do about it.

Cheves scored the Red and Black's only touchdown on a run in a 7–7 tie versus the University of Virginia in 1919. In his second and final season at Georgia, the starting quarterback scored five touchdowns during the year (third most on team), including the blocked field-goal return against Alabama.

Cheves also excelled on the hardwood, playing three seasons on Georgia's basketball team and captaining the 1920–1921 squad that achieved a 13–4 record.

After college, Buck Cheves was a noted college football official. For 33 years, he refereed mostly Southeastern Conference games until 1955.

November 14, 1959

TARKENTON TAMES TIGERS

Fran Tarkenton tosses a 13-yard touchdown on fourth down to defeat Auburn and capture SEC title

Perhaps the worst period in Georgia football was during the 1950s. As the decade forged on, the Bulldogs seemingly got worse with each passing season. However, the 1959 campaign was, if you will, a diamond in the rough—a rare successful year amidst 15 seasons of disappointment. The Bulldogs entered their game against Auburn with a surprising 7–1 record and a No. 12 national ranking—team bests in 11 years. On the other hand, the rival Tigers were considered one of the better squads in college football during the latter part of the decade. Since mid-November 1956, eighth-ranked Auburn had a spectacular 29–1–1 record, had won conference and national titles in '57, and needed a win over the Bulldogs in 1959 for a second Southeastern Conference crown.

With only 30 seconds remaining in the game, Georgia had the ball on Auburn's 13-yard line, trailing 13–7. It was fourth down, and the Bulldogs had only one final chance at victory and the conference championship. Quarterback Fran Tarkenton took the snap and rolled to his

right, decoying the defense and pretending to look to halfback Bobby Towns. Suddenly, Tarkenton turned and sailed a pass across the field to his left to end Bill Herron, who made an over-the-shoulder reception just beyond the reach of two Auburn defenders. Herron caught Tarkenton's toss at the 2-yard line and strolled into the end zone for the tying touchdown with the extra and winning point to follow.

Whereas the Bulldogs had been fortunate for most of the season, for the majority of the game, it was Auburn that was getting all the breaks. A 15-yard penalty and a fumble by Georgia quarterback Charley Britt had each led to Auburn field goals and a 6–0 halftime lead for the Tigers. Britt redeemed himself with a punt return for a touchdown late in the third quarter, but a possible 10–6 Georgia lead was later squandered with a missed field goal. Midway through the final stanza, Britt was blocked into the kick of his own punter, Bobby Walden. Auburn recovered the botched boot on Georgia's 1-yard line and scored on the next play to take a 13–7 lead.

The Tigers had the ball nearing midfield with only 2:35 remaining and looking to run out the clock. Georgia finally caught a break when guard Pat Dye hit Auburn quarterback Bryant Harvard, forcing a fumble recovered by Dye on the Tigers' 35-yard line.

On first down, Walden attempted a halfback pass that fell incomplete. Tarkenton followed that up with an incompletion of his own. On third and 10, Tarkenton completed a 16-yarder to halfback Don Soberdash down the middle for a first down. From the 19-yard line, Tarkenton passed to Soberdash again for an additional nine yards. However, Tarkenton's next pass fell incomplete, and on third down, his completion to Walden lost three yards.

On fourth down from the 13-yard line, a play came in from the sideline and coach Wally Butts. Tarkenton ignored Butts's called play, knelt on Sanford Stadium's turf, and diagramed the game-winning play.

"I knew we needed something different," Tarkenton later said.

As Tarkenton drifted back, Herron ran downfield, cut to left, ran past linebacker Jackie Burkett, and slid off defensive back Lamar Rawson. Herron angled into the clear as Tarkenton's pass was thrown to the wide-open receiver.

Durward Pennington, "the Automatic Toe," converted the extra point, and Georgia led 14–13. After the ensuing kickoff and an Auburn desperation pass falling incomplete, the Bulldogs had clinched their first bowl bid in nine years and the team's first conference title since 1948. Butts and Georgia's assistant coaches were carried to midfield in celebration on the shoulders of the victorious Bulldogs—victory rides that likely would not have occurred if Butts's play had not been disregarded and changed in the huddle by Tarkenton.

> **B**ill Herron came through like a champion on the winning TD pass, and so did Tarkenton.
>
> —WALLY BUTTS, GEORGIA HEAD COACH

Injured during the 1959 season, end Bill Herron caught only eight passes all year. However, his fourth-down touchdown reception from Fran Tarkenton to defeat Auburn is one of the greatest pass catches in the history of SEC football.
Photo courtesy of Hargrett Rare Book & Manuscript Library/University of Georgia Libraries.

BILL HERRON

Bill Herron likely would have had an outstanding career at Georgia, according to coach Wally Butts, but he was injured for most of the two seasons he was a Bulldog. A native of Sanger, California, Herron played at Fresno Junior College and was highly recruited to play major college football. Against Texas in the 1958 season opener, Herron injured his neck, an injury that persisted during his collegiate career.

In his senior season of 1959, Herron caught eight passes for 135 yards and two touchdowns, not including his two receptions for 26 yards against Missouri in the Orange Bowl.

Herron played one season in the Canadian Football League before suffering another injury. He returned to California, where he worked for a finance company for nearly three decades. Today, the retiree lives on a 20-acre ranch. Herron has traveled back to Athens just once, for the University of Georgia's 20th anniversary of its 1959 team during the 1979 Auburn game. He plans to return to Athens for only the second time since his illustrious catch when Georgia celebrates the 50th reunion of the 1959 SEC championship team in 2009.

After his touchdown catch clinched an SEC championship, Bill Herron and the rest of the 1959 Bulldogs earned a trip to the Orange Bowl to face Missouri. Pictured is Herron tackling Missouri's Fred Brossart on a punt return during a 14–0 Georgia win. *Photo courtesy of AP Images.*

Game Details

Georgia 14 • Auburn 13

Date: November 14, 1959

Site: Sanford Stadium

Attendance: 54,000

Records: Georgia 7–1; Auburn 6–1

Rankings: Georgia: No. 12 (AP); Auburn: No. 8 (AP)

Series: Georgia 29–27–6 (Auburn six-game winning streak)

> It was a makeup play, and Tarkenton simply told me to get open. The pass was perfect.
>
> —BILL HERRON, GEORGIA END

Fran Tarkenton

Fran Tarkenton's life both on and off the gridiron following his four years at Georgia has been well documented. During only his sophomore season as a Bulldog, Tarkenton already had begun to exhibit an innovative and risk-taking character that would eventually lead to his success in professional football, as a television personality, and in business.

In his first game on Georgia's varsity against Texas in 1958, Tarkenton, without consulting the Bulldogs coaching staff, substituted himself for reserve quarterback Tommy Lewis with Georgia trailing the Longhorns 7–0 midway in the third quarter. "They [the coaches] wanted to redshirt me, and I didn't want to...so I just bolted onto the field," Tarkenton said years later.

From his own 5-yard line, Tarkenton directed a 21-play, 95-yard drive lasting 8:40 and culminating in a three-yard touchdown pass to Jimmy Vickers. Following the touchdown, coach Wally Butts sent the kicking unit on to try the extra point. Similar to the '59 Auburn game, Butts called for one play but Tarkenton chose another. The sophomore quarterback waved the kicker off the field. Deciding instead to try for two points, Tarkenton passed to Aaron Box for the two-point conversion.

During his 18-season NFL career, the eventual Pro Football Hall of Fame inductee set many records and was regarded as one of the best quarterbacks in the history of the game. After football, Tarkenton appeared on television, wrote books, and became a pioneer in the computer-software business. Currently he markets several services and products, including Tarkenton Financial, Tarkenton Sports and Collectibles, and GoSmallBiz.

November 1, 1941

A Bulldogs Hail Mary

A Sinkwich-to-Racehorse bomb with no time remaining downs Plainsmen in 1941

Through five games of the 1941 season, the Bulldogs, led by a group of talented juniors, were considered Georgia's best gridiron edition in nearly a decade. The Bulldogs had tied a formidable Ole Miss team after trailing 14–0 at halftime, and a week later in New York, Georgia captured its first win ever against an Associated Press–ranked opponent with a 7–3 victory over No. 20 Columbia University.

The Bulldogs entered their contest against Auburn with a 3–1–1 record but with much of the team, including three starters, injured. Still, Georgia was nearly a three-touchdown favorite over the Tigers. As it turned out, a victory was dependent on a miracle.

Following a 1975 NFL playoff game, Dallas's Roger Staubach told reporters he said the Hail Mary prayer just as he threw a last-second, desperation, 50-yard touchdown pass to defeat Minnesota. More than 30 years prior to the term being coined, the Bulldogs had their own Hail Mary answered against the Plainsmen of Auburn. In a scoreless tie with only seconds remaining, Frank Sinkwich threw a long-shot pass downfield to Lamar "Racehorse" Davis for a 65-yard touchdown, stunning all witnesses. This play

is being acclaimed as the second-greatest play in Georgia football history.

During the game, Auburn constantly threatened to cross Georgia's goal line. Twice they reached the Bulldogs' 15-yard line, once the 18, and later the 16-yard line. Nevertheless, the Tigers never scored. Georgia had a couple of scoring opportunities, but on both occasions interceptions thwarted the drives. The last one ended on Auburn's 20-yard line when Plainsman Lloyd Cheatham intercepted a Bulldogs pass late in the contest. However, the Tigers were soon forced to punt, the kick rolling out of bounds on Georgia's 35-yard line.

With three seconds remaining in the game, both teams had combined for 359 rushing yards (117 on 26 carries by Sinkwich) but had scored no points. With time remaining to run only one play, the running game was not an option to Sinkwich and company as they stood 65 yards from Auburn's goal line. Up to that point, the Bulldogs' passing attack had struggled, with only three of 15 passes being completed for 34 yards, and two interceptions.

Sinkwich took the snap from center Bill Godwin and dropped back to pass. Sinkwich

Wearing a protective mask for a broken jaw he suffered in early October, Frank Sinkwich drops back to pass during a practice in 1941. Neither broken jaw nor Auburn's defense could prohibit Sinkwich from throwing a 65-yard "Hail Mary" to beat the Tigers on the final play of the game. *Photo courtesy of AP Images.*

threw a long heave down the middle of the field. At first, it appeared that Sinkwich's pass would not connect with anyone. Wingback Davis later recalled, "The play was designed to put pressure on the safety man and make him make a decision on which receiver to cover, which meant that somebody would be open."

Davis happened to be the open receiver. After eluding Auburn's Monk Gafford and Aubrey Clayton, he ran over to the lofted pass, gathered it in on the Tigers' 25-yard line, and raced untouched for the miraculous score. Place-kicker Leo Costa kicked the unnecessary extra point to give the Bulldogs a 7–0 victory.

FRANK SINKWICH

By the middle of the '41 season, junior Frank Sinkwich had already established himself as one of Georgia's all-time finest. As a sophomore, he led the Bulldogs in both rushing (five) and passing (six) touchdowns. Through the first five games of 1941, "Fireball" had been unstoppable, rushing for 553 yards and nearly six yards per carry. Sinkwich had done so playing with a broken jaw he had suffered against South Carolina during the second game of the year.

In the loss to Alabama that preceeded the Auburn game, Sinkwich gained more yards from scrimmage than the entire Crimson Tide team, despite the 13-point loss. In defeat, Sinkwich also passed for Georgia's only two touchdowns. Against the Tigers a week later, Sinkwich would again pass for the team's only touchdown—a play that goes down as the second greatest in Georgia football history.

Ears Whitworth, the line coach, was there first.... He even went so far as to kiss [Lamar] Davis. [Frank] Sinkwich escaped with his best run of the day—a sterling 75-yard sprint to the dressing room.

—JOHNNY BRADBERRY, ASSISTANT SPORTS EDITOR OF THE *ATLANTA CONSTITUTION*, AFTER THE TOUCHDOWN

Frank Sinkwich (No. 21, with football) rips off an eight-yard gain. Against Auburn, Sinkwich gained 117 rushing yards and threw for the only points Georgia needed in a 7–0 victory. *Photo courtesy of AP Images.*

Game Details

Georgia 7 • Auburn 0

Date: November 1, 1941

Site: Memorial Stadium

Attendance: 17,000

Records: Georgia 3–1–1; Auburn 2–3

Rankings: Georgia: No. 16 (Litkenhous Ratings)

Series: Tied 20–20–5 (Georgia one-game winning streak)

> The official came up to me to get the ball. I was so excited.... The game was over, there was no time left, but I reluctantly gave him the ball for the extra point.
>
> —LAMAR DAVIS, WINGBACK

Georgia had won the game on a 65-yard Hail Mary. Interestingly, the only people who knew the game was over were the players, coaches, and officials. The often indecipherable scoreboard clock at Columbus's Memorial Stadium was operated by hand and was not the contest's official time, which was kept on the field by the officials. By the end of the pass play, spectators could not tell how much time remained by the scoreboard clock. They finally got some indication when Georgia players and coaches swarmed the field in celebration.

The Bulldogs' win over Auburn in 1941 is not only memorable because of the Sinkwich-to-Racehorse game-winning play but because it was also the beginning of an extraordinary era in Georgia football. The victory was the first of 15 consecutive for the Bulldogs—the second-longest winning streak in school history. In addition, the win was part of the foundation that led to a national title the following year and three SEC titles in a seven-season span (1942–1948).

Lamar "Racehorse" Davis

While at Georgia, Lamar "Racehorse" Davis was known for making big plays. On the Bullpups freshman team in 1939, Davis returned successive punts against South Carolina for touchdowns in the third quarter. During the 1940 season, he returned both a kick and punt for scores while also catching two touchdowns. In his junior and senior seasons, Davis combined to catch 33 passes for 873 yards (26.5 average!) and 15 touchdowns while leading the Southeastern Conference in receiving both years. In 1941 he averaged 12.9 yards per punt return, 33.6 per kick return, and was second in the conference in scoring.

Davis's 145 career points still rank 23rd at Georgia in all-time modern career scoring. He scored 24 varsity touchdowns (12th in school history): 17 receiving, three rushing, and four on kick/punt returns, but none bigger than the 65-yard Hail Mary he hauled in from Frank Sinkwich to defeat Auburn.

November 8, 1980

THE PLAY

Belue-to-Scott 93-yard pass play beats Florida and keeps Georgia's national championship hopes alive

By November 1980, Georgia had soared to a No. 2 ranking in the national polls following eight consecutive victories to begin the season. The Bulldogs had their sights set on a Southeastern Conference title and a Sugar Bowl appearance, but even better, there was the possibility of playing for the school's first undisputed national championship. To be the No. 1 team in the nation and to play for a national title, often a team needs a little luck along the way. The '80 Georgia squad was no different. It needed a great deal of luck during the course of its title run, in particular, on a single play against the University of Florida. Without it, the greatest play in Georgia football history, there would be no top ranking or national championship in 1980.

With only 1:20 remaining in the game, the Bulldogs faced third down and 11 on their own 7-yard line, trailing 21–20 to the Gators. Many Georgia fans had either left or were in the process of departing the Gator Bowl in anticipation of the Bulldogs' first loss of the year. Georgia offensive coordinator George Haffner made the play call with the objective of only getting a first down, 15 to 20 yards at most, to keep the drive

alive so All-American kicker Rex Robinson could eventually be in a position to attempt a game-winning field goal.

Quarterback Buck Belue dropped straight back into the end zone, avoided pressure, and ran to his right nearing the 5-yard line. Split end Lindsay Scott, who had been lined up to Belue's right, had ran a simple curl pattern over the middle. Florida linebacker David Little positioned himself between Belue and Scott. Belue began running away from the pressure and motioned to Scott to slide a little from behind the linebacker. On the run, Belue threw a strike to a leaping Scott, who came down with the reception around the 25-yard line. The junior receiver stumbled a bit upon his catch, regained his balance, turned around, and began heading upfield. As Scott ran toward and then down his left sideline, it appeared several Gators defenders had angles on him to make a play. Scott simply outraced every one of them, and 93 yards later he was in the end zone for a touchdown. Georgia had somehow miraculously regained a 26–21 advantage over upset-minded Florida.

Because of "the Play," freshman phenomenon Herschel Walker for once was

As a corner of Jacksonville's Gator Bowl goes wild, Georgia's Chuck Jones (No. 1) runs in to congratulate and support teammate Lindsay Scott (No. 24), who is getting swarmed by some of the crowd. Scott just accomplished a 93-yard miracle pass play against Florida in 1980— the greatest play in Georgia Bulldogs football history. *Photo courtesy of Hargrett Rare Book & Manuscript Library/University of Georgia Libraries.*

THE PLAY

Needing a miracle, Buck Belue faked a handoff to Herschel Walker and dropped straight back behind his own goal line. Just as Mike Clark converged on the Georgia quarterback, Nat Hudson made a saving block on the Florida defender. The pressure forced Belue to roll out of the end zone and to his right. Spotting a wide-open Lindsay Scott, Belue threw a strike to the receiver at the 25. Running toward the sideline, Scott ran by and away from several Gators defenders, including fallen safety Tim Groves. Once he was near midfield, Scott outraced everyone into the end zone for a touchdown.

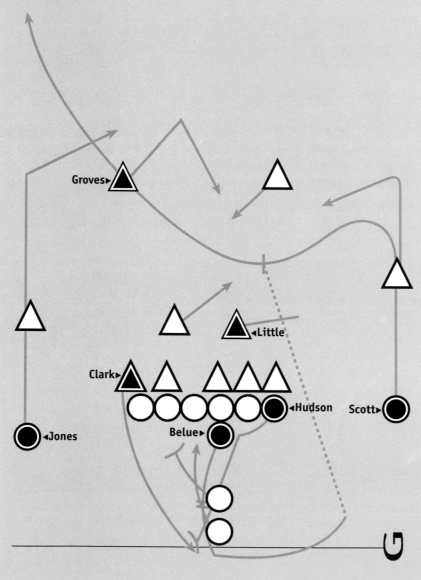

GAME DETAILS

Georgia 26 • Florida 21

Date: November 8, 1980

Site: Gator Bowl

Attendance: 68,528

Records: Georgia 8–0; Florida 6–1

Rankings: Georgia: No. 2 (AP)/ No. 2 (UPI); Florida: No. 20 (AP)/ No. 20 (UPI)

Series: Georgia 36–20–2 (Georgia two-game winning streak)

> **H**ow could we have given up? There was just too much at stake.
>
> —BUCK BELUE, QUARTERBACK

overshadowed, perhaps for the only time during his career at Georgia. Seventy-two of Walker's 238 rushing yards came on a run early in the game and gave the Bulldogs a 7–0 advantage. Georgia held a 20–10 fourth-quarter lead before the Gators, guided by freshman quarterback Wayne Peace, scored 11 consecutive points. Peace's 282 passing yards were the most thrown against the Bulldogs since California's Joe Roth passed for 379 in the 1976 season opener.

A Mark Dickert punt for Florida went out of bounds on Georgia's 8-yard line with 1:35 to play. On first down, Belue was forced to scramble and lost a yard. On second and 11, Belue's sideline pass to Charles Junior fell incomplete. Just when all hope was lost and the last nail was to be driven in the Dawgs' coffin, Georgia suddenly struck for its 93-yard wonder on third down and long.

The play, also called Left 76 or L-76, had been used by the Bulldogs a couple of times already in the game, but without success. That is, until Georgia tried to execute it one final time. The intent of the play was to only gain a first down, and it should have done just that. Safety Tim Groves covered Georgia's Chuck Jones as the flanker ran a long post route. After Belue threw short and Groves drew his attention from Jones to Scott, the Florida safety-man slipped to the Gator Bowl turf. After making the recep-

tion, Scott should have been immediately tackled by Groves, but instead, Scott ran by the fallen Gator eventually into the end zone.

As Scott crossed the goal line, bedlam broke out amongst the Bulldogs faithful. Fans, players, photographers, and the like jumped around in the end zone and/or on top of Scott. Items and substances were thrown onto the field in celebration. A sportswriter covering the "World's Largest Outdoor Cocktail Party" later reported it was the first time he had ever been caught in a "liquor storm." Georgia's play-by-play announcer, Larry Munson, got so excited he broke the chair he was sitting on, and the game temporarily went off the air.

Moments after the miracle, Georgia cornerback Mike Fisher intercepted Peace to secure a 26–21 victory.

Later, it was revealed that top-ranked Notre Dame had been tied; Georgia would be the new No. 1 team in college football the following Monday.

Florida head coach Charley Pell later described Belue-to-Scott as a "circus play," while disgruntled Gators receiver Cris Collinsworth added that it was merely a "fluke" and Florida deserved to win. Maybe so, but as defensive coordinator Erk Russell would often say, "I'd rather be lucky than good."

LINDSAY SCOTT

Lindsay Scott, a highly recruited receiver from Jesup, Georgia, quickly made an impression as a true freshman in 1978. Scott led the Bulldogs in receiving and the conference in kickoff returns and was selected first-team freshman All-American. As a sophomore, Scott again led the team in receiving and kickoff returns. Prior to the 1980 season, Scott's scholarship was rescinded because of an altercation with an academic counselor. By the Florida game, he

Once I caught it and got outside, I thought I'd go all the way.

—LINDSAY SCOTT, SPLIT END

was no longer the Bulldogs' primary receiver nor was he returning kickoffs. On "the Play," Scott, who later admitted he finally got winded at Florida's 30-yard line, scored his first points since catching a touchdown against the Gators the season before. Following the Florida game and while celebrating the victory, a delighted coach Vince Dooley rightfully said that he "may give it [the scholarship] back to him [Scott]."

Scott rode his wave of success into his senior season of 1981. His 728 receiving yards were a single-season school record until Andre Hastings's 860 in 1992. Scott was selected both AP and UPI first-team All-SEC. His 2,098 career receiving yards were a school record until 1995 and currently rank fourth.

Scott was the 13th overall pick of the 1982 NFL draft taken by New Orleans. In four seasons and 49 games with the Saints, Scott caught 69 passes, one for a

Buck Belue (left) and Lindsay Scott (right) embrace after their 93-yard completion stunned Florida and everyone watching. Georgia held on for a 26–21 victory over the Gators, and less than two months later, they capped a perfect 1980 season by winning the national championship. *Photo courtesy of Wingate Downs.*

Quarterback Buck Belue (with football) would have been sacked had it not been for a game-saving block by Nat Hudson (No. 65) against Florida's Mike Clark (No. 87). Belue rolled out to his right and completed a pass to Lindsay Scott on the run. *Photo courtesy of Wingate Downs.*

NAT HUDSON

As with other great plays in Georgia football history (see Number 8, B-E-L-U-E Spells Relief), Buck Belue was obviously an integral part of Georgia's winning play against Florida in 1980. However, it should be noted that without a spectacular block by lineman Nat Hudson, Belue likely would have been sacked in the end zone instead of Lindsay Scott streaking for a touchdown.

In his senior year of 1980, Hudson was in his third consecutive season as a Bulldogs starter along the offensive line. The left guard in 1978 and 1979, Hudson moved to right tackle in '80 and gained 15 pounds to weigh 265—the heaviest among all Georgia starters. Hudson was extremely strong, with lots of endurance and, despite his size, was considered quicker than most linemen.

The unsung hero of "the Play," Hudson slid off his block and to his left when his man dropped into pass coverage. Just as Florida defensive end Mike Clark closed in on Belue a couple of yards into the end zone, Hudson seemingly came out of nowhere to block the hard-charging Clark out of the play. Hudson would eventually be drafted by New Orleans in the sixth round of the 1981 NFL draft. He played 18 games with the Saints and Baltimore for two seasons (1981–1982).

Sources

Athens Banner-Herald (1895–2007).

Atlanta Constitution (1895–2007).

Atlanta Journal (1910–2007).

Augusta Chronicle (1913–2007).

Baseball-reference.com. "University of Georgia (Bulldogs)." http://www.baseball-reference.com/schools/georgia.shtml (accessed November 28, 2007).

Birmingham News (November 21, 1920).

Bolton, Clyde. *Silver Britches: Inside University of Georgia Football.* West Point, NY: Leisure Press, 1982.

College Football Data Warehouse. "Georgia Bulldogs." http://www.cfbdatawarehouse.com/data/div_ia/sec/georgia/index.php (accessed January 20, 2008).

Cornell University. *Football Media Guide*, 2007.

Cromartie, Bill. *Clean Old-Fashioned Hate.* Nashville: Rutledge Hill Press, 1987.

DatabaseFootball.com. "NFL Players Who Attended Georgia." http://www.databasefootball.com/players/bycollege.htm?sch=University+of+Georgia (accessed November 22, 2007).

Garbin, Patrick. *About Them Dawgs!: Georgia Football's Memorable Teams and Players.* Lanham, MD: The Scarecrow Press, Inc., 2008.

———. *"Then Vince Said to Herschel…": The Best Georgia Bulldog Stories Ever Told.* Chicago: Triumph Books, 2007.

Gay, Chris. "Munson Hunkers Down for One Last Season." *Savannah Morning News*, November 2, 2007. http://www.savannahnow.com/node/349443 (accessed November 2, 2007).

Hannon, Shane. "Fran Tarkenton." OnlineAthens.com. http://www.onlineathens.com/dogbytes/legends/tarkenton_02.shtml (accessed January 25, 2008).

Howell, Jim, and Sherri Howell. "Georgia." Jim and Sherri Howell's Home Page. http://www.jhowell.net/cf/scores/Georgia.htm (accessed January 29, 2008).

Martin, Charles E. *I've Seen 'Em All.* Athens, GA: The McGregor Company, 1961.

National Collegiate Athletic Association. *Official 2007 NCAA Divisions I Football Records Book.* Indianapolis: The National Collegiate Athletic Association, 2007.

New Georgia Encyclopedia. "Steadman V. Sanford (1871–1945)." http://www.georgiaencyclopedia.org/nge/Article.jsp?id=h-2623 (accessed November 14, 2007).

NoleFans.com. "Georgia Bulldogs." http://www.geocities.com/nolefan_fsu/team/035.html (accessed February 2, 2008).

OnlineAthens.com. "Spurgeon 'Spud' Chandler: No. 10 University of Georgia Athlete of the Century." http://www.onlineathens.com/dogbytes/legends/spud.shtml (accessed November 28, 2007).

OurSportsCentral.com. "USFL." http://www.oursportscentral.com/usfl (accessed February 8, 2008).

Randolph School. "Kurt Page Announces Move to Texas." http://www.randolphschool.net/news/news/default.asp?newsid=242101&from_nav=&from=archive (accessed November 22, 2007).

Red and Black [independent University of Georgia newspaper]1913–1976.

Rivalries: The Tradition of Georgia vs. Florida. DVD. New York: Hart Sharp Video, 2003.

Sanders, Jamie. "Jasper Sanks: Has It Really Been Nine Years?" Georgia Football Blog. http://2006. georgiabulldogfootball.blogspot.com/2006/02/jasper-sanks-has-it-really-been-9.html (accessed December 17, 2007).

Seiler, Sonny, and Kent Hannon. *Damn Good Dogs!: The Real Story of Uga, the University of Georgia's Bulldog Mascots.* Athens, GA: Hill Street Press, 2002.

Sewanee: The University of the South. *Football Media Guide,* 2007.

Smith, Loran. *Glory! Glory!* Atlanta: Peachtree Publishers Limited, 1981.

———. *Wally's Boys.* Athens, GA: Longstreet Press, Inc., 2005.

Stegeman, John F. *The Ghosts of Herty Field: Early Days on a Southern Gridiron.* Athens, GA: University of Georgia Press, 1997.

Thilenius, Ed, and Jim Koger. *No Ifs, No Ands, a Lot of Butts: 21 Years of Georgia Football.* Atlanta: Foote and Davies, Inc., 1960.

University of Georgia. *Football Media Guide,* 1948–2007.

University of Pittsburgh. *Football Media Guide,* 2002.

Woodruff, Fuzzy. *A History of Southern Football (1890–1928).* Vol. 1. Atlanta: Walter W. Brown Publishing Co., 1928.